TRUST
for Accoun

Mark Ockelton MA
of Lincoln's Inn, Barrister;
Lecturer in Law, The University of Leeds

London · Butterworths · 1987

United Kingdom	Butterworth & Co (Publishers) Ltd, 88 Kingsway, LONDON WC2B 6AB and 61A North Castle Street, EDINBURGH EH2 3LJ
Australia	Butterworths Pty Ltd, SYDNEY, MELBOURNE, BRISBANE, ADELAIDE, PERTH, CANBERRA and HOBART
Canada	Butterworths, A division of Reed Inc., TORONTO and VANCOUVER
New Zealand	Butterworths of New Zealand Ltd, WELLINGTON and AUCKLAND
Singapore	Butterworth & Co (Asia) Pte Ltd, SINGAPORE
South Africa	Butterworth Publishers (Pty) Ltd, DURBAN and PRETORIA
USA	Butterworths Legal Publishers, ST PAUL, Minnesota, SEATTLE, Washington, BOSTON, Massachusetts, AUSTIN, Texas and D & S Publishers, CLEARWATER, Florida

© Butterworth & Co (Publishers) Ltd 1987

All rights reserved. No part of this publication may be reproduced or transmitted in any form or by any means, including photocopying and recording, without the written permission of the copyright holder, application for which should be addressed to the publisher. Such written permission must also be obtained before any part of this publication is stored in a retrieval system of any nature.

This book is sold subject to the Standard Conditions of Sale of Net Books and may not be re-sold in the UK below the net price fixed by Butterworths for the book in our current catalogue.

British Library Cataloguing in Publication Data

Ockelton, Mark
   Trusts for accountants.
   1. Trusts and trustees——England——
   Accounting
   I. Title
   344.2065'9'024657   KD1495

ISBN 0 406 50090 8

Typeset by The Word Factory Ltd., Rossendale, Lancashire.
Printed and bound in Great Britain by Billings, Worcester.

Preface

Students of accountancy and banking sometimes ask why they have to study the law of trusts for their professional examinations. There are two reasons. The first is that the trust concept has been pervasive and influential. It may be that few of the readers of this book will ever have much to do with traditional large family trusts; but the chances are that most of them at one time or another will find that they are involved in some problem connected with pension funds, or charities, or the funds of a club, or the administration of a deceased's estate, or a profit made unlawfully by a director of a company, or a house owned by an unmarried couple: these are just a few of the areas in which the relevant legal rules are, to a greater or lesser extent, based on the law of trusts. It is therefore essential to have an elementary understanding of what a trust is and how it works. Secondly, accountants and bankers, by virtue of their professional positions, are likely to be asked to become trustees, and it is very desirable that they have some knowledge of what they are letting themselves in for if they accept appointment. In the following pages will be found many examples of the fate that befalls the trustee who is ignorant of the duties of his office.

This book is meant to provide a sufficient outline of the subject for those who meet trusts for the first time when studying for professional examinations: specifically, Chartered Accountants' P E 1 (Law), Certified Accountants' Executorship and Trust Law and Accounts, and the Trustee Diploma of The Institute of Bankers. I hope that it may also be of some use to any law students who find that the law of trusts seems to be entirely above their heads. It is not a textbook in the usual sense of that word. It is very short, and its balance between topics is rather peculiar. Angling the discussion towards those for whom the book is primarily intended, I have tried to give space to explanation where experience has shown that they most often tend to misunderstand; and I have dealt in broad concepts or dwelt on detail according to the usual requirements of their examiners. I have not avoided areas of difficulty and controversy, but here as elsewhere I have attempted to offer answers rather than indulge in casuistry. There is no doubt that trusts *can* be made difficult to understand, but most of the principles are quite straightforward, and beginners' confusions often arise from their being asked to cope with too much at once. For similar reasons I have mentioned tax only incidentally. Although it is true that one cannot fully appreciate the modern law of trusts without taking tax into account, it is much easier, and more effective in the long run, to learn the basics of trust law without trying to juggle with taxation problems at the same time.

I am very grateful to many people who have helped in various ways. In particular, Shelagh Gaskill provided the initial encouragement and has read most of the book in typescript; Kate Hornsby, Lesley McLean, Christine Taylor and Tina Wigley did the typing uncomplainingly and efficiently; the publishers have compiled the tables and the index. To all I offer my sincere thanks.

The law is stated as at 1 September 1986, except that the Insolvency Act 1986 is treated as though it were already in force.

C M G OCKELTON
Faculty of Law
The University of Leeds

Contents

Preface v
Table of statutes xi
Table of cases xv

PART I: THE CREATION OF A TRUST 1

Chapter 1 **Introduction** 3
    The trust concept 3
    The functions of trusts 6
    A note about exams 8

Chapter 2 **Formalities** 9
    Certainty of words 9
    Statutory requirements 11

Chapter 3 **The trust property** 14
    What can be the subject matter of a trust? 14
    Certainty of subject matter 16

Chapter 4 **Void and voidable trusts** 18
    The Rule against Perpetuities 18
    Other void trusts 27
    Voidable trusts: Setting trusts aside 29

Chapter 5 **The beneficiary** 35
    Who can be a beneficiary? 35
    The beneficiary principle 36
    Trusts and powers 41
    Certainty of objects 47
    Proprietary rights of the beneficiaries 52

Chapter 6 **Constituting a trust** 55
    Five ways of making a gift 56
    Exceptions to the rule that equity will not perfect an imperfect gift 67

Contents

Chapter 7   **Resulting trusts**   70
    Automatic resulting trusts   70
    Presumed resulting trusts   74
Chapter 8   **Constructive trusts**   78
    The nature of a constructive trust   78
    Situations in which a constructive trust arises   79
Chapter 9   **Secret trusts and mutual wills**   85
    Secret trusts   85
    Mutual wills   89
    Theoretical basis   91

PART II: THE ADMINISTRATION OF TRUSTS   93

Chapter 10   **The trustee**   95
    Who can be a trustee?   95
    Appointment, retirement and removal of trustees   98
Chapter 11   **General duties and powers of trustees**   105
    Standard of care   105
    Trustee Act 1925, s 69(2)   106
    The duty to be active   107
    The power to delegate   108
    A trustee may not profit from his trust   109
Chapter 12   **Duties and powers in relation to trust property**   114
    Trustees' duties in relation to the trust property   114
    Duties in choosing investments   117
    The power to invest   121
    Proposals for reform   126
Chapter 13   **Maintenance and advancement of beneficiaries**   127
    The power to maintain or accumulate   128
    The power of advancement   131
Chapter 14   **Variation of trusts**   135
    Informal variation   135
    Variation by authority of the court   136
Chapter 15   **Remedies for breach of trust**   144
    The personal liability of trustees   144
    Proprietary remedies   148
    Other remedies   152

PART III: TRUSTS FOR CHARITABLE PURPOSES 153

Chapter 16 Charity 155
          The advantages of charity 155
          The definition of charity 156

Chapter 17 The administration of charitable trusts 167
          The Charity Commissioners 167
          The trustees of a charity 170
          Cy-près 171

Index 177

Table of statutes

	PAGE
Administration of Estates Act 1925	7
s 17	11, 85
Adoption Act 1976	
s 45	117
Capital Gains Tax Act 1979	
s 145	155
Charitable Uses Act 1601	157, 160
Charities Act 1960	36, 167
s 1(3)	167, 169
(4)	167
3	168
4	168
5(1)	168
6	169
12	170
13	171, 172
(5)	172
14	174
16	168
17	168
18	169
20	170
22	168
23	169
24	167
28(1)	170
(6)	170
29	169
Sch 2	168
Charities Act 1985	
s 2	171
3	171
Civil Liability (Contribution) Act 1978	
s 2	148
Companies Act 1948	
s 14	36
Companies Act 1985	
s 183	58

	PAGE
Company Securities (Insider Dealing) Act 1985	147
Family Law Reform Act 1969	130, 131
ss 14–17	117
15(7)	27
Finance Act 1982	
s 129	155
Forfeiture Act 1982	80
General Rate Act 1967	
s 39	155
40	155
Income and Corporation Taxes Act 1970	
s 250(4)	155
360	155
(1)(c)	155
434(1A)	155
447	71
Inheritance (Provision for Family and Dependants) Act 1975	31
s 2(1)(f)	142
10–13	32
Inheritance Tax Act 1984	
s 23	155
58(1)(a)	155
76	155
Insolvency Act 1986	
s 283(3)	148
339	33
339–342	32
423–425	33
Judicial Trustees Act 1896	97
Land Registration Act 1925	
s 20	57
23	57
Law of Property Act 1925	14
s 1(6)	95
20	95

xi

Table of statutes

Law of Property Act 1925—contd.
- 25(1)(b) 81, 82
- 27(2) 97, 103
- 28 124
- (2) 121
- 52(1) 57
- 53 62
  - (1)(b) 11, 92
  - (c) 57, 58, 60, 61, 62, 139
  - (2) 61, 62
- 60(3) 75
- 105 80
- 136 58
- 164 26
- 175 129

Legitimacy Act 1976
- s 7 117

Limitation Act 1980
- s 8(1) 66
- 21(1)(a) 146
  - (b) 66, 146
  - (3) 146
- 22 146
- 32 146

Matrimonial Causes Act 1973
- s 24 .... 31, 80
  - (1)(c) 31, 142
  - (d) 31, 142
- 37(2)(a) 31
  - (b) 31
  - (c) 31

Mental Health Act 1983 101

Perpetuities and Accumulations Act 1964 ... 19, 23, 24, 25, 38, 133
- s 1 .... 24, 45
- 2(1) 23
- 3 24
- 4 24
- 5 24
- 13 26

Public Trustee Act 1906 95
- s 4 96
- (3) 110
- 7(1) 96
- 9 110
- 13 .... 115, 126

Public Trustee (Fees) Act 1957: 96, 110

Race Relations Act 1976 166
- s 34(1) 166

Recreational Charities Act 1958 .... 158, 162, 163

Settled Land Act 1925 ..... 14, 170

Settled Land Act 1925—contd.
- s 9 67
- 18(1) 103
- 27(1) 67
- 29(1) 170
- 64 .... 142, 143
- 73 124
- 94 103

Sex Discrimination Act 1975 ... 166

Stamp Act 1891
- s 54 62

Status of Aliens Act 1914
- s 17 35

Supreme Court Act 1981
- s 124 85

Theft Act 1968
- s 1 147
- 17 147
- 20 147

Trustee Act 1925 .... 106, 170
- s 7 115
- 8(1) 124
- 14 107
- 16 107
- 19(1) 115
- 21 115
- 22(4) 115
- 23(1) 108, 115
  - (2) 108
  - (3) 108
- 25 108
- 27 .... 107, 117
- 30(1) 108, 145
  - (2) 110
- 31 .... 128, 130, 131, 142
  - (1)(i) 129
  - (ii) 130
  - (2) 130
  - (3) 129
- 32 ..... 128, 131, 132, 134, 142
- 33 47
- 34 .... 103, 170
- 36 ..... 100, 101, 102, 103, 104
  - (2) 100
  - (3) 101
  - (6) 104
  - (7) 103
  - (8) 100, 101
- s 37(1)(a) 104
  - (d) 103
- 39 103
- 40 102

Table of statutes xiii

Trustee Act 1925—*contd.*	PAGE
(4)	102
41	100, 102
42	110
43	103
44	102
51	103
53	142
57	125, 137, 138, 143, 169
(3)	138
61	105, 145
62	146
69(2)	106, 107
Trustee Investments Act 1961	122, 124, 125, 126, 170
s 2(1)	123
(2)	123
(3)	123
(4)	123
3	123
5	122

Trustee Investments Act 1961—*contd.*	PAGE
6(1)	124
(a)	126
(2)	123
(3)	123
(4)	123
(5)	123
(6)	123
Sch 1	122, 123
Sch 2	123
Variation of Trusts Act 1958	125, 141, 169
s 1	137, 138
(1)	139, 143
(a)	139
(b)	140
(c)	140
(d)	140
Wills Act 1837	
s 9	11, 85, 91
15	72, 85, 86

Table of cases

	PAGE
Abbott Fund Trusts, Re, Smith v Abbott [1900] 2 Ch 326, 69 LJ Ch 539	74, 158
Abraham's WT, Re [1969] 1 Ch 463, [1967] 2 All ER 1175	133
Adams and The Kensington Vestry, Re (1884) 27 Ch D 394, 54 LJ Ch 87	10
Allcard v Skinner (1887) 36 Ch D 145, [1886–90] All ER Rep 90	30, 147
Arber, Re (1919) Times, 13 December	160
A–G v City of London (1790) 3 Bro CC 171	171
A–G Jacobs-Smith [1895] 2 QB 341, 64 LJQB 605	60
Baden's Deed Trusts (No 2), Re, Baden v Smith [1973] Ch 9, [1972] 2 All ER 1304	47
Baillie, Re, Fitzgerald v Noad (1886) 2 TLR 660	92
Baker, Re, Public Trustee v Baker [1924] 2 Ch 271, 93 LJ Ch 599	120
Ball's ST, Re [1968] 2 All ER 438, [1968] 1 WLR 889	139
Banque Belge Pour L'Etranger v Hambrouck [1921] 1 KB 321, 90 LJKB 322	149
Barclays Bank Ltd v Quistclose Investments Ltd [1970] AC 567, [1968] 3 All ER 651	73
Barlow's WT, Re [1979] 1 All ER 296, [1979] 1 WLR 278	52
Barnes v Addy (1874) 9 Ch App 244, 43 LJ Ch 513	84
Bartlett v Barclays Bank Trust Co Ltd (No 1) [1980] Ch 515, [1980] 1 All ER 139	105, 125
Bassett v Nosworthy (1674) Finch 102	151
Beale's ST, Re, Huggins v Beale [1932] 2 Ch 15, [1931] All ER Rep 637	138
Beatty v Guggenheim Exploration Co (1919) 225 NY 380	78
Belmont Finance Corp Ltd v Williams Furniture Ltd (No 1) [1979] Ch 250, [1979] 1 All ER 118	84
Beloved Wilkes's Charity, Re (1851) 3 Mac & G 440, 20 LJ Ch 588	106
Benjamin, Re, Neville v Benjamin [1902] 1 Ch 723, 71 LJ Ch 319	48
Bentley v Craven (1853) 18 Beav 75	111
Birch v Treasury Solicitor [1951] 1 Ch 298, [1950] 2 All ER 1198	68
Birmingham v Renfrew (1937) 57 CLR 666, 43 ALR 520	90
Blackwell v Blackwell [1929] AC 318, [1929] All ER Rep 71	87
Blathwayt v Lord Cawley [1976] AC 397, [1975] 3 All ER 625	28
Boardman v Phipps [1967] 2 AC 46, [1966] 3 All ER 721	78, 110, 112
Boulter, Re, Capital and Counties Bank v Boulter [1922] 1 Ch 75, [1921] All ER Rep 167	28
Boyce v Boyce (1849) 16 Sim 476	16, 17
Boyes, Re, Boyes v Carritt (1884), 26 Ch D 531, 53 LJ Ch 654	87, 88
Brassey, Re, Barclays Bank Ltd v Brassey [1955] 1 All ER 577, 99 Sol Jo 149	138

xv

xvi *Table of cases*

	PAGE
Brisbane City Council v A–G for Queensland [1979] AC 411, [1978] 3 All ER 30	160
British Museum Trustees v A–G [1984] 1 All ER 337, [1984] 1 WLR 418 ...	125
British Red Cross Balkan Fund, Re, British Red Cross Society v Johnson [1914] 2 Ch 419, [1914–15] All ER Rep 459	151
Brockbank, Re, Ward v Bates [1948] Ch 206, [1948] 1 All ER 287 ...	54, 100, 135
Brogden, Re, Billing v Brogden (1888) 38 Ch D 546, [1886–90] All ER Rep 927	115
Brown, Re, District Bank v Brown [1954] Ch 39, [1953] 2 All ER 655	28
Brown v Gould [1972] Ch 53, [1971] 2 All ER 1505	47
Broxtowe BC v Birch [1983] 1 All ER 641, [1983] 1WLR 314	160
Bull v Bull [1955] 1 QB 234, [1955] 1 All ER 253	75
Burns v Burns [1984] Ch 317, [1984] 1 All ER 244	81, 83
Buttle v Saunders [1950] 2 All ER 193, 66 (pt 1) TLR 1026	118
CL, Re [1969] 1 Ch 587, [1968] 1 All ER 1104	141
Cannon v Hartley [1949] Ch 213, [1949] 1 All ER 50	65, 66
Carly v Farrelly [1975] 1 NZLR 356	83
Caus, Re, Lindeboom v Camile [1934] 1 Ch 162, [1933] All ER Rep 818 ...	160
Chaine-Nickson v Bank of Ireland [1976] IR 393	116
Chapman v Chapman. See Downshire's Settled Estates, Re, Marquis of Downshire v Royal Bank of Scotland	
Chase Manhattan Bank NA v Israel-British Bank (London) Ltd [1981] Ch 105 [1979] 3 All ER 1025	79, 149
Chesterfield's (Earl) Trusts, Re (1883), 24 Ch D 643 [1881–5] All ER Rep 737	120
Chettiar v Chettiar [1962] AC 294, [1962] 1 All ER 494	77
Chillingworth v Chambers [1896] 1 Ch 685, 65 LJ Ch 343	146
Clayton's Case. See Devaynes v Noble, Clayton's Case	
Cleaver, Re [1981] 2 All ER 1018, [1981] 1 WLR 939	90, 91
Clore's ST, Re, Sainer v Clore [1966] 2 All ER 272, [1966] 1 WLR 955	133
Cochrane, Re, Shaw v Cochrane [1955] Ch 309, [1955] 1 All ER 222	71, 72
CIT v Pemsel [1891] AC 531, [1891–4] All ER Rep 28	157, 161
Cook's ST, Re, Royal Exchange Assurance v Cook [1965] Ch 902, [1964] 3 All ER 898	67
Cooper, Re, Le Neve Foster v National Provincial Bank Ltd [1939] Ch 811, [1939] 3 All ER 586	88
Coulthurst, Re, Coutts & Co v Coulthurst [1951] Ch 661, [1951] 1 All ER 774	157
Cowan v Scargill [1985] Ch 270, [1984] 2 All ER 750	118
Cradock v Piper (1850) 1 Mac & G 664, 1 H & Tw 617	110
Craig, Re, Meneces v Middleton [1971] Ch 95, [1970] 2 All ER 390	30
Cresswell v Cresswell (1868) LR 6 Eq 69	86
Crippen's Estate, Re [1911] P 108, [1911–13] All ER Rep 207	79
Currant v Jago (1844) 1 Coll CC 261, 8 Jur 610	76
Dean, Re, Cooper-Dean v Stevens (1889) 41 Ch D 552, 58 LJ Ch 693	40
Delamere's ST, Re [1984] 1 WLR 813, [1984] 1 All ER 584	131
Denley's Trust Deed, Re, Holman v H H Martyn & Co Ltd [1969] 1 Ch 373, [1968] 3 All ER 65	36, 38, 39, 40
Devaynes v Noble, Clayton's Case (1816) 1 Mer 572	151
Dillwyn v Llewelyn (1862) 4 De G F & J 517, 31 LJ Ch 658	69

Table of cases xvii

PAGE

Dingle v Turner [1972] AC 601, [1972] 1 All ER 878 .... 158, 162
Diplock, Re, Diplock v Wintle [1948] Ch 465, [1948] 2 All ER 318, CA,
   affd sub nom. Ministry of Health v Simpson [1951] AC 251, [1950] 2
   All ER 1137, HL 149, 151, 152
Downshire's Settled Estates, Re, Marquis of Downshire v Royal Bank of
   Scotland [1953] Ch 218, [1953] 1 All ER 103, CA, rvsd sub nom.
   Chapman v Chapman [1954] AC 429, [1954] 1 All ER 798,
   HL 137, 138, 141, 143
Dufour v Pereira (1769) 1 Dick 419 90
Duprèe's Deed Trusts, Re, Daley v Lloyds Bank [1945] Ch 16, [1944] 2 All
   ER 443 162
Dyer v Dyer (1788) 2 Cox Eq Cas 92, [1775–1802] All ER Rep 205 75

Egerton v Egerton [1949] 2 All ER 238, [1949] WN 301 28
Endacott, Re, Corpe v Endacott [1960] Ch 232, [1959] 2 All ER 562 .... 35, 41
Eves v Eves [1975] 3 All ER 768, [1975] 1 WLR 1338 82
Ewen v Bannerman (1830) 2 Dow & Cl 74 16

Finger's WT, Re, Turner v Ministry of Health [1972] Ch 286, [1971] 3 All
   ER 1050 174
Fletcher v Collis [1905] 2 Ch 24, 74 LJ Ch 502 .... 136, 145
Fletcher v Fletcher (1844) 4 Hare 67, 14 LJ Ch 66 67
Flinn, Re, Public Trustee v Flinn [1948] Ch 241, [1948] 1 All ER 541 164
Forster v Williams Deacon's Bank Ltd [1935] Ch 359, [1935] All ER Rep
   374 96
Fowkes v Pascoe (1875) 10 Ch App 343, [1874–80] All ER Rep 521 74

Gillingham Bus Disaster Fund, Re, Bowman v Official Solicitor [1958] Ch
   300, [1958] 1 All ER 37 74
Gilmour v Coats [1949] AC 426, [1949] 1 All ER 848 160
Gissing v Gissing [1971] AC 886, [1970] 2 All ER 780 .... 81, 83
Golay's WT, Re, Morris v Bridgewater [1965] 2 All ER 660, [1965] 1 WLR
   969 16
Gonin, Re, Gonin v Garmeson [1979] Ch 16, [1977] 2 All ER 720 68
Grainge v Wilberforce (1889) 5 TLR 436 59
Grant v Edwards [1986] 3 WLR 114, [1986] 2 All ER 426 .... 81, 82, 83
Grant's WT, Re [1979] 3 All ER 359, [1980] 1 WLR 360 38
Gray, Re, Todd v Taylor [1925] Ch 362, [1925] All ER Rep 250 162
Grey v IRC [1960] AC 1, [1959] 3 All ER 603 .... 57, 58
Groves v Groves (1829) 3 Y & J 163 76
Gulbenkian's ST, Re, Whishaw v Stephens [1970] AC 508, [1968] 3
   All ER 785 .... 47, 48, 50
Gwyon, Re, Public Trustee v A–G [1930] 1 Ch 255, 99 LJ Ch 104 157

Habergham v Vincent (1793) 2 Ves Jun 204, 4 Bro CC 353 89
Hallett's Estate, Re, Knatchbull v Hallett (1880) 13 Ch D 696, [1874–80]
   All ER Rep 793 150
Hamilton, Re, Trench v Hamilton [1895] 2 Ch 370, 64 LJ Ch 799 10
Hamilton-Snowball's Conveyance, Re [1959] Ch 308, [1958] 2 All ER 319 .. 80
Harvey, Re, Westminster Bank Ltd v Askwith [1941] 3 All ER 284, 85 Sol
   Jo 481 138
Harwood, Re, Coleman v Innes [1936] Ch 285, [1935] All ER Rep 918 174

xviii *Table of cases*

	PAGE
Hastings-Bass, Re, Hastings v IRC [1975] Ch 25, [1974] 2 All ER 193	133
Hawksley v May [1956] 1 QB 304, [1955] 3 All ER 353	116
Hay's ST, Re, Greig v McGregor [1981] 3 All ER 786, [1982] 1 WLR 202	45, 51
Hepplewhite's WT, Re (1977) Times, 21 January	27
Holder v Holder [1968] Ch 353, [1968] 1 All ER 665	111
Holmes v A–G (1981) Times, 12 February	160
Holmes v Dring (1788) 2 Cox Eq Cas 1	125
Holt's Settlement, Re, Wilson v Holt [1969] 1 Ch 100, [1968] 1 All ER 470	138
Hooper, Re, Parker v Ward [1932] 1 Ch 38, [1931] All ER Rep 129	40
Howe v Lord Dartmouth (1802) 7 Ves 137, [1775–1802] All ER Rep 24	119, 121
Hussey v Palmer [1972] 3 All ER 744, [1972] 1 WLR 1286	82
Industrial Development Consultants Ltd v Cooley [1972] 2 All ER 162, [1972] 1 WLR 443	79
IRC v Baddeley [1955] AC 572, [1955] 1 All ER 525	161
IRC v Broadway Cottages Trust [1955] Ch 20, [1954] 1 All ER 120	47
IRC v McMullen [1978] 1 All ER 230, [1978] 1 WLR 664, revsd [1980] 1 All ER 884	162
IRC v Yorkshire Agricultural Society [1928] 1 KB 611, [1927] 1 All ER Rep 436	161
James, Re, James v James [1935] Ch 449, [1935] All ER Rep 235	68
Jenkins's WT, Re, British Union for the Abolition of Vivisection [1966] Ch 249, [1966] 1 All ER 926	25, 172
Jones v Lock (1865) 1 Ch App 25, 35 LJ Ch 117	64
Josselyn v Josselyn (1837) 9 Sim 63, 59 ER 281	53
Kay's Settlement, Re, Broadbent v McNab [1939] Ch 329, [1939] 1 All ER 245	65, 67
Kayford Ltd, Re [1975] 1 All ER 604, [1975] 1 WLR 279	12
Keech v Sandford (1726) Sel Cas Ch 61, Cas *temp* King 61	112
Keeler's ST, Re, Keeler v Gladhill [1981] Ch 156, [1981] 1 All ER 888	112
Keen, Re, Evershed v Griffiths [1937] Ch 236, [1937] 1 All ER 452	87
Khoo Cheng Teow, Re [1932] Straits Settlement Reports 226	25, 40
Knight v Earl of Plymouth (1747) Dick 120, 3 Atk 480	105
Knocker v Youle [1986] 1 WLR 934	139, 140
Kolb's WT, Re, Lloyds Bank Ltd v Ullman [1962] Ch 531, [1961] 3 All ER 811	125
Lacey, Ex p (1802) 6 Ves 625	111
Laing(JW) Trust, Re, Stewards' Co Ltd v A–G [1984] 1 All ER 50, [1984] Ch 143	172
Lambe v Eames (1871) 6 Ch App 597, 40 LJ Ch 447	10
Leahy v A–G for New South Wales [1959] AC 457, [1959] 2 All ER 300	25
Learoyd v Whiteley (1887) 12 App Cas 727, 57 LJ Ch 390	117
Lipinski's WT, Re [1976] Ch 235, [1977] 1 All ER 33	39
Londonderry's Settlement, Re, Peat v Walsh [1965] Ch 918, [1964] 3 All ER 855	116
Lopes, Re, Bence-Jones v Zoological Society of London [1931] 2 Ch 130, [1930] All ER Rep 45	158

Table of cases xix

PAGE

Lucking's WT, Re, Renwick v Lucking [1967] 3 All ER 726, [1968] 1 WLR
  866 145
Lyell v Kennedy (1889) 14 App Cas 437, 59 LJQB 268 98
Lysaght v Edwards (1876) 2 Ch D 499, 45 LJ Ch 554 61

McGovern v A–G [1982] Ch 321, [1981] 3 All ER 493 165
McPhail v Doulton, Re Baden's Deed Trusts [1971] AC 424, [1970] 2 All
  ER 228 .... 47, 48
Maddock, Re, Llewelyn v Washington [1902] 2 Ch 220, 71 LJ Ch 567 86
Mallott v Wilson [1903] 2 Ch 494, [1900–3] All ER Rep 326 .... 69, 100
Mara v Browne [1896] 1 Ch 199, 65 LJ Ch 225 98
Milroy v Lord (1862) 4 De G F & J 264, [1861–73] All ER Rep 783 63
Molyneux v Fletcher [1898] 1 QB 648, 67 LJQB 392 134
Moncrieff's ST, Re [1962] 3 All ER 838, [1962] 1 WLR 1344 140
Morice v Bishop of Durham (1804) 9 Ves 399, on appeal (1805) 10
  Ves 522 .... 156, 157, 164
Moss v Cooper (1861) 1 John & H 352, 4 LT 790 88
Moyle v Moyle (1831) 2 Russ & My 710, 34 RR 186 115

National Anti-Vivisection Society v IRC [1948] AC 31, [1947] 2 All ER 217   165
National Deposit Friendly Society v Skegness UDC [1959] AC 293, [1958] 2
  All ER 601 163
National Westminster Bank plc v Morgan [1985] AC 686, [1985] 1 WLR 821 . 30
Nelson v Larholt [1948] 1 KB 339, [1947] 2 All ER 751 83
Neo (Yeap Cheah) v Neo (Ong Chen) (1875) LR 6 PC 382 160
Neville Estates Ltd v Madden [1962] Ch 832, [1961] 3 All ER 769 38
New, Re, Re Leavers, Re Morley [1901] 2 Ch 534, [1900–3] All ER
  Rep 763 .... 136, 137, 138
Norfolk's (Duke) ST, Re [1982] Ch 61, [1981] 3 All ER 220 110
Nottage, Re, Jones v Palmer [1895] 2 Ch 649, [1895–9] All ER Rep 1203 ... 163

Oatway, Re, Hertslet v Oatway [1903] 2 Ch 356, 72 LJ Ch 573 150
Oppenheim v Tobacco Securities Trust Co Ltd [1951] AC 297, [1951] 1 All
  ER 31 159
Osoba, Re, Osoba v Osoba [1979] 2 All ER 393, [1979] 1 WLR 247 73
O'Sullivan v Management Agency and Music Ltd [1985] QB 428, [1984] 3
  WLR 448 30
Ottaway v Norman [1972] Ch 698, [1971] 3 All ER 1325 92
Oughtred v IRC [1960] AC 206, [1959] 3 All ER 623 61

Palmer v Simmonds (1854) 2 Drew 221, 2 WR 313 16
Pardoe, Re [1906] 1 Ch 265 166
Parnall v Parnall (1878) 9 Ch D 96, 26 WR 851 17
Paul v Constance [1977] 1 All ER 195, [1977] 1 WLR 527 12
Pauling's ST, Re, Younghusband v Coutts & Co [1961] 3 All ER 713,
  [1962] 1 WLR 86, affd [1964] Ch 303, [1963] 3 All ER 1, CA 134, 145, 147
Pearse v Green (1819) 1 Jac & W 135 115
Pemsel's Case. See CIT v Pemsel
Pettitt v Pettitt [1970] AC 777, [1969] 2 All ER 385 .... 76, 80, 83
Pilkington v IRC [1964] AC 612, [1962] 3 All ER 622 .... 132, 133

xx *Table of cases*

PAGE

Pinion, Re, Westminister Bank Ltd v Pinion [1965] Ch 85, [1964] 1 All ER 890 .... 27, 158
Plumptre's Marriage Settlement, Re, Underhill v Plumptre [1910] 1 Ch 609, 79 LJ Ch 340 64
Power, Re, Public Trustee v Hastings [1947] Ch 572, [1947] 2 All ER 282: 124, 126
Pullan v Koe [1913] 1 Ch 9, [1911–13] All ER Rep 334 .... 64, 65, 66

R v Kneeshaw [1975] QB 57, [1974] 1 All ER 896 147
Ralli's WT, Re, Calvocoressi v Rodocanachi [1964] Ch 288, [1963] 3 All ER 940 62
Ransome, Re, Moberly v Ransome [1957] Ch 348, [1957] 1 All ER 690: 127, 131
Recher's WT, Re, National Westminster Bank, Ltd v National Anti-Vivisection Society Ltd [1972] Ch 526, [1971] 3 All ER 401 38
Rees' WT, Re, Williams v Hopkins [1950] Ch 204, [1949] 2 All ER 1003 ... 73, 86
Regal (Hastings) Ltd v Gulliver [1967] 2 AC 134, [1942] 1 All ER 378 113
Remnant's ST, Re, Hooper v Wenhasten [1970] Ch 560, [1970] 2 All ER 554 141
Rhodesia Goldfields Ltd, Re [1910] 1 Ch 239 146
Richards v Delbridge (1874) LR 18 Eq 11, 43 LJ Ch 459 .... 63, 64
Rochford's ST, Re, Rochford v Rochford [1965] Ch 111, [1964] 2 All ER 177 27
Roscoe (James) (Bolton) Ltd v Winder [1915] 1 Ch 62, 84 LJ Ch 286 150
Rose, Re, Rose v IRC [1952] Ch 499, [1952] 1 All ER 1217 .... 58, 68
Rowntree (Joseph) Memorial Trust Housing Association Ltd v A–G [1983] Ch 159, [1983] 1 All ER 288 .... 157, 163

Salusbury v Denton (1857) 3 K & J 529, 26 LJ Ch 851 17
Sanderson's Trust, Re (1857) 3 K & J 497, 26 LJ Ch 804 73
Satterthwaite's WT, Re, Midland Bank Executor and Trustee Co Ltd v Royal Veterinary College [1966] 1 All ER 919, [1966] 1 WLR 277 174
Saunders v Vautier (1841) 4 Beav 115, [1835–42] All ER Rep 58 .... 53, 135, 138
Scott, Re [1975] 1 WLR 1260, [1975] 2 All ER 1033 72
Scottish Burial Reform and Cremation Society v Glasgow City Corp [1968] AC 138, [1967] 3 All ER 215 161
Sharpe, Re [1980] 1 All ER 198, [1980] 1 WLR 219 79
Sinclair v Brougham [1914] AC 398, [1914–15] All ER Rep 622 149
Smith, Re, Public Trustee v Smith [1932] 1 Ch 153, [1931] All ER Rep 617 . 164
Smith's WT, Re, Barclays Bank Ltd v Mercantile Bank Ltd [1962] 2 All ER 563, [1962] 1 WLR 763 161
Snowden, Re, Smith v Spowage [1979] Ch 528, [1979] 2 All ER 172 91
Somerset,Re [1887] WN 122 102
South Place Ethical Society, Re [1980] 3 All ER 918, [1980] 1 WLR 1565: 159, 162
Speight, Re, Speight v Gaunt (1883) 22 Ch D 727 105
Stead, Re, Witham v Andrew [1900] 1 Ch 237, 69 LJ Ch 49 88
Stephenson v Barclays Bank Trust Co Ltd [1975] 1 All ER 625 54
Stickland v Aldridge (1804) 9 Ves 516 86
Stone v Stone (1869) 5 Ch App 74, 39 LJ Ch 196 66
Stratheden and Campbell (Lord), Re [1894] 3 Ch 265, 63 LJ Ch 872 161
Strong v Bird (1874) LR18 Eq 315, [1874–80] All ER Rep 230 68

Table of cases xxi

PAGE

Suffert's Settlement, Re, Suffert v Martyn-Linnington [1961] Ch 1, [1960] 3 All ER 561 140
T's ST, Re [1964] Ch 158, [1963] 3 WLR 987, 107 Sol Jo 981, sub nom Re Towler's ST [1963] 3 All ER 759 139
Tempest, Re (1866) 1 Ch App 485, 35 LJ Ch 632 99
Thomas v Howell (1874) LR 18 Eq 198 161
Thellusson v Woodford (1805) 11 Ves 112, 8 RR 104 26
Thompson's ST, Re [1985] 2 All ER 720 111
Thrupp v Collett (1858) 26 Beav 125 .... 27, 28
Thynn v Thynn (1684) 1 Vern 296, 1 Eq Cas Abr 380 91
Tilley's WT, Re, Burgin v Croad [1967] 2 Ch 1179, [1967] 2 All ER 303 151
Timmis, Re, Nixon v Smith [1902] 1 Ch 176, 71 LJ Ch 118 147
Tinker v Tinker [1970] P 136, [1970] 1 All ER 540 77
Tinker's Settlement, Re [1960] 3 All ER 85, [1960] 1 WLR 1101 142
Tito v Waddell (No 2) [1977] Ch 106, [1977] 3 All ER 129 .... 111, 146
Tollemache, Re [1903] 1 Ch 457, 72 LJ Ch 225 137
Turner v Turner [1983] 2 All ER 745, [1984] Ch 100 107

Utley, Re, Russell v Cubitt [1912] WN 147, 106 LT 858 115

Van Gruisen's WT, Re, Bagger v Dean [1964] 1 All ER 843, [1964] 1 WLR 449 141
Vandervell v IRC [1966] Ch 261, [1965] 2 All ER 37 .... 58, 71
Vickery, Re, Vickery v Stephens [1931] 1 Ch 572, [1931] All ER Rep 562 .. 108
Vinogradoff, Re, Allen v Jackson [1935] WN 68 .... 75, 95
Vynior's Case (1609) 8 Rep 8lb 90

Ward-Smith v Jebb (1964) 108 Sol Jo 919 145
Way's Trust, Re (1865) 2 De G J & S 365, 34 LJ Ch 49 10
Wedgwood, Re, Allen v Wedgwood [1915] 1 Ch 113, [1914–15] All ER Rep 322 161
Weston's Settlements, Re [1969] 1 Ch 223, [1968] 3 All ER 338 142
Wheeler and De Rochow, Re [1896] 1 Ch 315, 65 LJ Ch 219 101
White v Paine (1914) 83 LJKB 895, 30 TLR 347 14
Wilson v Turner (1883) 22 Ch D 521, 52 LJ Ch 270 130
Wilson, Re, Twentyman v Simpson [1913] 1 Ch 314, 82 LJ Ch 161 173

Young, Re, Young v Young [1951] Ch 344, [1950] 2 All ER 1245 86

Part I
The creation of a trust

Chapter 1
Introduction

THE TRUST CONCEPT

The invention of the trust is perhaps the most outstanding achievement of English law, and, like many great inventions, the idea is extremely simple.

If a person owns a farm, we may say that the rights he has as owner are of two different sorts. He has the right to have title to the farm, so that his name appears on the title deeds; and he has the right to enjoy the farm, so that he can live in the farmhouse, eat some of the produce and sell the remainder, or, if he prefers, let the farm and receive the rent. These two sorts of right are called respectively, the 'legal estate' and the 'beneficial interest', and both are normally comprised in ownership of an asset. A trust is simply the state of affairs which exists when the legal estate is separated from the beneficial interest. So if there is a trust of a farm, instead of there being one person who owns the farm, there will be one person (or group of persons) who owns the legal estate in the farm – the trustee or trustees – and one person (or group of persons) who owns the beneficial interest in the farm – the beneficiary or beneficiaries.

It is particularly important to notice the word 'owns' in the last sentence. A trust is not like a lease, where the tenant is living in the farm because the landlord (who owns the farm) allows him to by contract. When there is a trust, the beneficial interest is not the trustee's to dispose of: it *belongs to* the beneficiary. The beneficiary has the right to enjoy the farm or the income from it not because the trustee chooses to let him, but because he, not the trustee, *owns* that right. The legal estate owner does not, as such, have any right to benefit from the trust property, but must use his rights for the benefit of the beneficial owner only. If he occupies the farm himself, he holds the profits on behalf of the beneficial owner, and if he grants a lease of the farm, he receives the rent on behalf of the beneficial owner. In short, the trustee has a duty to manage the trust property for the benefit not of himself but of the beneficiary. We can no longer say that anyone owns the farm, because the trust divides the rights of ownership between trustee and beneficiary. What we can say is that trustee and beneficiary have rights in the farm, and the rights of both of them are real rights, proprietary rights, rights of ownership.

The rights of the trustee and the rights of the beneficiary are, however, rather different from each other. Anybody looking from outside the trust will see the trustee as owner of the property which is the subject matter of the trust. If it is land, it will be the trustee whose name is on the title deeds; if it is shares, they will be registered in the name of the trustee; if it is money, the bank account will be in the trustee's name. And a purchaser of the trust property will take a conveyance from, and will pay the purchase money to, the trustee. These are all consequences of the fact that the trustee has the legal estate.

At first, in the early Middle Ages, the legal estate was all that a court would recognise: the trust remained a matter of the trustworthiness of the trustee. If he recognised the rights of the beneficiaries, all was well; but if he chose to dispose of the trust property, or even to make use of it himself, there was nothing the beneficiaries could do. They did not have the legal estate, so they had no right that a court would enforce.

Gradually, however, it came to be realised that in taking this attitude the legal system was placing too much emphasis on rights at the expense of duties. Granted that the trustee had the rights appertaining to the legal estate, he also had a duty to hold that estate in such a way that the beneficiaries had the benefit of the property. The law courts would not recognise the duty; but surely in justice and fairness it had to be recognised. Disappointed beneficiaries began to appeal to the king as 'fountain of justice' for their rights to be enforced; he delegated the cases to his Chancellor. And so there grew up, parallel to the system of law administered in the courts of common law, a system of justice or 'equity' administered in the Chancellor's court. The Chancellor worked at first on broad principles of fairness which have become known as the 'maxims of equity'. We shall come across several of them in later chapters, but perhaps the most important for present purposes is 'equity acts on the person'. Whereas the law courts enforced a person's legal rights, equity would act against him and make him perform his duties, especially his 'fiduciary' duties arising from the fact that he had undertaken a trust.

The trust concept 5

The Chancellor's court was busy, and soon there was no need to rely greatly on principle because a body of precedent was building up as it had done in the law courts. The rules of equity, under which the duties of trustees were enforced, became as firm and predictable as the rules of law. Now as soon as it could be predicted what a court would do, it became possible to talk about rights. It could be said that whereas the trustee had legal rights the beneficiary had equitable rights. The trustee's legal rights would be enforced in a court of common law, but the beneficiary's equitable rights would be enforced by a court of equity's obliging the trustee to do his fiduciary duty. Although the two systems, law and equity, existed in parallel, equitable rights were in no way inferior to legal rights, and indeed since the early seventeenth century the position has been that where law and equity conflict, equity prevails: the equitable rights of the beneficiary of a trust take precedence over the legal rights of the trustee.

Since 1875, the rules of law and the rules of equity have been administered in the same courts, but they still retain their own identity. As this is a book on trusts, it is mostly concerned with rules of equity, but there are two areas in particular where common law interacts with equity. One is discussed in Chapter 4, where we shall see the common law Rule against Perpetuities is applied with rigour (and without any tempering of justice) to trusts which may last for too long. The other relates to the constitution of trusts, which is a difficult topic to understand precisely because the common law rules of contract and equity's recognition of the trust together produce such a hotchpotch of solutions to different situations.

Reverting, then, to the basic concept, we can now say that a trust has three characteristics. First, the legal estate and the beneficial interest in the trust property are separated; secondly, the trustee has an equitable fiduciary duty to hold the trust property for the beneficiary; thirdly, the beneficiary has an equitable proprietary interest in the property. In short, a trust is a combination of proprietary rights and fiduciary duties with respect to an asset.

Four matters require mention before we proceed further.

1 *Trustee–beneficiary.* There may be (and usually is) more than one trustee; there may be (and usually is) more than one beneficiary. There is nothing to stop the same person being one of the trustees and one of the beneficiaries. So *A* may hold on trust for *A* and *B*, or *A* and *B* may hold on trust for *A*, or *A*, *B* and *C* may hold on trust for *A*, *B* and *D*.

6 Introduction

2 *Sources*. The sources of the rules of equity are, as we have seen above, precedent and principle. There are also a number of statutes relating to trusts. It often happens, however, that a statute re-enacts either a previous statute or an established rule or practice of equity. There is therefore no cause for surprise if, in the discussion of a statutory rule, reference is made to a case decided before the statute was passed.

3 *Courts*. Matters relating to trusts come before the county court if the value of the trust property is less than £30,000, otherwise before the Chancery Division of the High Court. In either case there is a possibility of an appeal on a point of law to the Court of Appeal and again to the House of Lords.

4 *Deceased's estate*. When a person dies his estate passes to his 'personal representatives'. If he appointed personal representatives by his will they are 'executors'; otherwise they will need to be appointed by the court and are 'administrators'. Personal representatives owe fiduciary duties but they are not trustees. They have full ownership of the deceased's assets and their duties are to the estate as a whole, not to any particular persons entitled to it. Trusts are, however, often created by will, and the deceased may have appointed the same persons as his executors and trustees. Then their first duty is to act as executors, and on completion of the administration of the estate they take their duties as trustees, at which point beneficial ownership of the trust property passes to the beneficiaries of the will trust.

THE FUNCTIONS OF TRUSTS

Trusts vary according to the mode of their creation. They may be created expressly (intentionally) by a settlor, or implied by the rules of equity, or imposed by statute. The functions of the three types are different.

Express trusts. An express trust is created when the owner of an asset intentionally divides its legal title from its beneficial interest, either by keeping one and parting with the other, or by parting with both to different people (or groups of people). For an express trust to be valid, there must be certainty of words (Chapter 2), subject matter (Chapter 3) and objects (Chapter 5). The trust must comply with any requisite formalities (Chapter 2) and must be constituted (Chapter 6). There must be beneficiaries by whom or on whose behalf the trust can be enforced (Chapter 5) or else the trust must be for a charitable purpose (Chapter 16).

An express trust is an instrument of property management. By creating a trust the settlor can divide the beneficial interest in ways that would be impossible or undesirable if it remained attached to the legal estate. So he can, for example, provide that income from the property is to go to his wife while she is alive, and after her death the beneficial interest is to belong to his son: more technically this is 'on trust for his wife for life with remainder to his son'. Or he can give the beneficial interest in his farm to his four children equally, without having to divide up the farm itself: he will convey it to trustees to hold on trust for his children in equal shares. Or he can give the benefit of property to infants too young to manage it for themselves, or even to children not yet born; and he may further provide that children who die before attaining the age of majority should not receive any capital: 'on trust for such of the children of my daughter Amy as shall attain the age of 18'. The concept is infinitely flexible. In short, the purpose of an express trust is to give the beneficiaries the benefit of property without giving them the legal title to it.

Trusts implied by equity. In certain situations equity considers that a person who indubitably has the legal title to property should nevertheless not be allowed to benefit from it. Equity therefore imposes a trust upon him which, according to the circumstances, may be either a resulting trust (Chapter 7) or a constructive trust (Chapter 8). The outcome is that the legal owner, instead of holding for himself, holds on trust for those who ought to have the beneficial interest in the property. The function of trusts implied by equity is therefore quite different from that of express trusts. Instead of being created primarily in order to give the beneficial interest to the beneficiary, their primary purpose is to take the beneficial interest away from the owner of the legal estate.

The phrase 'implied trusts' should be avoided. It has been used to signify so many different concepts that it is hopelessly ambiguous and, as a result, almost meaningless.

Statutory trusts. Trusts are imposed by statute in a number of well-defined areas. The most important is in the administration of the estate of a person who dies intestate, where, after discharging debts and duties, the administrators hold on the trusts set out in the Administration of Estates Act 1925 as amended.

8   *Introduction*

The difference in function between express trusts and trusts implied by equity is seen most vividly in the fact that the former are intended to continue for some time whereas the latter are normally recognised only in order to be terminated. Once a legal owner realises that he is (or is declared by a court to be) a resulting or constructive trustee the next step will usually be for him to transfer the property to those entitled to the beneficial interest. Part II of this book, which deals with the administration of trusts, is directed mostly, therefore, to express trusts. Charitable trusts are the subject of Part III.

A NOTE ABOUT EXAMS

Experience shows that many candidates for professional examinations score low marks on their trusts questions although they appear to have learnt quite a lot of the law. The following words of advice, therefore, may be useful. First, in preparing for the exam, give greater priority to understanding each topic than to memorising every detail. A list of 'decided cases' will be marked at zero even if they are all relevant; but the candidate who writes a short, clear summary of the area in question will score a good mark even if he mentions no authorities at all. The examiner does not want to know whether you can learn by rote: he wants to know whether you have any acquaintance with the principles of the law. Besides, it is easier to remember material you understand than it is to memorise a meaningless list of names. Secondly, always confine yourself to answering the question set. Do not tell the examiner about the 'three certainties' or define a trust for him unless he has asked you to: you are wasting valuable time. You will be given no marks for irrelevant information. Thirdly, it may be a help to know that this book has been conceived with special regard to the mistakes most commonly made by candidates in professional examinations.

Dates. In the text, the name of each case is followed by the date when it was decided. This date is for information only, and need not be learnt, although you should be aware whether the case is old or recent. The date at the end of the name of a statute is, however, part of the name and should be included if you mention the statute.

Chapter 2
Formalities

A person who intends to create a trust may carry out his intention in one of two ways.

(1) If he himself, as well as being the settlor, is to be the sole trustee, he may make a declaration that he is henceforth trustee of property which he has hitherto held beneficially.
(2) Otherwise, he must part with the property by transferring it from his ownership to that of the trustees and declare that they are to hold as trustees, not as beneficial owners.

We shall see that problems can arise in the latter (and much more common) case. For the settlor must actually transfer the property, if that is what he is trying to do; and to transfer the property he needs to comply with the formalities for the transfer of that particular kind of property. These problems, however, are concerned principally with the transfer, and do not relate specifically to the creation of a trust. They are covered in Chapter 6. Here we are concerned with the formalities for the creation of the trust itself. What must the settlor do so that a court will recognise that he has created a trust, rather than (1) remained sole owner, or (2) made his transferees sole owners, as the case may be?

The answer is to be found in the maxim 'equity looks to the intention and not to the form'. There must be enough done for the court to be able to see that the settlor did indeed intend to create a trust; but, on the other hand, no particular form or method of declaration of trust is necessary except where required by statute.

CERTAINTY OF WORDS

Whatever means the settlor uses to create his trust, he must, by words or conduct, show an intent to create a present trust. So, first, an intention, however firmly and publicly expressed, to create a trust in the future, will not suffice because the settlor has not shown an intention to create a *present* trust (ie one to take effect immediately).

Secondly, an undeclared or secret intention to hold property on trust for another will not suffice, because the intention is not *shown*. As property rights change when a trust is created, it is obviously important that the existence of the trust is not something which is known solely to the settlor. The rule that the intention must be shown is, however, of the nature of a rule of evidence: there must be some evidence of the existence of the trust. It is not necessary that the existence of the trust be communicated to any *particular* person. In *Re Way's Trust* (1865) the settlor was beneficially entitled to an equitable interest under a trust, which she assigned by deed in 1852 to trustees on trust for her sisters, with remainders over. But she kept the deed herself, and apparently told nobody about it. The trustees of the settlement under which she held her interest, the trustees appointed by her, and even those named in her deed as beneficiaries, remained in ignorance of it. Later, she repented of her generosity, destroyed the deed, and made a will disposing of the property differently. Her solicitor was, however, able to give evidence of the contents of the 1852 deed, which was thus upheld as a valid declaration of trust although none of the people affected by it had known it existed. So the beneficiaries named in it, not those named in the settlor's will, were entitled to the equitable interest, because by the time she died the interest was no longer hers to dispose of.

Thirdly, what the settlor is required to show is an intention to create a *trust*. A trust is not a way in which the trustee may choose to deal with the property, but is the way in which he is obliged to deal with the property. So it is not enough that the settlor wished, or desired, or even that he intended his transferee to deal with the property in a particular way: it must be shown that he intended the transferee to be *obliged* to deal with it in that way. As Lindley LJ said in *Re Hamilton* (1895), 'we are bound to see that beneficiaries [of a will] are not made trustees unless intended to be made so by their testator'. This is the so-called rule of certainty of words. It is sometimes said to derive from *Lambe v Eames* (1871), but that case was, in fact, merely one of a number in which the rule was established. Another was *Re Adams and The Kensington Vestry* (1884) where a testator left all his estate to his widow 'in full confidence that she will do what is right as to the disposal thereof between my children'. It was held that the wording of the will was merely precatory (ie expressing a wish) and so the widow took free of any trust.

If, therefore, a testator leaves property by will to persons who are not obliged by the language of the will to take as trustees, those persons take beneficially. If a person makes an inter vivos (lifetime) gift to persons who are not obliged by the terms of the gift to take as trustees, those persons will, depending on their relationship to the settlor and the type of property, take either beneficially or on presumed resulting trust for the settlor himself. In neither case will they take on trust for others whom they were 'desired' to benefit.

STATUTORY REQUIREMENTS

The law requires writing in connection with the creation of express trusts of land, and trusts of any property taking effect on the settlor's death.

Land. 'A declaration of trust respecting any land or any interest therein must be manifested and proved by some writing signed by some person who is able to declare such trust or by his will' (Law of Property Act 1925, s 53(1)(b)). Notice that the declaration of trust does not have to be in writing: there merely has to be written evidence of it. If there is no writing, the trust is probably not void, but unenforceable. If an action is brought in which the existence of the trust is in issue, the trust will be found not to exist unless there is some written reference to it and its provisions, signed by the settlor and dating from before the commencement of the action. The writing need not be contemporaneous with the declaration of trust, but might be, for example, a later letter from the settlor, or, as the section expressly envisages, a reference in the settlor's will.

Testamentary dispositions. Any gift (including a gift by way of trust) which is to take effect at the settlor's death, and is to be revocable by him until death, must be made by will. The will must comply with the provisions of the Wills Act 1837, s 9 (as substituted by the Administration of Justice Act 1982, s 17). Broadly, there are three requirements: the will must be in writing, signed by the testator, and his signature must be witnessed by two witnesses who must also sign. If these provisions are fulfilled the will is properly executed and valid; otherwise it is totally void and the deceased's property will be distributed as on intestacy.

12 Formalities

There are two exceptions to the rule that trusts to take effect on death must be in a properly executed will. The first is that a soldier on actual military service, or a mariner or seaman at sea, may make a valid will without any formality. It does not even have to be in writing. The second exception relates to secret trusts. A testator may impose obligations of trusteeship on persons to whom he leaves property by will, without mentioning those obligations in the will itself. The conditions developed by the courts for enforcing such trusts are discussed in Chapter 9.

It follows that a settlor who wishes to create a lifetime trust of property other than land or an interest in land may do so without formality, provided he makes his intention clear. Not only is no particular form necessary; no particular words are necessary either. He does not have to use the word 'trust' if the notion of a trust can be construed from what he says or does. Two interesting modern examples of the informal creation of trusts, one by colloquial language, and one by conduct without words, are *Paul v Constance* (1977) and *Re Kayford Ltd* (1975).

In *Paul v Constance* the property in question was a bank account in the name of Mr Constance. It consisted largely of a sum which he had received as damages for injuries suffered at work; but there had been some other payments into the account, particularly joint bingo winnings of Mr Constance and Mrs Paul, his mistress, with whom he had lived since before the account was opened. There had been one withdrawal of £150 which was divided between the two of them. The evidence showed that frequently when they discussed the account, Mr Constance had said to Mrs Paul, 'the money is as much yours as mine'. After Mr Constance's death, it was necessary to decide whether he had during his life declared a trust of the account for himself and Mrs Paul in equal shares (in which case only half of the balance would go to his next of kin) or not (in which case it all would). The Court of Appeal, upholding the judge at first instance, held that, in the circumstances, the words 'the money is as much yours as mine' were an express declaration of a present trust. No technical language was used, but, as Scarman LJ pointed out, the case was concerned not with lawyers, but 'with simple people, unaware of the subtleties of equity, but understanding very well indeed their own domestic situation'.

Re Kayford Ltd concerned a company in voluntary liquidation. While it was trading it had carried on a mail-order business. Its managers realised that it might be about to be in financial difficulties and wanted to protect customers' money against a possible liquidation. Therefore they arranged that deposits and payments made by customers for goods which had not yet been delivered should be put into a separate bank account. The original intention was that the account should be entitled 'Customers' Trust Deposit Account', but that name was apparently not used by the bank until after the liquidation. Megarry J held that there had been an effective declaration of trust by the company's conduct. He said:

'I feel no doubt that here a trust was created. . . . The whole purpose of what was done was to ensure that the moneys remained in the beneficial ownership of those who sent them, and a trust is the obvious means of achieving this.'

The customers' money was held on trust for the customers, and was not available to the general creditors in the liquidation.

Although it is important to appreciate that express trusts can be, and sometimes are, created orally or by conduct, one may safely say that the vast majority of them are in fact made by written instrument. The reason is not only that if the trust is at all complex there will need to be something written down to which reference can be made in future years: it is also advisable to comply with the practical requirements of the Inland Revenue, which will want written proof of the terms of the trust and its date before it will be prepared to take the trust into account in reduction of the settlor's tax liability.

Chapter 3
The trust property

WHAT CAN BE THE SUBJECT MATTER OF A TRUST?

Anything capable of being owned may be the subject matter of a trust. There are very few exceptions to this rule. So the trust property may be realty (land) or personalty; it may be a chose in action, such as stock or shares, or the right to be paid a debt or to sue for one; if there is a contract for valuable consideration it may be a contractual right to an expectancy, where some asset has not yet come into existence or does not yet belong to the settlor; it may itself be an equitable interest. A trust of a person's interest under some other trust is often called a 'resettlement' or 'sub-trust'. How generous the courts are prepared to be in regarding property as capable of being the subject matter of a valid trust can be seen from *White v Paine* (1914), where part of the trust property was a herd of deer – not, it will be noted, the individual animals, but the herd as a whole, consisting of the animals which from time to time belonged to it.

Since, however, the creation of a trust necessarily involves the settlor's alienating some interest in the property, it is not possible to have a trust of property which the settlor is not permitted to alienate. Public policy prohibits the alienation of the right to alimony or maintenance granted by court order, or to any pension or salary granted to enable the recipient to perform public duties properly. Statutes prohibit the alienation of forces' pay and pensions and certain other pensions.

Land

When the trust property is a legal estate in land, the form of the trust is governed by special rules contained in the Law of Property Act 1925 and the Settled Land Act 1925. The principal purpose of the 1925 legislation was to simplify conveyancing. It requires that all interests in land, other than a fee simple absolute in possession or a term of years absolute (roughly speaking, a freehold or a leasehold completely owned in each case by one adult), exist only as equitable interests under trusts. Where there is only one beneficiary of the trust and he is adult and of full capacity and has an interest which is as large as the trustees', or where the land is given exclusively to charitable purposes, no problem arises. Where, however, a legal estate in land is to be given to a minor, or to several people together, or to persons in succession (to A for life remainder to B), or for an entailed interest (to A and the heirs of his body), or for a determinable interest (to A until he remarries), then the land must be settled in one of two specified ways. The two types of trust of land are as follows:

1 *Trust for sale.* The legal estate is conveyed to trustees, who have a duty to sell it and to hold the proceeds of sale upon the trusts declared by the settlor. Their duty to sell is normally coupled with a power to delay sale and any sale may be subject to certain conditions. But because they have a duty to sell, and 'equity looks on that as done which ought to be done', the land is regarded for most purposes as having already been sold, so that the beneficiaries' rights are, in principle, in the proceeds of sale of the land, not in the land itself. A purchaser of the land can therefore safely buy from the trustees, because the beneficiaries will have no rights against his land. On the other hand, because the trustees have a power to postpone sale, the beneficiaries may expect, as a practical matter, to remain in enjoyment of the land itself for as long as they wish to do so, particularly since the trust may require the consent of one or more of the beneficiaries before a sale takes place.

2 *Strict settlement.* The legal estate is conveyed by one document, the vesting deed, to the person presently entitled to possession of the land, the tenant for life. That document also contains the names of certain parties called the trustees of the settlement. A second document, the trust instrument, contains the details of the trusts of the land. The tenant for life has power to deal with the land, including power to sell it or mortgage it, and his power cannot be restricted in any way. A purchaser of the land takes a conveyance from the tenant for life (who has the legal estate), but must pay the purchase money to the trustees of the settlement. He is not concerned at all with the contents of the trust instrument and is not, in fact, entitled to see it. If a sale takes place, the trustees of the settlement hold the purchase money upon the trusts set out in the trust instrument.

The strict settlement formed an essential part of the old method of keeping land in a family. Since 1925 it has been possible to achieve the same results in almost every case by creating a trust for sale, and new strict settlements are rarely created today. The trust for sale is simpler and hence cheaper, and it has been suggested that little would be lost if the law were reformed to require all settlements of a legal interest in land to be by way of trust for sale. In the meantime, however, any conveyance of land for a limited interest, or for successive interests, or to a minor, takes effect as a strict settlement unless it is made on trust for sale either expressly or by law (as in the case of land in the estate of an intestate). It is certain that many strict settlements are created unintentionally by persons who indulge in such perilous pastimes as writing their own wills.

The rules just discussed apply only to trusts of a legal estate in land. There are additional formal requirements for the declaration of a trust respecting land or any interest in land, for example equitable interests under a trust for sale or strict settlement. These have been considered in Chapter 2.

CERTAINTY OF SUBJECT MATTER

The settlor of an express trust must make it clear what property is to be subject to the trust. If he does not do so, there is no trust as there is no property on which it can 'bite'. So where a testator left 'the bulk of my said residuary estate' upon trust, the trust failed for there was no way of telling what 'the bulk' was (*Palmer v Simmonds* (1854)). Likewise a gift with directions that a fund should accumulate interest until it amounted to   for building a hospital for   boys failed as regards the charitable trust. The court could not fill in the blanks (*Ewen v Bannerman* (1830)). However, if the settlor gives the court sufficient guidance it will strain to uphold the gift. So in *Re Golay's WT* (1965), where a testator directed that his executors should allow *A* a 'reasonable income' from his properties, the gift was held valid: the court could, if necessary, decide how much a 'reasonable income' was.

If the trust property is to be held variously for different beneficiaries, certainty is also required as to the extent of each beneficiary's interest. In *Boyce v Boyce* (1849) a testator devised his houses on trust to give to *M* whichever one she chose, and the others to *C*. *M* predeceased the testator without making a choice. It was clear that the houses were held on trust, but impossible to tell which were held on trust for *C*. Her interest therefore failed, and the trustees held all the houses on automatic resulting trust for the estate. Likewise, if property is given to *A* or on trust for *A*, and *A*'s interest is meant to be subject to a gift of an uncertain part of the property to *B* or on trust for *B*, the gift to *B* will fail and the gift to *A* will consequently be enlarged. In *Parnall v Parnall* (1878) a testator bequeathed certain property to his wife, with a direction that whatever might remain at her death be equally divided between his children. Because of the terms of the gift it would be uncertain during the wife's lifetime how much was hers absolutely and how much she held on trust for herself for life with remainder to the testator's children. The gift to the children therefore failed and the wife took absolutely.

When a certain amount of property is given to be divided among various beneficiaries for concurrent interests, but the proportions to be applied to each beneficiary are not stated, the court will make its own division, unless there is a clear, contrary indication from the settlor (as there was in *Boyce v Boyce*). It is particularly apt to do so where an uncertain part is to be applied to charitable purposes. The division will be into equal parts, applying the maxim 'equality is equity', unless that would produce an absurd result. So in *Salusbury v Denton* (1857) the gift was to the trustee to apply 'part' for a charitable endowment for the poor and 'the remainder' for the testator's next of kin. Half was applied under a charitable scheme and half went to the next of kin. A common type of trust with a clear indication that the property should not be divided equally is the discretionary trust, where the amounts of the beneficiaries' interests are fixed by the trustee in his discretion. The court works on the principle that that is certain which is capable of being made certain; so the trust does not fail for uncertainty of subject matter, because the trustee cures the defect.

Chapter 4
Void and voidable trusts

A trust which is created with the purpose of contravening some principle of public policy or morality or which will result in doing so may be void or voidable. If it is void, it is of no effect. If it is voidable, it will remain in force unless it is cancelled or modified, normally by court order. Of void trusts the most important are those which contravene the Rule against Perpetuities, which was evolved many years ago with reference to dispositions of land, but is, in practice, nowadays largely concerned with trusts of personalty. Trusts which tend to promote a purpose which is criminal or immoral, and some trusts restraining marriage, are also void. A trust is likely to be voidable if it attempts or tends to place the settlor's property beyond the reach of those who have a just claim upon it – his creditors, his spouse upon divorce, or his dependants upon his death – or if for some other reason it is inequitable that the settlor should be held to it.

THE RULE AGAINST PERPETUITIES

One of the settlor's principal purposes in setting up a trust, whether during his lifetime or at his death, is likely to be to control the disposition of his property for some time into the future. By giving a life interest he can ensure that a beneficiary obtains the income without being able to squander the capital and so prejudice his heirs; by creating a discretionary trust he can enable a group of people to receive what they each need without leaving them to fight over their inheritance; and so on. It is, however, against the policy of the law for a person to be able to control property for too long a period after his death. There are two reasons for this. First, control by a settlor 'from the grave' prevents the beneficiaries from having full power over the property, and this state of affairs may not be appropriate for more than a couple of generations after the settlor. Secondly, a trust ties up the property itself, because while the trust is in existence the trust property has to be in the trustee's hands to satisfy the claims of the beneficiaries. The amount of property available is finite; so unless there were some rule to prevent it we might reach a situation where the economy ground to a halt because too great a proportion of the country's wealth was taken out of commerce by being bound by trusts. In particular, if perpetual trusts were allowed it is probable that by now there would be no piece of land in England not held under some trust. Therefore from the seventeenth century onwards the courts developed a system of rules to prevent property of any kind from being tied up indefinitely. Those rules have been modified by a number of statutes. The result is the system known (collectively) as the Rule against Perpetuities, the effect of which is that any gift or direction which breaches the Rule, or any part of it, is void.

It must be admitted that experience shows that parts of the Rule are difficult to apprehend; and the learning associated with some of its details is, to say the least, abstruse. Experienced lawyers sometimes draft settlements which (accidentally) break the Rule, thus wasting both their efforts and their fees. For present purposes we do not need to trouble about the details, but we must establish the basic structure and principles of the Rule.

As mentioned above, the Rule derives from both precedent and legislation. The most notable statute from this point of view is the Perpetuities and Accumulations Act 1964, which made a number of far-reaching but piecemeal changes. It did not, however, replace or even restate the Rule; it merely modified it, and with two important restrictions. First, the Act only applies to instruments taking effect after 15 July 1964. There are many trusts still in existence which derive from an instrument which took effect well before that date, for example the will of a settlor who died in 1952. Secondly, the Act only applies to gifts and directions which would be void if it were not for the Act. A gift or direction which would be void under the common law (i e pre-1964) Rule may be saved by the Act; but the Act has no application to a gift or direction which is valid under the common law Rule.

It follows that to determine whether a trust or a direction in a trust infringes the Rule against Perpetuities it is necessary to be familiar both with the Rule as it was before the passing of the Perpetuities and Accumulations Act 1964, and with the Act itself, and then to ask three basic questions:

1 At what date did the instrument creating the trust take effect? (If the trust is a lifetime trust the relevant date will be when

the instrument was executed; if a will trust, the date of the settlor's death.) If the instrument creating the trust took effect before 16 July 1964, it must be judged *solely* by the common law Rule. Otherwise:
2   Is the trust valid under the common law Rule? If so, the Act is not needed, and does not apply to it. Otherwise:
3   Is the trust, though void by the common law Rule, saved by the Act?

The Rule against Perpetuities has three quite separate parts: the rule against remoteness of vesting; the rule against inalienability of income; and the rule against accumulation of income. We shall treat each in turn. To be valid, a trust must not infringe the Rule in any of its aspects.

1   *The rule against remoteness of vesting*

The rule against remoteness of vesting is the rule which prohibits too long a period elapsing between the time the trust takes effect and the time when the beneficiaries attain a realistic interest in the property. As its name suggests, this rule does not allow an interest to 'vest' at a date which is too remote from the date of the relevant instrument. An interest is said to be vested when the person who is to take it is alive and identified, his share of the property is ascertained, and all conditions have been fulfilled so that he is ready to take subject to any prior interests. So if A is alive and aged 14, a gift to 'A for life' is vested but a gift to 'A for life if he shall attain the age of 21' is not (yet); if the remainder is 'to such of X's children as shall attain the age of 25 in equal shares' it will not vest in interest in any of them until (i) X is dead (so that he can have no more children) and (ii) all X's children have either attained the age of 25 or died under that age. Only then will the share of each beneficiary be ascertained. Notice the use of the phrase 'vest in interest'. A gift may vest in interest even though the person in whom it vests has no present right to the propery: he is ready to take *subject to any prior interests*. A gift to 'A for life with remainder to B if he attains the age of 25' is vested in A straightaway and is vested in interest in B as soon as B attains the age of 25 even though A is still alive. B is ascertained, as is his share (100%), all necessary conditions are fulfilled (B has attained the age of 25), and B is ready to take, subject to A's prior life interest. B's remainder is a vested interest. Speaking very broadly, an interest is vested when it is (subject to actuarial valuation) saleable. In the last example B has nothing to sell until he has celebrated his 25th birthday; thereafter, although he has no immediate right to benefit from the property he has a saleable future interest in it.

At common law the rule against remoteness of vesting is as follows: *To be valid, each interest under a trust must be defined in such a way that it cannot vest later than 21 years after the death of a life in being.* A 'life in being' is a person (anyone) alive, or at any rate conceived, at the time the trust instrument takes effect; and a life in being plus 21 years is often called 'the perpetuity period'. A period of gestation may be added to the 21 years whenever necessary. Look at the rule again: 'each interest must be *defined* in such a way that it *cannot* vest' outside the perpetuity period. We are concerned with definition – the words of the instrument – and with possibilities – 'cannot'. We are not concerned with probabilities or practicalities. The gift must be defined so that, because of the way it is expressed, it is *logically impossible* for an interest to vest more than 21 years after the death of a person alive at the date the instrument took effect. If it is logically possible (however unlikely) for an interest to vest outside the perpetuity period, the gift is void.

Let us consider some examples.

(a) A gift in X's will 'to such of my grandchildren as shall attain the age of 21 years'.

We saw above that this gift will not vest until X's grandchildren have all either attained the age of 21 or died under that age. It must now be considered when that might happen. The gift is in a will, so X is dead when it takes effect. All X's children are therefore already born (or, at any rate, conceived). They are either alive, or have already died. Suppose they are alive. Then they are lives in being. Any child of theirs (who would be X's grandchild) must be born (or conceived) within his parents' lifetimes, that is, during the life of at least one life in being. So their children must, if they attain the age of 21 at all, do so within 21 years after the death of a life in being. Suppose on the other hand that X's children (or some of them) are dead. Then *their* children (X's grandchildren) are already born (or conceived). These grandchildren are themselves lives in being and obviously must attain the age of 21 within their own lifetimes, if at all. Therefore any grandchild of X who attains the age of 21 is bound to do so within 21 years after the death of a life in being. It is logically impossible for this gift to vest outside the perpetuity period. It is therefore valid by the common law rule.

22 Void and voidable trusts

(b) The same gift, but in a trust made during X's lifetime.

The reasoning of example (a) depended on the fact that as X was dead his children must all be either lives in being or themselves already dead. The present example differs because as X is still alive at the date the instrument takes effect he may subsequently have a child who, of course, would not be a life in being. That child might have a child (X's grandchild) at a time when all those alive at the date the instrument took effect were dead. Here, then, is a *logical possibility* of a grandchild of X attaining the age of 21 outside the perpetuity period. The gift is void by the common law rule. It does not matter that X is extremely unlikely to have another child because he is aged 104 or has had a vasectomy (or both), for the rule is not concerned with probabilities or practicalities. As the interest is not defined in such a way as to make it logically impossible for it to vest outside the perpetuity period, the gift is void.

(c) 'to the first man to set foot on Mars'.

This gift is clearly void as it is not limited to any period at all, and so is not defined in such a way that it cannot vest outside the perpetuity period. But suppose a wealthy but eccentric testator who has always had a keen interest in astronomy wants to leave a gift in terms similar to these. His task is to amend (c) so that it is defined in such a way that it cannot vest outside the perpetuity period. He might choose

(c 1) 'to the first person to set foot on Mars provided he does so within 21 years of my death'; or
(c 2) 'to the first person to set foot on Mars provided he does so within 21 years of the death of the last survivor of my grandchildren alive at my death'; or
(c 3) 'to the first person to set foot on Mars provided he does so within 21 years of the death of the last survivor of the descendants of King George V alive at my death'.

(c 1) gives a rather short period and (c 3) is usually preferred to (c 2) because royal persons usually live long lives and their deaths are widely reported. The advantage of (c 3) is therefore that it will give a long perpetuity period which will be relatively easy to calculate. This type of condition is called a 'Royal Lives' clause; it can be relied upon to give a perpetuity period of rather over a century.

The pre-1964 rule against remoteness of vesting had a number of disadvantages. The main one was that there was no relationship between the question whether the gift was valid or void and the likelihood of anyone actually managing to satisfy its conditions. Look again at example (c). Suppose these words were contained in the will of a testator who died in 1963. If someone had landed on Mars in 1964 he could not have claimed the gift because it was void: void because of the logical possibility that it might have vested in the far distant future. On the other hand, if the testator had used the words in example (c 3), the money would have to be kept by the trustees for the long period, in case somebody qualified. They could not dispose of it to the remaindermen until 21 years after the death of the last survivor of all the descendants of King George V who were alive at the testator's death. So in the first case the astronaut failed to benefit even though he qualified very soon after the testator's death; in the second the property was tied up uselessly for a long time even though in the end it might be that nobody qualified. There is no link between the theoretical question 'valid or void?' and practical question of what is going on in the world (or beyond it).

The Perpetuities and Accumulations Act 1964 was passed in order to correct this unsatisfactory position. It makes basic changes to the rule against remoteness of vesting, in order to save many gifts which would have been void under the pre-1964 rule. In the case of such a gift:

First we are allowed to presume that a man cannot beget a child until he is 14, and a woman cannot bear a child except between her 12th and 55th birthdays; and we are allowed to investigate in the case of a living individual whether he is capable of having a child or not (Perpetuities and Accumulations Act 1964, s 2(1)). This provision may be enough to save the gift. Example (b) above was void because of the possibility (never mind the practicality) that the donor might have another child. If a lifetime gift is made in these words after 15 July 1964 by a woman who is over 55 or by a man who has had a vasectomy for example, it will be valid.

Secondly, if the gift is still not valid, instead of striking it out straightaway, we *wait* for the perpetuity period specified by the Act. If the gift vests within that period it is good; if it does not, and as soon as it becomes established that it cannot, it is void. the perpetuity period specified by the Act is the lives of the donor and (broadly speaking) all the beneficiaries or potential beneficiaries,

24 Void and voidable trusts

and their parents and grandparents, plus 21 years. There are two reservations. The lives must be of people alive, or at any rate conceived, and ascertainable at the date of the gift; and the whole of a class of potential beneficiaries is to be disregarded if it is so numerous as to render it impracticable to ascertain the death of the survivor. So in example (b) we are allowed to wait until 21 years after the death of the survivor of (i) the donor, (ii) all his grandchildren alive at his death, and (iii) their parents and grandparents. In example (c) we are allowed to wait until 21 years after the death of the donor if it is a lifetime gift, or simply 21 years if the gift is in a will. We cannot use the beneficiaries or potential beneficiaries or their parents or grandparents as measuring lives because the class of people, one of whom might be the first man to set foot on Mars, is so numerous as to render it impossible to ascertain the death of the survivor.

The principle of waiting during the statutory perpetuity period is often called the 'wait and see' rule. It is to be found in s 3 of the Act. Sections 4 and 5 contain a number of provisions to save some gifts which are still void even after applying 'wait and see'. For example, an age of 25 could be reduced if necessary, but not to lower than 21.

In addition to saving many gifts which would otherwise be void because of the theoretical possibility that they would vest too far in the future, the Act gives the donor another alternative. He can specify as the perpetuity period for his gift any number of years not exceeding 80. For example

(c 4) 'To the first man to set foot on Mars provided he does so within 75 years of the date hereof which period is hereby specified as the perpetuity period applicable to this disposition'.

This provision, in s 1 of the Act, may be regarded as the modern equivalent of a Royal Lives clause.

Since the passing of the Perpetuities and Accumulations Act 1964 a donor may therefore either choose to draft his gift so that it is valid under the pre-1964 rule (as in examples (a), (c 1), (c 2) and (c 3)); or he may make use of the new-style perpetuity period (as in example (c 4)) or he may leave the gift to take its chances under 'wait and see' (examples (b) and (c) will be treated in this way). The overall effect is that gifts to the next generation but one in a family (like (b)) are, since 1964, almost certain not to be void for remoteness. Other gifts (like (c)) are at least given the chance of succeeding.

2 The rule against inalienability of income

The rule against inalienability of income is the rule which prohibits property from being tied up for too long in a trust under whose terms nobody can dispose of the income or the right to the income. When trustees hold property on trust for a person or persons with an interest in the income – most commonly a life interest – the problem does not arise, because a person who has a right to the income can dispose of that right. But if trustees hold property on trusts which oblige them to use the income for a particular *purpose*, there is no person or group of persons with a right to the income, and therefore no one who can dispose of it. The income is inalienable. The rule against inalienability of income does not apply to charitable purposes, so trustees may hold property on trust to use the income for a charitable purpose for ever. But where property is to be held on trust for a purpose which is not in law charitable, the length of time during which it may be so held is limited by the rule.

The rule against inalienability of income may be stated as follows: *A trust under which property is to be held for a non-charitable purpose must be expressed in such a way that it cannot last for longer than 21 years after the death of a life in being.* The maximum period during which the income may be inalienable is, in other words, the same as the pre-1964 perpetuity period for the rule against remoteness of vesting; and a Royal Lives clause may be used in the same way: *Re Khoo Cheng Teow* (1932). Indeed the 1964 Act has no application at all to this rule, so there is no 80-year alternative period and no possibility of 'wait and see'. The trust must be expressed in such a way that it is logically impossible for the income to be inalienable for longer than the perpetuity period. It is common for trusts to fail on this ground where a testator has made a gift for a purpose which he thought, wrongly, was charitable. Because he thinks (or is advised) that it is charitable, for example, to support a purely contemplative order of nuns (*Leahy v A-G for New South Wales* (1959)), or to promote the cause of the British Union for the Abolition of Vivisection (*Re Jenkins' WT* (1966)) the testator expresses no perpetuity period. It would not be appropriate for him to do so, since the rule against inalienability of income does not apply to charities. In fact, however, these purposes are not charitable, so his trusts are subject to the rule. Therefore, since they are not expressly limited to the perpetuity period, they are void.

3 The rule against accumulations of income

The rule against accumulations of income is the rule which prohibits a direction in a trust that income, instead of being paid out to beneficiaries, is to be accumulated at compound interest for a long time. Up to the end of the eighteenth century it was lawful to direct that income be accumulated for the perpetuity period (a life in being plus 21 years). But a wealthy banker, Peter Thellusson, who died in 1797, put this rule to the test by directing that his entire estate be held on trust to accumulate during the lives of all his descendants living or conceived at his death, and only after the death of all of them to be divided into three parts and paid to the eldest male lineal descendant then living of each of his three sons. The House of Lords decided (*Thellusson v Woodford* (1805)) that the direction to accumulate was valid, being limited to the perpetuity period. Parliament, however, considered it against public policy to use this device to make a modest fortune into an enormous one. A statute was therefore passed limiting accumulations to periods much shorter than the perpetuity period.

The rule against accumulations of income today is as follows: *Any direction, express or implied, that any income is to be accumulated must limit the period of such accumulation to one of the periods allowed by s 164 of the Law of Property Act 1925 or (only in the case of an instrument taking effect after 15 July 1964) s 13 of the Perpetuities and Accumulations Act 1964.* The periods in the 1925 Act are:

(a) the life of the donor;
(b) 21 years from the donor's death;
(c) the duration of the minorities of any persons living or conceived at the date of the donor's death (ie until the last of them is 21 years old if the instrument in question takes effect before 1970, otherwise until the last of them is 18 years old);
(d) the duration of the minorities of any persons who would be entitled under the trust to the income if it were not directed to be accumulated.

The periods added by the 1964 Act are only relevant to lifetime trusts. They are:

(a) 21 years from the date of making the instrument;
(b) the duration of the minorities of any persons living or conceived at the date of making the instrument.

A settlor or testator who wishes any income to be accumulated for any purpose must choose one of these periods and expressly limit the accumulation to it. If he does express a period which, though within the common law perpetuity period, exceeds the statutory periods, the trust will be treated as though it directed accumulations for the nearest lawful period (*Re Ransome* (1957)). If, however, he fails to express any period, the direction to accumulate is wholly void. A good example of the operation of this rule is *Re Rochford's ST* (1964). Under the terms of the settlement, estate duty was to be paid from trust income. When a liability to estate duty arose, it was discovered that one year's trust income was grossly inadequate to pay it; so the direction to pay it from income was, in effect, an implied direction to accumulate income. But the settlement did not limit this accumulation of income to any period. It was therefore void; and the estate duty could thus be paid from trust capital.

This example completes our study of the Rule against Perpetuities. It must be emphasised that we have barely scratched the surface of the topic. Those who require further details are recommended to read the chapter entitled 'Future Interests' in Cheshire and Burn *Modern Law of Real Property* (13th edn, 1982).

OTHER VOID TRUSTS

A trust to promote a purpose which is illegal or contrary to public morals is void. There are few reported cases, but a memorable one is *Thrupp v Collett* (1858) which concerned an attempt to set up a trust to pay the fines imposed on convicted poachers. In *Re Pinion* (1965) Harman LJ suggested that trusts to provide 'a school for prostitutes or pickpockets' or a library 'devoted entirely to works of pornography or of a corrupting nature' would not be allowable. A trust under which a beneficiary was to be entitled to certain property if he became destitute was held to be void in *Re Hepplewhite's WT* (1977) on the ground that it might encourage him to behave irresponsibly. It used to be that a trust for future illegitimate children was void as tending to promote immorality. This rule was reversed by the Family Law Reform Act 1969, s 15(7), but is still of interest as an illustration of the approach of the courts to the question of illegality.

The law on trusts which contain conditions relating to marriage and divorce is complex and probably outdated, and need not be learnt in detail. To take the extreme cases, it is certainly legitimate to make a gift on trust to a person until marriage, with a remainder in the event of his marriage. It is common for a testator to leave a substantial gift to his widow 'for her life or until her remarriage' with a gift over to his children. On the other hand if a trust contains a gift worded in such a way as to give an interest without limit of time (that is, without using the word 'until'), but has also a condition which purports to take away the interest in the event of the beneficiary's marriage, the condition will be void if the attempted restraint of marriage is too wide; thus the beneficiary will keep the property despite his marriage. It has been held, however, that conditions which divest the beneficiary of his property only on a second marriage, or a marriage with a particular person, or a person of a particular religion, are not too wide and so are valid. A trust, or a condition in a trust, which may induce a married couple to become separated or divorced is void, but, as Denning LJ said in *Egerton v Egerton* (1949), terms that merely provide what should happen to the property in the event of a divorce are not contrary to public policy. Likewise, a trust or a condition in a trust which will tend to promote a separation between parent and child is void, as in *Re Boulter* (1922) where, under the terms of the trust, the beneficiaries were to forfeit their interests if they continued to live with or be under the custody, guardianship or control of their father. However, the House of Lords decided in *Blathwayt v Lord Cawley* (1976) that a condition that any tenant for life should forfeit his interest if he became a Roman Catholic was valid, even though it might affect or influence the parents of the beneficiaries in the exercise of their parental duties.

It is generally a contradiction to give somebody property with the condition that he never dispose of it, for his rights as owner include the right to dispose of it. We have seen that some property is rendered inalienable by statute or on public policy grounds (Chapter 3). In all other cases a condition which prevents alienation or which restricts it very gravely is void: see *Re Brown* (1954) where a condition that each of the testator's sons could alienate only to the others was held void.

In all these cases if the trust is void there is an automatic resulting trust for the settlor or his estate; but if a condition is void it is struck out and the gift takes effect free of it. In cases where the trust is not merely void but fraudulent (as in *Thrupp v Collett*) the court will refuse to hear any action based on it. So if the settlor has already transferred his property to the trustees they will not be compelled to return it to him: 'When the parties are equally in the wrong, the defendant's position is the stronger'.

VOIDABLE TRUSTS: SETTING TRUSTS ASIDE

Once a trust has been validly made it cannot be revoked by the settlor unless there is in the settlement a clause empowering him to revoke it. Such a clause is extremely rare because almost all express trusts are made, if not for tax-planning purposes, at any rate with a view to their tax implications; and if the settlor reserves a power to revoke the trust, the trust property will be treated for tax purposes as though he still owned it.

It sometimes happens, however, that although a trust is formally perfectly valid, it was made in such circumstances that it is tainted and so may be set aside (that is, cancelled) or modified either by the settlor or by the court.

1 By the settlor on general equitable principles

Suppose a trust has been obtained by fraud, or duress, or undue influence, or the settlor was acting under a fundamental mistake when he made it. In each of these cases it would be inequitable for the trust to be enforced against the settlor; so he may set it aside, and if necessary the court, exercising its inherent power to dispense justice according to established principles of equity, will uphold his right to do so. The fact of the matter is, though, that a trust has been created, so the rule is that the settlor must be prepared to prove that it is tainted in some recognised way. The burden is upon him. He must show that there was duress, or fraud, or a fundamental mistake arising through no fault of his own. Where he alleges that he was acting under undue influence the rule is slightly different. There are some relationships which equity regards with particular circumspection, for they are relationships in which one party is particularly likely to come to depend on the other for help and advice. Solicitor and client, parent and child, guardian and ward are obvious examples: if one of these relationships exists and the settlor, being the weaker party, has conferred some benefit on the stronger party, a court will presume that the weaker party was acting under the undue influence of the stronger party and so will allow the gift or trust to be set aside. The presumption can be rebutted by the stronger party; normally he will have to show that the weaker party had adequate independent advice.

If, on the other hand, the relationship alleged is not one which normally gives rise to influence and reliance, the settlor may nevertheless show that he was acting under the undue influence of the other. Here the burden of proof is on the settlor to show that the relationship was one of undue influence, leaving the other party to prove he did not abuse it. In *Re Craig* (1971) an employee was said to have had undue influence over her employer. This may seem unlikely at first glance, but on behalf of the settlor it was shown that the employer was an aged widower who had come to rely wholly on his secretary. It was held that a relationship of undue influence had been proved. This was similarly the case in *O'Sullivan v Management Agency and Music Ltd* (1984), where the relationship was between a young and inexperienced pop-singer and his manager.

All that has been said above about undue influence applies to lifetime gifts. Where the gift is by will, those challenging it must prove affirmatively not merely that a relationship of undue influence existed, but also that undue influence was actually exerted by the stronger party: in other words, the rule is exactly analogous to that for fraud or duress or mistake. And in any event, a transaction will not be set aside on the ground of undue influence unless it was, at the time it was made, to the manifest disadvantage of the weaker party: *National Westminster Bank plc v Morgan* (1985).

The settlor has power to set his trust aside in these circumstances because, although validly made, it is tainted and it would be inequitable to enforce it. But equity also imposes limitations: the settlor will not be allowed to set his trust aside if it would be inequitable to do so. In particular, first, if a trust is to be set aside it must be possible to put all the parties back into their original position. If this cannot be done the trust will remain in full force. Examples of the latter are where someone has innocently acted on the faith of the gift and where the trust was made in consideration of a marriage which has now taken place. Secondly, it is a maxim of equity that 'delay defeats equity'. A settlor who is entitled to set a trust aside must do so reasonably quickly or he will lose his right and the trust will become irrevocable: it would be inequitable for the possibility of avoidance to be hanging over the trust for ever. In *Allcard v Skinner* (1887), a nun acting under the undue influence of the mother superior made a gift of all her property to the convent. In 1879 she left the convent, and so ceased to be under the mother superior's influence. In 1885 she tried to recover her property. The Court of Appeal held that she was too late. She had had a right to set her gift aside, but she had lost it by delaying.

2 By the court under a statutory power

So far, we have dealt with those circumstances in which a trust can be set aside by the settlor, with the court's support if necessary: the trust is voidable on general principles of equity, and the court has jurisdiction to see equity done. Some trusts however may be voidable not on

Voidable trusts: setting trusts aside 31

principle but simply because a particular statute gives the court power to set them aside. There are various occasions when a person's assets fall to be divided in favour of others according to a scheme laid down by the law. Bankruptcy and the break-up of a marriage are obvious examples. Another such situation is where a person dies leaving a will which does not make proper provision for his dependants. In each of these cases it is against the policy of the law to allow him to frustrate a proper division by giving his property away to those he chooses, in advance of the court order. Statutes, therefore, give the court power to cancel or modify otherwise valid transactions, including trusts, in appropriate cases.

Matrimonial proceedings. Under s 24 of the Matrimonial Causes Act 1973, the court has a wide jurisdiction to make orders relating to property belonging to either party to a marriage which has ended by divorce, judicial separation or decree of nullity. Either party may be required to transfer any property of his, or to make a settlement of it. And under s 24(1)(c),(d) any settlement made on the parties to the marriage may be varied by the court, so as to benefit the parties to the marriage and the children of the family, or so as to extinguish or reduce the interest of either of the parties to the marriage. If one party is about to dispose of property so that it will not be available for financial relief under s 24, the court may make an order prohibiting the disposition (s 37(2)(a)). If he has already made the disposition, it may be set aside by the court (s 37(2)(b),(c)). In either case, the court must be satisfied that the disposition was intended to defeat the claim under s 24: but if it was made within three years before the application to the court it is presumed to have been so intended unless the contrary is shown. A disposition cannot be set aside if it has already been made to a bona fide purchaser for value without notice of the intention to defeat the claim.

Family provision. English law (unlike systems based on the Roman law) adheres in general to the principle that a testator may dispose of his estate to whomsoever he wishes. The main exception is contained in the Inheritance (Provision for Family and Dependants) Act 1975. The deceased's spouse, children and other dependants may apply to the court on the ground that the disposition of the estate (whether by will or intestacy or a combination) is not such as to make reasonable financial provision for them. If they do apply, the court has a discretionary power to make an order in favour of any of them. It will normally be an order for provision out of the estate, but in a suitable case the court may vary an existing settlement so as to make provision for an applicant. Suppose a settlement made on the marriage of *A* and *B* was 'to *A* for life with remainder to the children of *A* and *B* with remainder to the *C* charity'. *A* and *B* have no children but *X*, who is severely disabled, comes to live with them and is treated as one of the family. *A* dies, leaving no will, or leaving one which makes little or no provision for *X*. If an application was made to the court on behalf of *X*, the court might, in its discretion, order payments to *X* out of *A*'s estate or it might vary the settlement so as to treat *X* as if he were a child of *A* and *B*.

Obviously the family provision legislation would lose a great deal of its effect if the person dying could part with his property (whether by gift or by setting up a trust) before his death so as to leave little in his estate to satisfy claims under the Act. It is therefore provided in ss 10-13 that if the deceased disposed of property within six years before his death, and with the intention of defeating a claim under the Act, the court may order that financial provision be made out of the property disposed of. Thus, the donee (or in the case of a trust created by the deceased, the trustee) will be ordered to provide for the applicant. If the person against whom the order is made is a trustee, the amount he can be ordered to pay is limited to the value of the trust property at the time of the court order. Again, an order cannot be made against a bona fide purchaser for value who had no notice of the intention to defeat a claim under the Act.

Bankruptcy. When a person is adjudged bankrupt, it is sometimes necessary for the court to investigate and rearrange his recent transactions. It is likely that he foresaw that he would become bankrupt, and he may have tried to dispose of such assets as he had in order to keep them from his creditors. The new law dealing with such a situation is contained in ss 339-342 of the Insolvency Act 1986. It covers transactions at an undervalue and preferences. A 'transaction at an undervalue' is a transaction in which the other party does not pay full value for what he received from the bankrupt; and marriage does not count as valuable consideration for these purposes. A 'preference' is an act by which the bankrupt's creditor or surety or guarantor is put in a better position in the bankruptcy than he would have been if the act had not been done; and the sections only apply to acts done with the intention of having that effect. A simple example would be the conversion of an unsecured loan into a secured loan, intending to better the position of the creditor by making it more likely that he would be repaid. To be subject to ss 339-342, the transaction at an undervalue or the preference must have been during the 'relevant time', which is calculated backwards from the date of the presentation of the bankruptcy petition. It varies from six months in the case of giving a preference to someone who was not an associate of the bankrupt, up to a maximum of five years in the case of a transaction at an undervalue if the bankrupt was insolvent at the time he entered into it, or became insolvent as a result of it.

Where an individual is adjudged bankrupt, and within the relevant time he has entered into a transaction at an undervalue or given a preference, the trustee of the bankrupt's estate may apply to the court. The court then has a discretionary power to make 'such order as it thinks fit for restoring the position to what it would have been' but for the transaction at an undervalue (in which case the order is under s 339) or preference (s 340). Thus a businessman who, foreseeing his impending bankruptcy, transfers assets to his wife on trust for herself for life with remainder to their children, may well find that the trust is set aside by the court. Notice, though, that this may happen even if he makes the trust not to keep the assets from his creditors but with a motive of pure generosity; for when a transaction at an undervalue, as distinct from a preference (see above), is under consideration, s 339 does *not* require the court to be satisfied that it was entered into with the intent of avoiding the provisions of the Act. It is enough that it has the effect of altering the bankrupt's position vis-à-vis his creditors.

General powers. If, however, the court *is* satisfied that a person has entered into a transaction at an undervalue for the purpose of putting assets beyond the reach of someone with a claim against him, it has a similar discretion under ss 423-425 of the Insolvency Act 1986: that is, it may make an order designed to restore the position to what it would have been but for the transaction and to protect the interests of those who are prejudiced by it. The order (like one under ss 339-340) may be made against the other party to the transaction, even though he was a bona fide purchaser, but not against a subsequent bona fide purchaser for value and without notice of the circumstances. The remedy of an order under ss 423-425 is not limited to cases where the person in question is bankrupt. Although it will clearly be of great relevance in

Void and voidable trusts

bankruptcy and insolvency cases, the power is quite general and (unlike ss 339-342) there is no time limit: it is enough that the dishonourable motive is proved. So a trust set up to avoid the claims of creditors may at any time be set aside by the court under this section.

Chapter 5
The beneficiary

'No principle perhaps has greater sanction or authority behind it than the general proposition that a trust, not being a charitable trust, to be effective, must have ascertained or ascertainable beneficiaries' (*Re Endacott* (1960) per Lord Evershed MR). In this chapter we analyse the implications of this principle. These are, broadly speaking, that (1) every non-charitable trust must have a beneficiary or beneficiaries (sometimes called 'the beneficiary principle'); and (2) the beneficiaries must be ascertained or ascertainable ('the rule against uncertainty of objects'). We begin by considering who may be a beneficiary. Then we look at the beneficiary principle, and examine the ways courts have been prepared to construe gifts so as to avoid their failing for lack of a beneficiary. At the other end of the scale are trusts with lots of beneficiaries: we discuss how they are set up in order to be properly manageable. But it is trusts of this type that are most prone to fail because the beneficiaries are not 'ascertained or ascertainable', so the next topic is certainty of objects. Finally we set out the property rights which people acquire by being the beneficiaries or potential beneficiaries of a trust.

WHO CAN BE A BENEFICIARY?

Any person may be a beneficiary of a trust. An infant may be a beneficiary of a trust of land, even though he is not able to hold the legal title to land. A corporation (whether or not a trading company), being a juristic person, may be a beneficiary. The settlor may be a beneficiary. The exceptions to the general rule are unlikely to cause difficulty. An alien cannot be a beneficiary of a trust of a British ship (Status of Aliens Act 1914, s 17). A company incorporated under the Companies Acts cannot be a beneficiary of a trust of land unless it is expressly or impliedly empowered by its memorandum of association to hold an equitable interest in land (Companies Act 1948, s 14, which gave companies an automatic power to hold land, was repealed by the Charities Act 1960). The same person cannot be both sole trustee and sole beneficiary, because his interests would merge, thus extinguishing the trust.

Notice, however, that, although the list of those who may be beneficiaries of a trust is a long one, it includes only persons. Animals and things may not be beneficiaries of a trust, nor (save in the case of charitable trusts) may a trust be purely for the benefit of a purpose.

THE BENEFICIARY PRINCIPLE

Every non-charitable trust must have a beneficiary, that is, a person, human or corporate, in whose favour the trust is created, and in whose favour the court can decree performance of the trust. Without such a person, the trust would be unenforceable (as nobody would have standing to sue) and hence, as an obligation imposed on the trustee, could not be said to exist at all. Many trusts do indeed have beneficiaries all of whom are humans, and then the beneficiary principle causes no problems. It is only where property is given for the furtherance of some non-charitable purpose that there may be difficulty. Even so, the trust may be valid, for the beneficiary principle does not cause every non-charitable trust for a purpose to fail. The principle does not say 'look for a purpose; if you find one the trust is void', but 'look for a beneficiary; *unless* you find one the trust is void'.

In the landmark case of *Re Denley's Trust Deed* (1969), the trust property was a piece of land which was to be held and maintained as a sports ground 'primarily for the benefit of the employees of Martyn & Co Ltd, and secondarily for the benefit of such other person or persons as the trustees may allow to use the same'. Goff J held that the trust was valid: 'where the trust, though expressed as a purpose, is directly or indirectly for the benefit of individuals, it seems that it is in general outside the mischief of the beneficiary principle'. A non-charitable purpose trust will fail for lack of a beneficiary if the purpose is pure or general; but it will not fail (on this ground, anyway) if the purpose is clearly intended primarily for the benefit of some ascertained or ascertainable individuals. For if the trustees fail to carry out the purpose and so fail to benefit those individuals, the latter clearly have standing to sue to enforce the trust. Remember, though, that non-charitable purpose trusts do not have the advantages of charity: they must be limited to the perpetuity period, so that those who have locus standi to enforce the purpose are ascertained within the period; and the income must not be rendered inalienable by being committed to the purpose for longer than the perpetuity period.

Unincorporated associations
Now we are in a position to discuss the fate of a very common type of gift. Settlors (and particularly testators) often wish to make a donation to further the purposes of an association with which they have been connected, or which they have supported in the past. If the association's purposes are charitable, the gift will take effect as a charitable gift and it is not necessary to find a beneficiary. If the association's purposes are not charitable, but the association is a corporate body, the association will itself be the beneficiary, and the gift will take effect as an absolute gift to the corporation. But if the purpose is not charitable, and the association is not incorporated, the gift runs the risk of failing for lack of a beneficiary. For although it is usual to speak of an unincorporated association as though it existed, in law it has no existence except as a group of people. It cannot be a beneficiary. However, it is sometimes possible to construe gifts to unincorporated associations as being for the benefit of ascertainable individuals. There are three ways in which this may be done.

(1) The gift may be interpreted as a gift to the present members absolutely, or to the trustees of the association on trust for the present members beneficially. The donor is thus seen as having used the name of the association simply as a shorthand for the names of its members. The effect of this interpretation is that each member may, if he wishes, demand to be paid his share, and there can be no restriction upon what he does with it. It follows that this interpretation is not possible if either (a) the rules of the association prevent a gift given to the association from being divided among the members, or (b) the words of the gift indicate that the members were not intended to take beneficially, for example 'to the *X* Association for its general purposes', or 'to the *Y* golf club to build a new club house'. On the whole, the court is unlikely to interpret the gift in this way unless the association is of a sort whose purpose is to provide financial, or quasi-financial, benefits to its members, like a mutual benefit association or a dining club.

(2) The gift may be interpreted as a gift on trust for the present and future members beneficially. This interpretation has all the

disadvantages and restrictions of the last, and one other in addition: there may be a perpetuity problem. If the trust is really for present and future members absolutely, the difficulty caused by the fact that every time a new member joins a new interest vests will normally be cured by the 'wait and see' provisions of the Perpetuities and Accumulations Act 1964. But if the trust is of the *Re Denley's Trust Deed* type, then it is not a trust for present and future members, but a trust for purposes which indirectly benefit present and future members. A trust for purposes infringes the rule against inalienability unless it is limited by the settlor to the common law perpetuity period (as *Denley's* trust was): there is no 'wait and see' for inalienability (see p 29 above).

(3) The gift may be interpreted as a gift to the present members absolutely, but so that in their hands it is bound by the implied (or express) terms of the contracts they have with each other as members of the association. Each member is not entitled to demand to be paid his share, but is deemed to have agreed to allow it to remain in the association's hands. Thus, in the result, the gift will be added to the general funds of the association. This brilliant formulation, which will normally cause the gift to be used exactly as the donor intended (despite the vagaries of the beneficiary principle and the Rule against Perpetuities), derives from the judgments of Cross J in *Neville Estates Ltd v Madden* (1962) and Brightman J in *Re Recher's WT* (1972). It is important to realise that interpretation (3) is quite different from interpretation (2) and is, in fact, a variation of interpretation (1). If interpretation (3) is looked at closely, it will be seen that, as far as the donor is concerned, he has made a gift for the present members for them each to use as they wish. But as far as the members are concerned, the gift is to be dealt with in a particular way – not by the donor's instructions, but by the members' own choice. By becoming members of the association they contract not to demand their share of any such gift but to allow it to be added to the association's funds. It follows that interpretation (3) cannot be used where treating the gift in that way is not a free choice by the members, but is forced on them, either because the words of the gift indicate that the donor intends it not to be available for the present members' own use, or because the rules of the association prohibit distribution of the funds among the members and cannot be changed by the members to allow it. *Re Grant's WT* (1979) concerned a gift for the purposes of the Chertsey Labour Party headquarters. The rules of the local Labour Party did not allow distribution of funds to its members, and the rules could not be

changed by its members without the consent of the National Executive Council of the party. The Council itself could also change the local party's rules. If the gift had gone to the local party's funds it would have stayed there, not necessarily because the members would have chosen to allow it to do so, but because they would have been compelled to allow it to. Interpretation (3) was therefore not available.

When none of these three interpretations can be used, the gift must be seen either as an endowment for present and future members for ever (in which case it may fail for perpetuity) or as a gift in trust for the purposes of the association. In the latter case too, the duration of the trust must be limited to a suitable period to satisfy the rule against inalienability, but it will still fail (for lack of a beneficiary) unless the association's purposes are such as to give ascertainable individuals standing to enforce the trust: see the discussion of *Re Denley's Trust Deed* above.

It will be apparent by now that gifts to unincorporated non-charitable associations pose a number of complex legal problems. We conclude by looking at the judgment of Oliver J in *Re Lipinski's WT* (1979) as an illustration of how the courts approach the construction of such gifts. *Re Lipinski's WT* concerned a will in which half the residue was left on trust 'for the Hull Judeans (Maccabi) Association in memory of my late wife to be used solely in the work of constructing the new buildings for the association and/or improvements to the said buildings'. In the course of his decision, the learned judge had to consider very nearly all the principles outlined in this section and the last. First he examined the objects of the association and determined that, although some of them were charitable, the association as a whole was a non-charitable sports and recreation club existing for the benefit of its members. Next, looking at the rules, he found that they did not permit the distribution of the association's funds among the members, but that the rules could be changed (by a 75% majority of the members) to allow it. As regards the reference to 'my late wife' he held that the testator merely 'wished the association to know that his bounty was a tribute to his late wife'. The words of the gift clearly negatived any intention to create a perpetual endowment in his wife's memory, since it was obvious that the association was to be at liberty to expend both capital and income for the specified purpose. There was thus no perpetuity problem. However, the fact that a purpose had been expressed made it impossible to apply interpretation (1), as we have called it above. It was not the testator's intention that the gift take effect as one to the members for them each to take free of any trust or contractual obligations. On the other hand, the application of interpretation (3) seemed also to be hindered by the purpose: the members were not to be free to use the gift as they pleased, subject only to the contracts between them as members. At this point, the judge took aid from the principle of *Re Denley's Trust Deed*.

Looking at the business of the association at the time of the will and the testator's death, it was apparent that 'the new buildings for the association' did not refer to any particular buildings. The phrase had to be construed to mean no more than 'whatever buildings the association may have or may choose to acquire. . . . The association was to have that legacy to spend in this way for the benefit of the members'. Thus the purpose specified by the testator was not a pure or general purpose, but one for the benefit of ascertainable persons, who were, in fact, the members of the association. As the members were also the beneficiaries they did have a free choice whether to use the gift for the specified purpose, thus carrying out the trust, or to use it for something else, by choosing not to enforce the trust. In the result, therefore, Oliver J held the trust valid under interpretation (3) and enforceable under the *Denley* principle. The beneficiaries, as members, could choose to enforce it, or the members, being the sole beneficiaries, could choose to terminate it and (by changing their rules) distribute the capital.

Trusts without a beneficiary

Charitable trusts, that is, trusts for purposes which the law regards as charitable, need not have any ascertainable beneficiary as they benefit the public in general; and the public's interest will, if necessary, be enforced by the Attorney General. Charitable trusts are considered in Part III. There is in addition a small number of types of case in which a trust for a pure non-charitable purpose has been held valid, even though there was no person with standing to enforce it. These trusts are therefore genuine exceptions to the beneficiary principle. They are as follows: trusts for the erection or maintenance of tombs (see *Re Hooper* (1932)); trusts for the maintenance of specific animals (*Re Dean* (1889)); and trusts for purposes which, though religious, are not charitable – for example ancestor worship (*Re Khoo Cheng Teow* (1932)). To be valid, any trust of this type must be restricted to the perpetuity period, otherwise it will contravene the rule against inalienability.

It will be noticed that each of these three types of trust is on the very edge of charity, for a trust for the maintenance of a churchyard or part of it is charitable, as is a trust to promote the interests of animals in general. It has sometimes been argued that all these cases of unenforceable trusts or 'trusts of imperfect obligation' for non-charitable purposes are wrongly decided. In any event it is clear that, as Harman LJ said in *Re Endacott*, they are 'troublesome, anomalous and aberrant' and 'ought not to be increased in number, nor indeed followed, except where the one is exactly like another'. So except for cases 'exactly like' these, we may say that every non-charitable trust must have a human beneficiary.

TRUSTS AND POWERS

Most trusts have more than one beneficiary. Even a simple family trust may have several: Jack may bequeath his estate to trustees on trust for his widow Joan for life, thereafter for his son John for life, with remainder to his grandchildren in equal shares absolutely. Notice that he specifies his widow and his son by name, but defines the remaindermen by describing them, 'my grandchildren'. This is good sense, because he can only name those who are already born, and there may be more to come. A group of people defined by description in this way is called a 'class' and a gift in their favour is called a class gift. Here are some more classes: the male children of my cousin Edith; the members of the Drones Club; this year's candidates for Professional Examination I; the officers and employees and ex-officers and ex-employees of ICI plc and their dependants. The first is probably quite small, the last is almost unimaginably large. But any of them might be the beneficiaries or 'objects' of a trust.

It is the settlor's privilege to decide how to distribute the trust property between the members of a class. In the first example in this section, the settlor decreed that after the death of his son John, his grandchildren were to take equally. He could instead have given his grandsons twice as much as his granddaughters (or vice versa), or he might have given a larger share to grandchildren who were already married at the time of John's death. Any of these options would be perfectly reasonable, and valid. The settlor would have exercised to the full his power of disposing of his property by laying out exactly how it is to pass to his descendants; and John and the grandchildren would each have a clear entitlement to a share, even though the grandchildren might have to wait until John was dead before they knew precisely how much each would get. The settlor and the beneficiaries could feel safe. But a trust in which the settlor has laid down the shares of the beneficiaries many years in advance has a disadvantage, because nobody can predict what the future will bring. It may be that on John's death there are three grandchildren. One is a brain surgeon, so successful that he does not need any money from the family trust: it will only increase his tax liability. One was convicted of smuggling heroin into Russia and is serving a life sentence in Siberia: he will not be able to gain any benefit from his entitlement under the trust. The third is severely disabled and in need of constant nursing attention and expensive medicines. Yet under the terms of the trust, each of the three gets an equal share of the capital. In retrospect it would have been better for Jack, instead of playing safe, to have given to somebody else the authority to decide how much each grandchild should get. Then the decision, instead of being made long in advance, could have been made when the relevant facts were known.

Consider now the very large classes of which we gave examples. Clearly it would be entirely unreasonable (though not necessarily impossible or invalid) for the settlor to direct what share each member should have. The purpose of setting up a trust for a very large class is not that each member shall receive a tiny sum of money. The purpose is to set up a fund from which payments will be made only to those members of the class who merit them. Keith, perhaps, wants to set up a trust to pay a prize of £25 to the candidate who writes the best law paper in Professional Examination I; Leonard's idea is to endow a fund which will provide public school education for the dependants of officers, employees, ex-officers and ex-employees of ICI plc who would benefit from such an education but cannot afford it. In each case the settlor cannot predict who will qualify next year, let alone in future years. He therefore must give someone authority to decide which members of the class should receive a payment from the trust. This authority, to choose beneficiaries from a class (large or small) or to fix the amounts of their entitlements, is called a 'power of appointment', and the person who has it is called the 'donee' of the power.

A person has a power when he can dispose of or deal with property, not because he owns it, but because he has been given the authority to do so. Trustees (who own only the legal estate) may be given a power to dispose of the beneficial interest; a person with no interest in property may be given a power to deal with it. When the donee of a power is authorised to choose from a class someone to receive a benefit he cannot *give* the benefit because it is not his to give. We say instead that he *appoints* the benefit to the person: hence, 'power of appointment'. Generally speaking, trustees have many powers, for example the power to appoint new trustees, the power to invest, the power to appoint a professional agent. These we shall consider in detail later. They are all *administrative* powers. The power we are discussing here is a *dispositive* power. It is only if a person has a power of appointment that he has authority to choose beneficiaries of the trust. A trustee without a power of appointment might have authority to deal with the property, for example by moving it from one investment to another, but that would be the exercise not of a dispositive but of an administrative power. Notice that several of the administrative powers are powers *to* appoint persons to offices. Rather confusingly, they are *never* called 'powers of appointment'. A power of appointment is a power to choose beneficiaries. And where a class is covered by a power of appointment, so that a person can choose which of the members is to receive a benefit, it is better to call them not 'beneficiaries' but 'potential beneficiaries' – or, more simply, 'objects', a word which has the advantage of including in its meaning both the actual and the potential beneficiaries of a trust.

It seems, then, that Jack, Keith and Leonard would all wish to grant a power of appointment. Before any settlor decides to whom he will grant a power, there are a number of factors to be considered. The first is this. A power is by its nature the converse of a duty. Power implies choice; duty implies obligation. A power of appointment gives authority to choose beneficiaries; but does the settlor want the donee of the power to have also the choice of whether to exercise the power? Is he to be allowed only to choose beneficiaries, or is he also to be allowed to decide whether to select any beneficiaries at all? In Keith's trust it might be advisable to grant to the donees of the power authority not only to decide who should have the prize, but also to decide that in any particular year the prize should not be awarded as no paper is of a high enough standard. A power that is coupled with authority not to exercise it is called a 'mere power'. A properly-drafted grant of a mere power will include a gift in default; that is, the instrument creating the power will say what is to happen if the power is not exercised. On the other hand, Leonard may well feel that there will always be some member of the class who are the objects of his trust, who merits a payment. He may therefore grant a power of appointment, but oblige the donee of the power to choose a beneficiary or beneficiaries to have the benefits under the trust as they become available. A power coupled with a duty to exercise it is called a 'trust power'. There is no need to have a gift in default: if the donee of the power does not perform his duty to choose, he will be compelled by the court to do so, or replaced.

The second matter to be considered is what duties of acting responsibly the settlor wishes to impose on the donee of the power. Is he to be entirely free to choose within the class, motivated perhaps by personal like or dislike? Or is he to be obliged to make a decision on impersonal, rational, grounds, having made a proper survey of potential beneficiaries? If a power of appointment is given to someone who has fiduciary duties in relation to the property in question (most commonly a trustee) he will be obliged to exercise the power too in a fiduciary manner. But if the power is given to someone in a purely personal capacity (the settlor's wife, for instance) the donee has only to exercise the power without actual fraud. This is a 'personal power'.

Thirdly, by how many people should the power be exercised? Unless the settlor directs otherwise, a power can only be exercised unanimously. (The one exception is that trustees of a charity may act by majority.) So although the settlor may seek security by vesting the power in more than one person, if he chooses too many, it may be found that the power cannot be exercised at all.

Taking all these factors into account, it is likely that Jack would grant a mere power to his son John to appoint the capital of the trust to Jack's grandchildren in such proportion as he may in his absolute discretion see fit. As it is a mere power there should be a gift in default, probably to the grandchildren equally, and it should also be stated in the trust instrument that John may exercise the power by executing a deed or by his will. A personal power such as this is appropriate for a family trust with capital to be shared out, and by giving the power to the last life tenant Jack would ensure that it could be exercised with the maximum possible knowledge of the relevant circumstances.

Keith's trust is more ambitious. It is clear that a personal power would not be appropriate, because there is no connection between the settlor and the objects; and, besides, the power would have to be exercised each year: a professional approach is therefore required. Keith should be advised to grant a power to his trustees (so it would be a fiduciary power) to pay the prize to the most deserving candidate. We suggested earlier that a mere power would be suitable in this case, and the provision in default would be that, if the power were not exercised, the income for that year should be added to the capital. Keith's trust is, in fact, a charitable trust. Should he take advantage of the rule that trustees of a charity may act by majority, and give the power to a larger body – perhaps his trustees and the board of examiners? It would probably be better from an administrative point of view to have the power vested in the trustees alone but oblige them to consult the board of examiners before making their award. The charitable nature of Keith's trust does, however, mean that no problems of perpetuity arise, although the income of the trust is inalienable and no limit is placed on its accumulation.

Leonard's trust is not charitable and so must be restricted to the perpetuity period: a period not exceeding 80 years specified under s 1 of the Perpetuities and Accumulations Act 1964 would be suitable, or he might prefer to use a Royal Lives clause. We have already suggested that a trust power would be apt here. It would need to be enforceable, so it would be a fiduciary power, vested in the trustees. They would therefore be given power during the perpetuity period to pay the income of the trust in each year 'to such of the objects as they shall in their absolute discretion determine to be able to benefit from a public school education but unable to afford one'. Notice the word 'shall', which is a hallmark of a trust power as the gift in default is a hallmark of a mere power. This very common type of arrangement, in which property is vested in trustees who have a duty to distribute it, but with a discretion enabling them to select beneficiaries from a class, is called a 'discretionary trust'.

Thus, we have discovered four solutions to the problems of how to set up a trust in favour of a class of objects. First, the fixed trust, in which the settlor fixes the share of each beneficiary, then a trust coupled with a personal power, a trust coupled with a mere power vested in the trustees, and a discretionary trust. Each of the last three is based firmly on the notion of a power of appointment; they differ in the duties imposed on the donee of the power. A useful summary of those duties is set out, as follows, in the judgment of Megarry V-C in *Re Hay's ST* (1981).

Anybody who has a power of appointment is bound to obey the trust instrument, and in particular may make no appointment that is not authorised by it. A person not in a fiduciary position has no further duty: he 'is free to exercise the power in any way that he wishes – or to refrain from exercising it at all'. A trustee of a discretionary trust must exercise it, and if need be will be compelled by the court to do so. He 'is bound by the duties of his office in exercising the power to do so in a responsible manner according to its purpose. It is not enough for him to refrain from acting capriciously: he must do more'. He must not 'simply proceed to exercise the power in favour of such of the objects as happen to be at hand or claim his attention' but must make 'such a survey of the range of objects as will enable him to carry out his fiduciary duty. He must find out the permissible area of selection and then consider responsibly, in individual cases, whether a contemplated beneficiary is within the power and whether, in relation to other possible claimants, a particular grant is appropriate'.

A trustee who has a mere power is not bound to exercise it, but that 'does not mean he can simply fold his hands and ignore it, for normally he must from time to time consider whether or not to exercise the power'. So he has a threefold duty: he 'must first, consider periodically whether or not he should exercise the power; second, consider the range of objects of the power; and third, consider the appropriateness of individual appointments'.

Protective trusts

A beneficiary of a fixed trust has an interest in the trust property, vested in possession (e g a life interest), vested in interest (e g a remainder while the life tenant is still alive) or contingent (e g if he attains the age of 25). An object of a power of appointment has no interest in the trust property until the power is exercised in his favour. In the meantime he has only a hope that it will be so exercised. This difference may be exploited. Suppose Michael wants to create a family trust. He is tempted to do so in the usual form, with a life interest for Nicholas, (his son or son-in-law), followed by a life interest for Nicholas' widow, with remainder to the children of their marriage. He is, however, rather worried about giving Nicholas a vested interest. Perhaps Nicholas is running a rather unsuccessful business, and if it fails and he becomes bankrupt, his income from the trust will be intercepted by his trustee in bankruptcy to pay his creditors. Or perhaps Nicholas is a spendthrift and Michael is afraid he will sell his life interest and fritter away the capital he receives. In either case, Nicholas' wife and family will be without the benefit of the income of the trust during Nicholas' life. The solution is to create a protective trust. Instead of giving a life interest to Nicholas, Michael will give him an interest lasting for his life or until he does or allows anything which would cause him to lose his right to the income. So if Nicholas goes bankrupt or attempts to sell his interest, the interest simply ceases, as it would do at his death. If the interest ceases in this way during his life, it is replaced under the terms of the protective trust by a discretionary trust, under which Nicholas is one of the objects, as are his wife and their children. Thus Nicholas has the security of a vested life interest so long as he does not abuse it; if he does, the trust property and the other beneficiaries are still protected. Protective trusts require careful drafting, but there is a model in s 33 of the Trustee Act 1925 which can be imported into any settlement by using the words 'on protective trusts'. If this is done, the provisions of that section apply as if they were contained in the trust instrument.

One cannot settle property on protective trusts on oneself. That would amount to avoiding completely the claims of one's creditors and the scheme of the bankruptcy legislation, so the attempt would be void on public policy grounds. Notice also that a protective trust is not the same as the American device called a 'spendthrift trust'. In a spendthrift trust the life interest is made inalienable but continues to pay income to its holder regardless of his creditors. Such a scheme is impossible in England, as although an interest can be made determinable, it cannot be inalienable.

CERTAINTY OF OBJECTS

The larger the class of beneficiaries and potential beneficiaries, the more care is needed to ensure that the trust does not fail for uncertainty of objects: uncertainty, that is, as to the ambit of the class. The history of this topic in the courts is complex and unedifying. The account that follows is based chiefly on the decisions of the House of Lords in *IRC v Broadway Cottages Trust* (1955), *Re Gulbenkian's ST* (1968) and *McPhail v Doulton (Re Baden's Deed Trusts)* (1970), and the decision of the Court of Appeal in *Re Baden's Deed Trusts (No 2)* (1972).

A *Fixed trusts*

A trust in which the interests are not subject to any power of appointment but are fixed by the settlor has a very simple rule as to uncertainty of objects. The trust is void unless it is possible to draw up a complete list of those entitled. This is the *Broadway Cottages* test for certainty.

A court examining a trust of this nature will operate on the principle that 'it is better for a thing to be valid than void' and therefore will strain in favour of holding that a list can be compiled. As Megarry J said (in an entirely different context) in *Brown v Gould* (1972), one should approach the issue with

48 The beneficiary

'reasonable goodwill'. 'The question is not whether the clause is proof against wilful misinterpretation, but whether someone genuinely seeking to discover its meaning is able to do so'. In particular, words of rather uncertain ambit may be construed in a restrictive way, for example 'my relatives in equal shares' might be interpreted as 'my next of kin in equal shares'; but 'my family' would probably be too vague. Further, if a list of potential or probable beneficiaries can be drawn up, but the only problem is that the trustees are unable to discover the facts that determine one person's entitlement, the court may grant a *'Benjamin* order'. This will allow them to distribute on the basis that the facts are as they assume, and may require them to insure against the assumption's being wrong. In *Re Benjamin* (1902) itself, the testator had left a substantial estate to be equally divided between his children living at his death or predeceasing him leaving issue. P D Benjamin, one of the 12 relevant children, had disappeared some ten months before the testator's death. It was admitted that the evidence was that he had not married and had children before the testator's death; but had he himself survived the testator? When last seen he had been about to set off on a skiing holiday, and had no reason to engineer his own disappearance. The probability was that he had died some months before the testator, and Joyce J ordered that the testator's executors be at liberty to distribute the estate on the basis that P D Benjamin had not survived the testator.

If uncertainties of language cannot be cured by interpretation, or uncertainties of entitlement cannot be cured by a *Benjamin* order, it will not be possible to draw up a complete list. As a result, no beneficiary's share can be known, because it is not known how many beneficiaries there are. The gift to each beneficiary fails for uncertainty.

B *Where the trustees have a power of appointment*

Where the beneficial interests are subject to a power of appointment, the rule for uncertainty of objects is very much more complicated. It is clear that it is not necessary to be able to compile a complete list of potential beneficiaries: see *Re Gulbenkian's ST* for mere powers and *McPhail v Doulton* for trust powers. There are, however, three ways in which the existence of a class of beneficiaries may cause a trust to fail for uncertainty. Each of the three categories of uncertainty is quite different from the others, and each has its own test. For the trust to be valid, the class must pass the test in all three categories.

1 *The class must be linguistically certain.* Linguistic certainty is sometimes called 'semantic' or 'conceptual' certainty. As all these names suggest, the key to linguistic certainty is to be found in the language of the trust instrument. *Test*: Evidential problems apart, it must be possible to say with certainty whether any individual is or is not a member of the class. In other words, the words used in defining the class must be apt to split the world into two categories: those in the class, and those not in the class. There must be nobody of whom it would have to be said 'it is uncertain whether he is in the class or not'. Note that this is 'evidential problems apart': in looking at linguistic certainty we are dealing with a theoretical or conceptual problem, and we can reach a conclusion by looking at the words of the trust instrument without worrying about the practicalities. So we can tell instantly that 'my grandchildren' and 'people who own Rolls-Royce cars' are classes that are linguistically certain; and, as in the case of a fixed trust, the court will be eager to construe words so as to avoid uncertainty. But, with the best will in the world, 'my friends' and 'people with red hair' remain linguistically uncertain classes. Some people are certainly my friends and others certainly are not; some people certainly have red hair and others certainly have not: but in each case there are people of whom it cannot be said with certainty whether they are in the class or not. There may be difficulty in tracing Rolls-Royce owners, or even my grandchildren, but the *concept* is clear. The words 'friends' and 'red' on the other hand are inherently vague. They are not precise enough to divide the world into two groups. They are linguistically uncertain.

2 *The class must be evidentially certain.* Linguistic certainty is not about practicalities: evidential certainty is. Evidential certainty is concerned with the relationship between the group of people who *are* (theoretically) in the class and the group of people who (in practice) can be *shown to be* within the class. We can appreciate that conceptually, every owner of a Rolls-Royce is a member of the class, but in practice the trustees will only consider those who are shown to be owners of a Rolls-Royce. Fred did own a Rolls-Royce but it has been stolen, and the papers with it, and whether he is still its owner depends on whether it has been sold by the thief in circumstances which give the transferee ownership. Theoretically, it is clear that he is either in the class of owners or not in it: there is no vagueness about the definition. But practically, we do not know whether he is in the class or not.

Now for the class to be certain it cannot be necessary for every person to be able to be *shown* to be a member or not a member. For if the class is linguistically certain, and if everyone who is in the class could be shown to be in the class, it should be possible to draw up a list of those in the class; and the House of Lords has told us that we do not have to be able to draw up a list (see above). On the other hand, the House of Lords (specifically overruling Lord Denning MR's suggestion in the Court of Appeal in *Re Gulbenkian's ST*) has also decided that it is not enough to be able to say of just one person that he is shown to be within the class. We therefore suggest the following. *Test*: *Of those within the class, it must be possible to say with certainty of a substantial proportion that they are shown to be within the class.* In other words, it does not matter that a few of the members of the (linguistically certain) class cannot be shown to be members. It *does* matter if a large proportion of those within the class cannot be shown to be within it. Suppose the class is 'all those who travelled on public transport in West Yorkshire during 1983'. This is a vast class, but it is linguistically certain: the world divides itself neatly into those who did and those who did not. Evidentially, however, this class is hopeless. Only a tiny proportion of those who are members of the class will be able to be shown to be members of the class. The trustees have an impossible task. The class they are directed by the settlor to consider is very large; but, because of the problems of evidence, the class of people they actually can consider is quite small. The class fails the test for evidential uncertainty, so the trust will fail for uncertainty of objects.

3 *The trust must be administratively workable.* Linguistic and evidential certainty are concerned with identifying those whom the trustees *may* choose for benefits. Administrative workability is concerned with how the trustees go about their job: not who is in the class, but whom to choose from the class. *Test*: *If the class is very large the donee of the power of appointment must either (a) be permitted by the settlor not to exercise it or (b) given some guidance by the settlor as to how he should exercise it.*

If the trustees are obliged to make a choice from a very large class ('all the residents of Greater London' was Lord Wilberforce's example in *McPhail v Doulton*) the settlor must give them some guidance as to how to make that choice. If he does not, but leaves property simply 'on trust for such of the residents of Greater London as my trustees shall in their absolute discretion think fit' the trustees again have an impossible task. As donees of a trust power they are obliged to make a choice; as fiduciaries they are prohibited from making a choice on capricious grounds, unrelated to the settlor's purpose; but they have no information enabling them to make a proper choice. The trust must fail because, although the class is linguistically and evidentially certain, it is administratively unworkable. Where, however, a large class is subject to a mere power rather than a trust power it will not cause the trust to fail for administrative unworkability. For if the power is a mere power, the trustees can fulfil their duty by deciding from time to time that (as they are unable to exercise it in a rational manner) they will not exercise it (*Re Hay's ST* (1981)).

C *Where there is a personal power of appointment*
Nearly all the litigation about certainty of objects has concerned trusts where there was a fiduciary power of appointment. It will be remembered that the duties of the holder of a fiduciary power are much greater than those of the holder of a personal power. In particular, the former must consider the range of objects, and appoint on a rational basis. It is because of these greater duties that the rules as to linguistic and evidential certainty and administrative workability have been developed: the holder of a fiduciary power cannot carry out his duties unless the class passes the three tests. None of these restrictions should apply to a class which is subject to a personal power. The holder of a personal power does not have to survey the field, or appoint on a rational basis. So where a class is subject to a personal power of appointment, there should be no objection on grounds of uncertainty. Even a class which is linguistically grossly uncertain can probably be the object of such a power: 'to such of my friends as my dear wife may by deed or will appoint'. The settlor's wife can validly exercise the power by appointing to persons who definitely are his friends: it does not matter that there are thousands who might or might not be, since she does not have to consider the whole class. She should, however, avoid making any appointment to those of doubtful status: her sole duty is to adhere to the terms of the trust, and she should therefore confine herself to appointees who are definitely within the terms of the trust.

D *Series of gifts each subject to a condition*
In the same way, the rules as to certainty of object appear to have little application in a case where the settlor, instead of giving a block of property to be distributed under a power of appointment, has made a series of separate gifts to persons fulfilling a particular

description. A fiduciary power of appointment of which the class of objects is 'my friends' is, as we have seen, void; but a direction to trustees to give '£10 to each of my friends' is valid. The reason is that, in the case of the power, the trustees have to survey the whole range of possible beneficiaries, which they cannot do as 'friends' is linguistically uncertain: but to administer the series of separate gifts the trustees have only to consider the qualifications of individuals coming forward. Provided that they take a conservative view of what constitutes being a friend, so that they are definitely within the terms of the gift, they can administer the trust. If they are in doubt, they should seek the directions of the court. In *Re Barlow's WT* (1979) the testatrix directed her trustees to allow 'any members of my family and any friends of mine' to purchase pictures from her collection at a discount. Browne-Wilkinson J held that the effect of the clause was to confer on the family and friends a series of options to purchase. It was not, therefore, necessary to draw up a list of those who might be entitled: all that was required was for the executors to be able to say of any individual whether he had proved that he was a member of the family or a friend. The learned judge went on to give guidance on how 'family' and 'friends' should be interpreted.

We conclude this section by summarising the rules for certainty of objects in ascending order of severity. If there is a personal power of appointment or a series of separate gifts one needs to be able to say of individuals who come forward that they have or have not shown that they are within the class or description respectively. A class subject to a mere power vested in trustees must be linguistically and evidentially certain. A class subject to a discretionary trust must be linguistically and evidentially certain and administratively workable. A class subject to a fixed trust must be listable.

PROPRIETARY RIGHTS OF THE BENEFICIARIES

The whole beneficial interest in the trust property is owned by the beneficiaries. That is to say, all the beneficiaries of a trust – present and future beneficiaries, actual beneficiaries, beneficiaries with an interest subject to contingency, people who may become beneficiaries if a discretion is exercised in their favour, a charity which is to take as remainderman at the end of the perpetuity period – all who might possibly become entitled to an interest, together, as a group, own the beneficial interest. And, as a group, the beneficiaries may assert their ownership of the beneficial interest: they may terminate the trust. But the beneficiaries can only act in this way if every member of the group is of full capacity and wishes to do so. So unless all the beneficiaries are ascertained, over 18 and not mental patients, the trust continues. But if all the possible beneficiaries of a trust are of full age and sound mind they may together require the trustees to transfer to them the legal title to the trust property, thus extinguishing the trust. This is the rule in *Saunders v Vautier* (1841).

The rule applies regardless of the wishes of the settlor expressed in the trust instrument. In *Josselyn v Josselyn* (1837) the trustee was to retain the trust property, accumulating interest until the beneficiary reached the age of 24. There was a gift over to somebody else if he should die before reaching the age of 21. When the beneficiary was 21 he demanded the capital of the trust fund, and it was held that the trustee was bound to pay it to him. He was of full age and sound mind; he was now the only person possibly entitled as beneficiary; he therefore owned the whole beneficial interest and was entitled to terminate the trust now, despite the direction to accumulate until he was 24. So whenever a trust has only one possible beneficiary and he is not under any disability it may be terminated at any moment. Such a trust is called a 'bare trust'. A bare trust may be intentionally created as such, in order that a person be relieved of the responsibility of the management of his investments; or it may arise, for example, when the last life tenant dies leaving a remainderman solely beneficially entitled; in addition, many resulting and constructive trusts are bare trusts.

If there is more than one beneficiary the principle is exactly the same. Regardless of the terms of the settlement, the beneficiaries may together terminate the trust if they are all of full age and sound mind. So if a testator leaves his estate to trustees on trust for his widow for life with remainder to his three children in equal shares, then as soon as the children are 18 the four beneficiaries together can demand the capital from the trustees and split it up in any way they choose. Obviously, the more possible beneficiaries there are, the less practicable this course of action will be, and in the case of some trusts it is either impracticable or impossible. In the case of a discretionary trust, it would be necessary to obtain consent from all possible beneficiaries; in the case of a mere power, one would need consent not only from all the objects of the power, but from those entitled in default of exercise of the power as well.

54 The beneficiary

It sometimes happens, however, that although, for one reason or another, the rule in *Saunders v Vautier* cannot be applied, there is yet one beneficiary (or sub-group of beneficiaries) who can say that he has become indefeasibly entitled to part of the trust property. Suppose Fred left property on trust for his sons George and Harry in equal shares absolutely. George has now reached the age of 18. Although the trust cannot be terminated, because Harry is still only 14, George is definitely entitled to half the trust property. However, because the trust as a whole will continue, George can demand his share only of those parts of the trust property which will easily divide, like money and shares. As regards property which cannot be easily divided (land for example), George will have to be content with his rights under the trust until the property is sold and he can share the proceeds: *Stephenson v Barclays Bank Trust Co Ltd* (1975).

It must be emphasised that the proprietary rights of the beneficiaries enable them *only* to terminate the trust. They cannot control the trustees, by, for example, requiring them to appoint a particular new trustee or to make a particular investment. The reason is that it is a contradiction to use a power to terminate a trust as a means of keeping it going (*Re Brockbank* (1948)). The trustees may agree to do whatever it is the beneficiaries want, but they cannot be compelled to do so, even by the owners of the whole beneficial interests. If the latter are dissatisfied, their remedy is to demand the trust property and resettle it on trustees more amenable to their will.

Chapter 6
Constituting a trust

A valid express trust must, as well as being properly declared, be constituted. A trust is constituted if either (a) the trust property is in the hands of the trustee, when the trust is said to be *completely constituted*; or (b) the beneficiary is in a position to ensure that the property is transferred to the trustee: in this case the trust is *incompletely constituted*. If the trustee does not have the property, and the beneficiary cannot compel the settlor to transfer it, there is no trust at all.

In order to understand why this is so, let us stand back and, forgetting trusts for the moment, see how a person may cause another to enjoy the advantages of a particular piece of property. The law enforces rights of ownership and bargains, but not bare promises. So if S wants B to have certain property, S must carry out one of two courses of action. Either he actually transfers the property to B (in which case B becomes owner and his rights as owner have legal protection) or he contracts with B to transfer the property to him. In the latter event, provided B has given consideration (that is, that the contract is a bargain, not a bare promise), B can sue S on the contract and either obtain a decree of specific performance, compelling S to transfer the property to him, or obtain damages for S's failure to carry out his side of the bargain. If B has not given consideration, so that there was no contract but merely a promise by S to make a gift to B, B is powerless. If S keeps his promise, all is well, but, if he does not, B cannot compel him to. And the doctrine of privity of contract prevents any but the parties to the contract from suing on it; so, if S contracts with T to give property to B, T may sue S (though his damages are likely to be nominal), but B has no standing to sue S as he was not a party to the contract.

Now the principles under which transfers in trust are enforced are precisely the same. Equity recognises the rights of a person to whom a gift has actually been made, and the rights of a person to

55

sue on a contract; but equity will not allow a person who has not given consideration to enforce a bare promise to make a gift. The maxim is 'equity will not assist a volunteer' – a 'volunteer' being one who has not given consideration – or 'equity will not perfect an imperfect gift'. The only two extra pieces of information we need in order to work out the rules of constitution of trusts are the following. First, equity's conception of what may be regarded as consideration for a promise is different from the common law's. Secondly, equity regards a transfer to B as complete not only where B has the property but also where somebody else has the property and is holding it on trust for B. Thus equity likewise protects rights of ownership and rights under contracts; but it has a slightly different idea of contract and a wider concept of ownership.

FIVE WAYS OF MAKING A GIFT

So, using the trust concept, if S wants B to have the benefit of certain property, S must carry out one of five courses of action.

(1) He may transfer the property to B; this is a complete gift, without the imposition of a trust.
(2) He may declare himself a trustee of the property for B. This is a completely constituted trust. The property is in the hands of the trustee (S) and B has equitable ownership.
(3) He may transfer the property to T to hold on trust for B. This too is a completely constituted trust. The property is in the hands of the trustee (T) and B has equitable ownership.
(4) He may make a contract with B, for which B provides consideration, under which he promises to transfer the property to B. This is an incomplete transfer but B, having given consideration, can sue on the contract.
(5) He may make a contract with B, for which B provides consideration, under which he promises to transfer the property to T on trust for B. This is an incompletely constituted trust, but B, having given consideration, can sue on the contract.

We will now consider each of these five methods in more detail, and throughout, we shall for brevity's sake refer to 'method (1)' and so on, and shall denote the settlor, trustee and beneficiary as S, T and B respectively. The treatment of method (1) is long, because it includes a discussion of how to transfer various types of property. After method (4) there is a section comparing the first four methods; and after method (5) there is a section showing how method (3) may be used in order to avoid some difficulties of the last two methods. The chapter concludes by examining some exceptions to the principle that equity will not complete an imperfect gift.

Method (1): Complete gift

In order to make a gift of property to *B*, *S* must transfer the property to him. If he fails to transfer it, whether because he changes his mind, or because he does not use the method of transfer appropriate to the type of property involved, there is no gift. *B* does not have the property and cannot sue for it: he has not given consideration, and equity will not assist a volunteer.

It therefore becomes necessary to set out the methods of transfer appropriate to various types of property.

1 *Land.* A conveyance of a legal estate in land must be by deed (Law of Property Act 1925, s 52(1)). If the title to the land is registered, or is to be registered, the transfer is not complete until the new owner is registered as the proprietor (Land Registration Act 1925, ss 20, 23).

2 *Equitable interests.* An equitable interest (normally an interest under another trust) may be the subject matter of a gift or a trust; but 'a disposition of an equitable interest or trust subsisting at the time of the disposition, must be in writing signed by the person disposing of the same or by his agent thereunto lawfully authorised in writing or by will' (Law of Property Act 1925, s 53(1)(c)). The application of this rule has caused some difficulty in practice. In *Grey v IRC* (1959), *G* held shares on presumed resulting trust for *H*. On 18 February *H* orally directed *G* to hold the shares on trust for *B*. On 25 March *G* executed documents, which *H* also signed, declaring that since 18 February *G* had held on trust for *B*, not *H*. In the House of Lords it was held that the transfer of the equitable interest in the shares took place on 25 March, not 18 February. The intention of the parties was that the situation in which *G* held on trust for *H* should be converted to the situation in which *G* held on trust for *B*. A comparison reveals that if *G* holds on trust for *B*, that must be because *H* has disposed of his equitable interest to *B*. A disposition of an equitable interest must be in writing signed by (in this case) *H*. The only writings signed by *H* were the documents of 25 March, so it was by virtue of those documents that *H*'s interest passed to *B*.

Constituting a trust

Section 53(1)(c) does not apply where the intention is to vest the whole legal and equitable title in a donee, even if immediately before the transfer the legal and equitable interests were held by different persons. So in *Vandervell v IRC* (1965) *G* held on trust for *H*; and on *H*'s instructions *G* transferred the *legal* title to *B* intending *B* to take as beneficial owner. The legal title had clearly passed to *B*; but the question for the House of Lords was, had *H*'s equitable interest passed with the legal title, or did it need to be transferred to *B* separately in writing? It was held that s 53(1)(c) had no application in these circumstances. Looking at the case in the same way as we looked at *Grey v IRC*, the situation in which *G* holds on trust for *H* has been converted to the situation in which *B* is absolute beneficial owner. A comparison does not reveal a disposition of *H*'s subsisting equitable interest but its extinguishment by merger with the legal estate in the hands of *B*.

3 *Company shares.* The ownership of shares or debentures in a company is transferred by the entry of the new owner's name in the company's books, after receipt by the company of a proper instrument of transfer (Companies Act 1985, s 183).

4 *Other choses in action.* Statutes prescribe methods of transfer for some special types of chose in action, for example policies of assurance, patents, copyrights. Other choses in action may be assigned using the statutory method under the Law of Property Act 1925, s 136, which requires the assignment to be written, and written notice of it to be given to the debtor or other person from whom the assignor would, but for the assignment, be entitled to claim. Alternatively a valid assignment in equity may be made if there is clear intention to assign, however evidenced. Writing will, however, still be needed if the nature of the property demands it. A cheque or other bill of exchange must be indorsed.

5 *Chattels.* Chattels must be transferred by actual delivery to the transferree or by constructive delivery or by deed of gift.

It is sometimes said that equity will regard an incomplete transfer as complete, provided that the transferor has done all that he could do to complete it. That does not appear to be true as a general rule; but *Re Rose* (1952) seems to indicate that the courts may take such an approach where to do otherwise would cause undue hardship. The donor in that case executed instruments of transfer of shares in a private company and handed them together

Five ways of making a gift 59

with the share certificates to the donee on 30 March 1943. The donee sent them to the company, which registered the transfer by entry of the transferee's name in the books of the company on 30 June. The donor died on 10 April 1947. More estate duty was payable if the transfer had been made within four years of his death. The Court of Appeal held that the gift was complete on 30 March (not within four years of the death) because on that date the donor had done all he could do in order to transfer the shares: the remaining acts were to be done by parties over whom he had no control. It should be noted that in *Re Rose* the transfer was, in the end, completed on 30 June; the court was merely back dating a complete transfer to the date when the transferor had done all he could do to effect the transfer. It does not follow that, if the transfer had *not* been completed by registration of the new owner, the court would nevertheless have held the transfer complete in equity. So it is better to say as a general rule that, for the gift to be effective, there must be a completed transfer of the property to the donee; but, provided there is a complete transfer, the court may be prepared to hold that it took place at the time when the donor had done all that he could do in order to effect the transfer.

Method (2): Settlor declares himself trustee

We have seen already, in Chapter 2, that for S to declare himself trustee of property, he must clearly and unambiguously show his intention that the property is henceforth to be held by him as trustee. Provided he has done so, the trust is complete. There is no need for any transfer to take place, since S is to continue to hold the property, and no form is necessary except as set out in that chapter. To these rules we must add a postscript; for there is one set of circumstances in which a declaration of trust has the effect of a transfer, and, what is more, a transfer which is ineffective without writing. Suppose T holds property on trust for S, who declares himself a trustee of his interest for B. If S, on declaring this subtrust, reserves for himself some powers or duties (for example a power to appoint new trustees of the sub-trust), then there has indeed been a declaration of trust by S; the position now is that T holds on trust for S who holds his interest on trust for B. But if S does not reserve any powers or duties when declaring himself a trustee of his interest for B, then in reality he 'drops out of the picture', leaving T holding on trust for B: *Grainge v Wilberforce* (1889). If we compare the situation before the declaration by S (T holds on trust for S) with the situation after (T holds on trust for B) we see that the effect of S's declaration of trust of his whole equitable interest in favour of *B* has been to transfer that interest to *B*. In other words, *S* has disposed of an equitable interest subsisting at the time of the disposition; and we have seen that such a disposition must, by the Law of Property Act 1925, s 53(1)(c), be in writing, signed by the disponer (see p 57 above). So if a person wishes to declare himself a trustee of his equitable interest, he should be aware that the declaration must be in writing if the effect is to be that he 'drops out of the picture'.

Method (3): Settlor transfers property to trustees

In order to carry out this method of benefiting *B*, *S* must fulfil the requirements of both method (1) and method (2). He must transfer the property to *T* so that *T* holds the title to it, and he must use clear and unambiguous words showing his intention that *T* is not to take beneficially but is to hold on trust for *B*. If he fails to transfer the property to *T* using the appropriate method of transfer for the type of property involved, there is no trust. *T* does not have the property and (there being no consideration) *S* cannot be compelled to transfer it.

Method (4): Incomplete transfer supported by consideration

If *S* promises to transfer property to *B* and, for one reason or another, fails to carry out his promise, *B* can sue *S* if and only if *B* gave consideration for the promise. At common law consideration may be found in the fact that the promise was by deed ('the seal imports consideration', as it is said). Otherwise the consideration must be some valuable act or promise detrimental to *B* or advantageous to *S*. 'Equity looks to the intention and not to the form', so in equity a promise made in the form of a deed is no better than any other bare promise. Apart from that, everything that would be consideration at common law is consideration in equity, with one important addition. When a promise is made in consideration of marriage, equity regards the husband and wife and the issue of the marriage as having given consideration. They are all said to be 'within the marriage consideration': *A-G v Jacobs-Smith* (1895).

B has an action for damages for breach of contract if he has given consideration of any kind. If, however, he has given consideration of a kind recognised by equity, and the property which *S* promised to transfer to him is unique, or if for some other reason damages would not be adequate to compensate *B* for *S*'s failure to carry out his promise, then the court will grant *B* an order for

Five ways of making a gift 61

specific performance of the contract: that is, it will order *S* to carry out his promise. In these circumstances, therefore, although the transfer is incomplete, the court will order it to be completed. The principle goes further. Suppose that the circumstances (type of consideration, type of property) which would lead to a grant of specific performance do exist: until *S*'s promise to transfer to *B* is carried out, equity will regard *S* as holding the property on constructive trust for *B*. 'Equity looks on that as done which ought to be done'; *S* ought to transfer to *B* and would, if necessary, be compelled by a court to do so; therefore equity looks on the benefit of the property as having been already transferred to *B*: that is, *S* holds on trust for *B*. This is the usual position between contract and conveyance in the sale of a house. The purchaser gives consideration by his promise to pay; the property, being a parcel of land, is unique; therefore specific performance would, if necessary, be ordered; so pending completion the vendor holds on constructive trust for the purchaser (*Lysaght v Edwards* (1876)). Thus *B*, having given consideration, is in much the same position as if *S* had declared a trust in his favour using method (2).

If the property which *S* promises to transfer to *B* is an equitable interest, it is not clear whether writing is necessary because of s 53(1)(c) of the Law of Property Act 1925, or whether the general law imposing a constructive trust upon *S* (and so passing the equitable interest to *B* when *S* 'drops out of the picture') takes effect without writing. One would suppose the latter solution to be the correct one, as s 53(2) provides: 'This section [i e s 53] does not affect the creation or operation of resulting, implied or constructive trusts'. It would seem that as *B* by giving consideration causes the creation of a constructive trust in his favour, s 53(1)(c) would have no effect. This view is probably correct, though it may need modification in the light of the enigmatic case of *Oughtred v IRC* (1959).

In that case, trustees held 200,000 shares in a private limited company on trust for *B* for life with remainder to *S*; *B* also held 72,700 shares absolutely. On 18 June 1956 *S* and *B* agreed orally that *S* would cede his remainder interest in the 200,000 (an equitable interest) to *B*, in exchange for *B*'s transferring her 72,700 to *S*. On 26 June *B* transferred the 72,700 to *S* and then the trustees conveyed the 200,000 to *B* on the basis that since 18 June she had been owner of the whole beneficial interest (the life interest under the original trust; the remainder by the constructive trust arising out of the contract) and so was entitled to have the legal estate. The Inland Revenue sought to charge the conveyance of 200,000 to ad valorem stamp duty as a 'conveyance on sale', which 'includes every instrument whereby any property or any estate or interest in any property upon the sale thereof is transferred to or vested in a purchaser or any other person on his behalf or at his discretion' (Stamp Act 1891, s 54). *B* argued that the document was not a 'conveyance on sale': *S*'s equitable interest had become vested in her either on 18 June or, at latest, when she transferred the 72,700 to *S* (at which point she had paid for *S*'s interest and was entitled to have it). The Inland Revenue argued that the conveyance was nevertheless a 'conveyance on sale'; or alternatively that *S*'s equitable interest could not have passed by the oral contract on 18 June because of s 53(1)(c) and so must have been transferred, if at all, by the writing on 26 June. The House of Lords held against the taxpayers by a majority of 3 to 2. Lord Jenkins (with whom Lord Keith agreed) held that, even if *B*'s argument was correct, the conveyance was a 'conveyance on sale'. Although it might be that the beneficial interest had already vested in her, the conveyance was executed in order to carry through the purpose of the contract. Just as the conveyance of a house is a 'conveyance on sale' even though the beneficial interest already belongs to the purchaser because of the constructive trust, so here too the document was stampable. Lord Radcliffe and Lord Cohen, the minority, held that the beneficial interest had indeed passed to *B* by the contract: s 53(2) made writing unnecessary to achieve this effect. Therefore the conveyance was not 'on sale': the purpose of the sale had already been completed and *B* was merely exercising her right to have the legal title vested in her as she now owned the whole equitable interest. Only Lord Denning, who gave judgment in favour of the Inland Revenue, held that s 53(2) did not do away with the need for writing when an equitable interest to is to pass in these circumstances. He gave no reasons for his view.

Although the taxpayers lost in *Oughtred*, it would appear that, as far as s 53 is concerned, their oral contract probably was effective to transfer *S*'s equitable interest to *B*: the trouble was that even so the conveyance was subject to ad valorem stamp duty.

A comparison of the first four methods

We have seen now that methods (1) and (3) require an actual transfer of property and methods (2) and (3) require a declaration of trust. Method (4) requires neither, but will not apply unless there is consideration in equity. Where the gift or trust is complete, as in methods (1), (2) and (3), there is no need for consideration. In *Re Ralli's WT* (1964) the settlor covenanted (that is,

Five ways of making a gift 63

promised by deed, there being no consideration other than that imported at common law by the seal) that she would transfer property to T on trust for B. Part of the property was a reversionary interest under another trust. In the covenant the settlor also declared that all the property comprised within the terms of the covenant should be subject in equity to the trusts of the settlement pending transfer of the property to T. The reversionary interest was never transferred to T. Nevertheless Buckley J held that from the date of the covenant the settlor had held her reversionary interest on trust for B because the terms of the covenant were tantamount to a declaration of trust. It was irrelevant that T was a volunteer because the gift was complete by method (2). Likewise, in the more obvious cases where S has actually transferred property to B or to T on trust for B, no consideration is necessary.

But where S intends to use method (1) or method (3) but fails to transfer the property, equity will not regard him as having declared himself to be a trustee of the property. There are two reasons for this rule. First, to regard his actions in this light would be contrary to what he actually intended. There is a world of difference between on the one hand declaring oneself to be a trustee and thereby taking upon oneself all the duties and liabilities of trusteeship, and, on the other hand, getting rid of the property altogether. A person who attempts unsuccessfully to do the latter cannot possibly be seen as having intended to do the former. 'For a man to make himself a trustee there must be an expression of intention to become a trustee, whereas the words of the present gift show an intention to give over property to another, and not retain it in the donor's hands for any purpose, fiduciary or otherwise' (*Richards v Delbridge* (1874) per Jessel MR). Secondly, to hold that in cases of this sort S holds on trust for B would be to enforce a bare promise, which would run counter to the maxim that equity will not assist a volunteer.

In the classic case, *Milroy v Lord* (1862), Turner LJ, after setting out methods (1), (2) and (3), said:

'In order to render the settlement binding one or other of those modes must be resorted to, for there is no equity in this court to perfect an imperfect gift. The cases I think go further to this extent, that if the settlement is intended to be effectuated by one of the modes to which I have referred, the court will not give effect to it by applying another of those modes. If it is intended to take effect by transfer, the court will not hold the intended transfer to operate as a declaration of trust, for then every imperfect instrument would be made effectual by being converted into a perfect trust'.

Milroy v Lord concerned an attempted transfer of shares which was incomplete because the transferee's name was never entered in the company's books. In *Richards v Delbridge* the intending donor wrote on the back of a lease 'this deed and all thereto belonging I give to Edward Benneto Richards from this time forth, with all the stock-in-trade'. Another well-known case on this topic is *Jones v Lock* (1865), in which *S*, to show his affection for his baby, put a cheque for £900, payable to himself, into its hand, and said 'Look you here, I give this to baby, it is for himself'. He then took the cheque back. None of these gifts was complete: a transfer of shares requires registration by the company; a transfer of a lease requires a deed of assignment and the stock-in-trade could not be transferred without a deed or delivery; a cheque needs indorsement. The result in each case was the same. *S* had attempted to transfer property to *B* and had failed; he would not be regarded as having made himself a trustee for *B*. The intended donee, being a volunteer, therefore obtained nothing. The same would have applied if *S*, instead of attempting to transfer to *B*, had in each case attempted to transfer to *T* on trust for *B*. But if in any of the cases *B* had given consideration the position would have been entirely different: he would not be a volunteer, so equity would assist him, and, provided that the promise was of a type to be specifically enforced, equity would regard *S* as holding on trust for *B* pending transfer.

Method (5): Incomplete transfer to trustees supported by consideration

If *S* promises or attempts to transfer property to *T* on trust for *B* but the transfer is not made, then *B* can enforce the promise if he has given consideration; if he has not, he cannot. The contrast between the volunteer and the person whom equity regards as a purchaser is well illustrated by two cases with similar facts. *Pullan v Koe* (1913) concerned a settlement made in consideration of a marriage in 1859, in which the wife covenanted that any property she might in the future acquire in her own right would be settled by her on the trusts of the marriage settlement in favour of herself, her issue and her next of kin. In 1879 she acquired £285 which, for various reasons, was never settled but was in the husband's control on his death in 1909. It was held that, as the wife and the children of the marriage were 'within the marriage consideration' they could sue to enforce the covenant, and for that reason the £285 was to be regarded as trust property the moment it came into the wife's hands in 1879. In *Re Plumptre's Marriage Settlement* (1910) the settlement was made in consideration of marriage in 1878, and similarly contained a covenant to settle after-acquired property. Some stock was given by the husband to the wife, which she sold and reinvested, and at her death in 1909 it had still not been settled but remained in her name. There were no children of the marriage, and so, the wife being dead, those suing to enforce the covenant were the next of kin. The next of kin are not 'within the marriage consideration' but are volunteers. The covenant therefore could not be enforced.

If *B* had not given consideration in equity he may still be able to sue if the promise was made in a deed to which he was a party. He will not, however, be able to *enforce* the promise because specific performance is an equitable remedy and is only available to those who have given what equity regards as consideration. Instead he will obtain damages for breach of the promise, as illustrated by *Cannon v Hartley* (1949). *S* covenanted to settle certain after-acquired property on trustees for himself for life, with remainder to his wife for life with remainder for his daughter (*B*) absolutely. Unlike the last two cases discussed, the covenant was not made in consideration of marriage, but quite the contrary: it was a deed of separation. Thus there was no consideration in equity. But *S*, his wife and *B* were all parties to the deed. In 1944 *S* became entitled to an equitable interest under his father's will. His wife died in 1946. *S* refused to carry out the terms of the covenant, and *B* sued. It was held that as *B* had in equity given no consideration she could not enforce the promise; yet since she was a party to the deed she was entitled at common law to damages for its breach. If *B* had not been a party to the deed she could have obtained neither specific performance nor damages.

The question sometimes arises whether the intended trustees can enforce a promise on behalf of the intended beneficiaries. The answer is that the trustees can sue if there is a beneficiary who is not a volunteer. Indeed, the trustees were the plaintiffs in *Pullan v Koe*. But where *S* covenants with *T* to transfer property to *T* on trust for *B*, and *B* gives no consideration and is not a party to the covenant, *T* will not be allowed to enforce the covenant in *B*'s favour, because to do so would be to assist a volunteer. In *Re Kay's Settlement* (1939) a spinster covenanted with *T* to settle after-acquired property on *T* on the usual marriage settlement terms, although the covenant was not made in consideration of marriage. Subsequently she married, had three children, acquired property and refused to settle it. *T* sought directions from the court on whether he should sue on the covenant. Simonds J held that he should not, as the children were volunteers both at law and in equity.

We saw from *Cannon v Hartley* that where *B* has not given consideration in equity he will not obtain the equitable remedy of specific performance, but at best only the common law remedy of damages. The same applies where the equitable remedy is unavailable for some other reason. Specific performance will only be granted where the property is unique (which may be because it is already impressed with a trust, as in *Pullan v Koe*) or where damages would not be an adequate remedy for non-performance of the contract. So where the promise is not to transfer any particular piece of property but merely to pay a sum of money from *S*'s general funds, specific performance is not available; the only possibility is an action for damages: *Stone v Stone* (1870). The particular disadvantage of this is that a plaintiff suing for damages for breach of covenant is subject to a limitation period of 12 years, after which the action cannot be brought, whereas a plaintiff suing on the grounds that the defendant is in possession of trust property is not so limited (Limitation Act 1980, ss 8(1), 21(1)(b)).

Completely constituted trust of the benefit of a covenant

There is a refinement of method (3) which may occasionally allow a trust to be regarded as fully constituted although the intended trust property has not been transferred to the trustee. Suppose *S* covenants with *T* that he will transfer certain property to *T* on trust for *B*. We have seen that *B* cannot sue *S* on the covenant if he has given no consideration, and *T* cannot sue on *B*'s behalf. But *T* has acquired something by the covenant: he has acquired a contractual right against *S*. A contractual right may be the subject matter of a trust. So perhaps *T* holds his contractual right on trust for *B*. In that case there would be a completely constituted trust, but the trust property, instead of being the property which *S* covenanted to transfer, would be *T*'s right to enforce the covenant against *S*. As the trust of that right was completely constituted, *B*'s proprietary right to the benefit of the trust property would be recognised in equity and hence *B* could sue on *T*'s contract.

This is an inviting solution from *B*'s point of view. It is certainly open to *S* and *T* to declare expressly in their covenant that it is made 'to the intent that the benefit of this covenant shall be held by *T* on trust for *B*'. But where there is no such express declaration *B* will normally not be able to persuade a court to assist him, a volunteeer, by interpreting the transaction between *S* and *T* in such a way as to imply such a term. *B* will have a heavy burden to

Five ways of making a gift 67

discharge, and it seems to be almost impossible to predict how the court would react. In *Fletcher v Fletcher* (1844) Wigram V-C held that *S* must have intended *T* to hold his contractual right on trust for *B* since otherwise the covenant would be totally ineffectual; but it seems unlikely that his argument would have force today. In a more recent case, *Re Cook's ST* (1965), Buckley J refused to find that the benefit of the covenant was held on trust for *B* and so decided that the rule exemplified by *Re Kay's Settlement* (above) prevented either *T* or *B* from suing. Thus it appears that the arcane notion of a completely constituted trust of the benefit of the covenant may be imported by an express term in the covenant, but otherwise cannot be exploited by a volunteer.

EXCEPTIONS TO THE RULE THAT EQUITY WILL NOT PERFECT AN IMPERFECT GIFT

In a number of special situations, none of them at all common, an incomplete transfer will be regarded as complete, thus giving proprietary rights even to a volunteer. These situations are therefore exceptions to the rule that equity will not perfect an imperfect gift. There are two statutory exceptions (both concerned only with land) and five deriving from the cases.

Statutory exceptions

1 *Incomplete settlement of land.* A settlement of land has to be made by two documents, the trust instrument and the vesting deed (see Chapter 3). If an intending settlor only executes one document, the settlement is therefore incomplete. However, s 9 of the Settled Land Act 1925 provides that in such circumstances the one document takes effect as the trust instrument, and the tenant for life is entitled to have a vesting deed executed in his favour.

2 *Conveyance of land to an infant.* A legal estate in land cannot be held by an infant, so any attempt to give a legal estate in land to an infant would be an incomplete gift, unenforceable by the intended beneficiary. However, s 27(1) of the Settled Land Act 1925 provides that a conveyance of a legal estate in land to an infant shall take effect as (a) an agreement for valuable consideration to settle the land on trustees in favour of the infant, and (b) in the meantime, a declaration that the settlor holds on trust for the infant. Thus the statute turns a failure of method (1) into method (2) and method (5) successively.

68   Constituting a trust

Equitable exceptions

1 *Donatio mortis causa.* Where a person (a) has a settled contemplation of his impending death, and (b) intends to make a gift which is conditional upon his dying and will be ineffective if he recovers, and (c) delivers to the donee either the property to be given or documents representing it, then (d) provided that he dies, equity will in many cases regard the gift as complete even though the proper mode of transfer was not used. So courts have allowed the contents of a bank account to be transferred by delivery of the passbook (*Birch v Treasury Solicitor* (1951)) and a cheque to be transferred by delivery without indorsement. But certain types of property, particularly land and shares, cannot pass by this method, and, for any property, the conditions for a donatio mortis causa will be strictly applied. In particular, it is essential that the gift was intended not to be absolute, but to be conditional upon the donor's death.

2 *The rule in* Strong v Bird *(1874)*. Where *S* intends to transfer any specific property to *B* or to *T* on trust for *B*, and continues in that intention right up to the moment of his death, and is found to have appointed the intended transferee as his executor (so that the executor acquires title to the property by virtue of his office), the transfer is regarded as complete. The rule has been extended to cases where the intended transferee was appointed (by the court) to be *S*'s administrator on his intestacy (*Re James* (1935)) and where the intended transferee acquired title to the property on his appointment by a third party to be trustee of another trust (*Re Ralli's WT*). Both these extensions of the rule were recently doubted by Walton J in *Re Gonin* (1979). The principle of *Strong v Bird* is that dying and appointing someone, to whom you intend to give property, as your executor is a sort of transfer, just as is delivery of a chattel to someone to whom you intend to give it. But the analogy only operates if the donor, not the court or a third party, chooses the eventual recipient. It is suggested therefore that Walton J's reservations are well-founded, and the rule should be confined to cases where the intended transferee takes as executor.

3 *The rule in* Re Rose *(1952)*. When the transferor has done all in his power to effect a transfer, a court may be prepared to treat the transfer as complete at that moment, at any rate if the transfer is eventually properly completed. *Re Rose* is discussed at p 58 above.

Exceptions to the rule 69

4 *Disclaimer*. Where *S* attempts to create a trust by deed, by vesting property in *T* on trust for *B*, it may be that *T* does not wish to accept the office of trustee. If *T* disclaims, as he is entitled to do, the property vests in *S* as if it had never left him, but he holds on trust for *B*: *Mallott v Wilson* (1903).

5 *Proprietary estoppel*. If *S* makes an imperfect gift to *B* and *B* then expends money on improving the property while *S*, knowing that *B* is under a misapprehension, does nothing to stop him, equity will sometimes compel *S* to perfect *B*'s title to the property. The leading case is *Dillwyn v Llewelyn* (1862). *S* allowed *B* (his son) to take possession of certain land, and signed an informal memorandum purporting to give the land to *B*. *B* built a house on it. It was held by Lord Westbury LC that after *S*'s death his heir could not claim the land against *B*.

CONCLUSION

The law contained in this chapter may be summed up in two sentences. Save in the rare cases where one of the exceptions is applicable, a court will only enforce a gift or trust when the gift is complete or the trust is completely constituted, or when the beneficiary has given consideration. That is what it means to say that 'equity will not assist a volunteer'.

Chapter 7
Resulting trusts

A resulting trust is a trust implied by equity in favour of the settlor or (if he is dead) his estate. Of course it is possible to have an express trust in favour of the settlor, where the settlor names himself as one of the beneficiaries. A resulting trust, however, being implied, arises not from the expressed intentions of the settlor but by operation of the rules of equity. The word 'resulting' comes from the same root as 'resilient' and in this context means 'springing back'. We are to imagine that in a resulting trust the beneficial interest 'springs back' to the settlor. It may do so for one of two reasons. In an automatic resulting trust the beneficial interest springs back because there is nowhere else for it to go: there is no person, other than the settlor, beneficially entitled to the property. In a presumed resulting trust the beneficial interest springs back because, in the absence of evidence to the contrary, equity presumes that a person who gives property to a stranger intends the latter to hold on trust for him.

AUTOMATIC RESULTING TRUSTS

The principle of automatic resulting trusts is simple and is well stated by Snell (*Principles of Equity* (28 edn, 1982)): 'What a man does not effectively dispose of remains vested in him'. Where a trust is created, but, for one reason or another, the beneficial interest in the trust property is not wholly disposed of by the settlor, a resulting trust arises to fill the gap. Any part of the beneficial interest which the settlor has not disposed of is held by the trustees on resulting trust for him. The cause is often bad drafting, where the draftsman of the original settlement has not foreseen the possibility of the events which actually happened, or where the declared trusts fail, for illegality (for example, perpetuity) or for some other reason, such as uncertainty of

Automatic resulting trusts 71

beneficiaries. *Re Cochrane* (1955) is a simple illustration. Property was settled by a marriage settlement on the wife for her life or so long as she should live with her husband. On the termination of her interest, the income was to be paid to the husband for his life. On the death of both parents, the property was to go to the children of the marriage. The wife ceased to live with the husband, so her interest terminated. The husband died (thus terminating his life interest) in 1953, at which time the wife was still alive. The children were not to take until both parents were dead, so the beneficial interest for the remainder of the wife's life had not been disposed of. Therefore, after the death of the husband, the trustees held on automatic resulting trust for the settlor, who received the income until the wife's death, when the property went to the children.

The automatic nature of this type of resulting trust means that it comes into existence regardless of the fact that, if the settlor had realised what was going to happen, he would certainly not have wanted the property to be held on trust for him. This factor is particularly important in view of the Income and Corporation Taxes Act 1970, s 447, which makes a taxpayer liable to tax on the income of any property in which, or in the income of which, he retains any interest. In *Vandervell v IRC* (1967) the combination of the automatic resulting trust and the predecessor of s 447 had disastrous results for a wealthy philanthropist. The settlor wished to endow a chair at the Royal College of Surgeons and, naturally, intended to do so in the most tax-efficient way possible. The scheme arranged was that certain shares belonging to the settlor should be transferred to the College. The College would receive dividends, which would be, in its hands, free of tax; but the College would also grant to the trustees of the settlor's family trust an option to repurchase the shares at an undervalue. The option was the undoing of the scheme. The benefit of it was to be held by the trustees, but, on trust for whom? The settlement did not say. The automatic effect was that the option was held by the trustees on resulting trust for the settlor, who had thus failed to divest himself of all interest in the shares. The income received by the College was therefore deemed to be his, and he was obliged to pay surtax on about a quarter of a million pounds.

Although the resulting trust is automatic it will only arise if the express trusts do indeed fail to exhaust the beneficial interest. Two possible situations need to be considered.

Acceleration. Normally, if a gift to a life tenant fails because he is dead at the date of the gift, the remainder takes effect straightaway. The same applies if the gift to the life tenant fails for some other reason. For example, a testator bequeaths property to *A* for life, remainder to *B*. The will is signed by the testator and by two witnesses, one of whom is *A*. A witness can take no beneficial gift under the will (Wills Act 1837, s 15) so the gift to *A* fails. Even though *A* is still alive, *B*'s remainder takes effect straightaway: it is accelerated. So what might have appeared to be a gap in the declared trusts is filled by the acceleration of a later interest, and there is no room for a resulting trust.

Sometimes, however, it is not possible to accelerate. One possibility, as in *Re Cochrane* (above), is that the settlor may have made it clear that the remaindermen are not to take until those named as life tenants are actually dead. Alternatively, it may not be possible until then to tell who the remaindermen are. In *Re Scott* (1975) the gift (in a will) was to the testator's sister and brother during their lives and then to the survivor of them for life; and after the death of both, to such children of the brother as should attain the age of 21 or (if female) marry under that age. If there were no children who fulfilled the contingency, the remainder was to go to two named charities. The brother and the sister, comfortable with their income and having no desire to incur further liability to taxes, disclaimed their gifts under the will. At that time the brother was aged 78 and had no children. But the remainder could not be accelerated. Although the brother was unlikely to father children before his death, not until he died childless (or until any children of his died without attaining the age of 21 or (if female) marrying) could it be said for certain that the charities were entitled as remaindermen. There being no acceleration, the property was to be held on automatic resulting trust for the testator's estate until such time as the identity of the remaindermen became certain; that is, in all probability, until the brother's death.

Gift or Trust? Suppose there is a gap in the declared beneficial interests which cannot be filled by acceleration: a resulting trust for the settlor will fill it unless it can be shown that somebody other than the settlor was intended to take beneficially. Generally, those who hold the legal estate, or are entitled to call for it, argue that they are also beneficially entitled in the absence of declared trusts. Their argument will be unsuccessful unless the true construction of the gift is that the settlor intended to give the beneficial interest to them in the events which have happened. Otherwise, as he did not

Automatic resulting trusts 73

intend to give it away, he retained it himself, and a resulting trust arises. The following are the most important rules of construction which are used to decide whether there is a gift to the holders of the legal estate.

First, persons named only as trustees by the settlor cannot claim that they were intended to hold beneficially: *Re Rees' WT* (1949).

Secondly, 'if a gross sum be given, or if the whole income of the property be given, and a special purpose be assigned for that gift, the court always regards the gift as absolute, and the purpose merely as the motive of the gift, and therefore holds that the gift takes effect as to the whole sum or the whole income as the case may be'. This is the rule in *Re Sanderson's Trust* (1857). It was recently applied in *Re Osoba* (1979), which provides a useful example of its operation. A testator left the major part of his property to his wife 'for her maintenance and for the training of my daughter Abiola up to university grade and for the maintenance of my aged mother'. By the time the matter came to court the daughter had finished her university education and the wife was dead, the mother having predeceased the testator. The Court of Appeal held that the *Sanderson* rule applied and on its true construction the gift was to the wife on trust for herself, the mother-in-law and her daughter jointly; so that, now that the others were dead, the daughter was solely beneficially entitled. Thus the rule prevented an automatic resulting trust. If the words quoted above had been interpreted as part of the gift, rather than as the motive for it, there would have been a resulting trust for the settlor's estate now that the expressed purposes were all fulfilled.

Thirdly, where the transferor receives a contractual right as consideration for parting with his property, no trust in his favour will result. A trust is not a contract, and a contractual right will not be automatically converted into a right under a trust. It is, however, possible for a person making a transfer of property pursuant to a contract to agree with the transferee that the property is only to be used for a specific purpose: if so, and the purpose becomes impossible or is carried out, the property or the remainder of it is held by the transferee on trust for the transferor. It is better not to think of this situation as a resulting trust: it depends on agreement between the parties and so is more like an express trust. In *Barclays Bank Ltd v Quistclose Investments Ltd* (1968) *R* Ltd declared a dividend on its shares but had not sufficient cash to pay it. It therefore borrowed nearly £300,000 from *Q*. It was agreed on both sides that the money would only be used for paying the dividend, and for no other purpose. Before paying the dividend, *R* went into liquidation. It was held by the House of Lords that, because of the agreement, now that the sole purpose of the loan had become impossible, the money was held on trust for Q and was therefore not part of R's assets. If there had been no specific agreement there would have been no trust for Q, who would have had to take their place with R's general creditors to enforce their contractual right.

In many cases none of the rules of construction will assist, and it will be necessary simply to look at the circumstances of the gift and decide whether the legal owner is intended to benefit or not. A classic example is *Re Abbott Fund Trusts* (1900). Subscriptions were raised for the benefit of two aged, deaf-and-dumb spinsters. After the death of both of them, some money remained. The court held that it was clear that the object had been to benefit them, not their estates; so the remaining funds were held on automatic resulting trust for the subscribers (or their estates) in proportion to their original contributions. If the subscribers cannot be traced in such a case, the money must be paid into court: it cannot be claimed by the Crown as bona vacantia. When a number of boy cadets were killed in a road accident, the mayors of three towns opened a fund to defray the funeral expenses and assist the injured. There was a substantial surplus after all possible assistance had been given; and most of the donors had made their gifts anonymously in street collections and the like. The money was paid into court on trust for the donors and, because they cannot be traced, it is there now: *Re Gillingham Bus Disaster Fund* (1958). Note that neither of the last two cases discussed concerned charitable trusts. If they had, a different outcome would have been possible.

PRESUMED RESULTING TRUSTS

Equity is suspicious of gifts to strangers. So where A transfers personal property to B, and A is under no obligation to maintain B, then, unless there is some evidence that A intended B to have the beneficial interest, equity will presume that B holds on resulting trust for A. The presumption will thus cause what was probably intended as a gift to have no real effect, in the absence of actual evidence of intention to make a gift. It was roundly criticised by the Court of Appeal as long ago as 1875, in *Fowkes v Pascoe*, where James LJ asked: 'is it possible to reconcile with mental sanity the theory that she put £250 into the names of herself and her companion and £250 into the names of herself and the defendant, as trustees upon trust for herself? What object is there conceivable in doing this?' Mellish LJ added 'could anything be more absurd?' Perhaps the high-water mark of absurdity came in *Re Vinogradoff* (1935). The deceased had, during her lifetime, transferred £800 of War Loan Stock into the joint names of herself and her granddaughter, who was then aged four. She continued to receive the dividends. At her death, as there was no evidence that the granddaughter was to have the beneficial interest, the latter was declared to be holding on trust for her grandmother's estate. Despite the fact that it occasionally produces such odd results, the principle is still good law as regards gratuitous lifetime transfers of personalty. If the gift is made in a will, the transferor knew that by the time it took effect he would not be in a position to benefit from the property and so he is presumed to have intended an outright gift. As regards transfers of realty, the presumption was abolished in 1925, by the Law of Property Act 1925, s 60(3).

A presumed resulting trust also arises where *A* purchases property and has it conveyed by the vendor to *B*, or to *A* and *B* jointly; and here the presumption applies to all types of property, both real and personal. 'The clear result of all the cases without a single exception is that the trust of a legal estate, whether freehold or leasehold, whether taken in the names of the purchasers and others jointly, or in the names of others without that of the purchaser, whether in one name or several, whether jointly or in succession – results to the man who advances the purchase money'. (*Dyer v Dyer* (1788) per Eyre CB). However many people provide the purchase money, the person (or persons) to whom the property is conveyed is presumed to hold on resulting trust for the purchasers in proportion to their contributions. Where the purchasers make equal contributions it is presumed that the equitable interest results to them as joint tenants, with right of survivorship; otherwise they take as tenants in common. So in *Bull v Bull* (1955) where a mother and her son together paid for a house, the son provided most of the money and the conveyance was into his name alone: there was a resulting trust for mother and son as tenants in common in the proportions in which they had contributed. Commonly, even today, a husband and wife, or man and mistress, may buy a house jointly and have it conveyed into the name of the man. The same rule applies: in the absence of agreement to the contrary, the man holds on resulting trust for the two of them in proportion to their contributions. Shared homes are discussed in more detail in the next chapter.

The presumption of advancement. Equity is suspicious of gifts to strangers, but it is a maxim that 'equity looks on that as done which ought to be done'. So where *A* transfers property to *B*, or purchases property in *B*'s name, and *A* is under an obligation to maintain *B*, unless there is some evidence that *B* was not intended to benefit, it will be presumed that the transfer was in partial performance of *A*'s obligation. The presumption is called the presumption of advancement: *A* is presumed to be acting so as to advance *B*'s position in life. There is an equitable obligation to maintain, giving rise to the presumption, in two situations only: where *A* is *B*'s father, and where *A* is *B*'s husband.

The presumption of advancement between father and child extends to the relationship between a man and a child to whom he is in loco parentis, that is where he has taken upon himself the duty to provide for the child. So, in *Currant v Jago* (1844) money was invested by a man in the name of his wife's nephew. At first sight one would have expected a resulting trust for the settlor; but, upon evidence that he had assumed the role of father to the boy, the presumption of advancement applied and the nephew was held entitled to the investment beneficially. The presumption does not, however, extend to the relationship between father and remoter issue, mother and child, or child and parent, for in these circumstances there is no equitable obligation of the first to maintain the second.

The presumption of advancement between husband and wife does still exist, but in modern cases the courts have been eager to find evidence that the parties in fact intended to share the beneficial interest. Three members of the House of Lords remarked in *Pettitt v Pettitt* (1970) that the presumption is based upon old-fashioned considerations of the relative roles of husband and wife, and that its force is now much diminished. The presumption has no application where property is transferred by a wife to her husband, nor where the parties are not married to each other (unless the gift is in contemplation of marriage).

Rebutting the presumptions. Either presumption may be rebutted by evidence. If there is evidence that the transferor did intend to make a beneficial gift to the transferee, there will be no presumed resulting trust. If there is evidence that the transferor did not intend to make a beneficial gift to his wife or his child, there will be no presumed advancement.

The presumptions will, in addition, be ignored if to apply them would produce a result contrary to public policy. So in *Groves v*

Groves (1829) *A*, who had no duty to maintain *B*, purchased property in the name of *B* in order to give *B* the land-owning qualifications he needed in order to vote for *A* at a Parliamentary election. Instead of finding a presumed resulting trust in favour of *A*, the court held that it was against public policy to allow *A* to obtain an extra vote in this way and retain the beneficial interest in the land as well. Besides, the purpose of the electoral qualifications was to ensure that voters had a real interest in the constituency. *B* therefore took beneficially. *Chettiar v Chettiar* (1962) was somewhat similar in spirit, but in that case *A* did have an obligation to maintain *B* and public policy prevented him from adducing evidence to counter the presumption of advancement. *A* owned 139 acres of rubber plantation in Malaya. The government proposed to nationalise all estates of over 100 acres, so *A* conveyed 40 acres to his son *B*. To allow him to adduce evidence that *B* was not intended to benefit would have been to allow *A* to evade the legislation. It was therefore against public policy to hear the evidence and so the presumption of advancement could not be rebutted. *B* was entitled beneficially to the 40 acres. Likewise in *Tinker v Tinker* (1970) where the husband conveyed the matrimonial home to his wife in order to protect it from his creditors if his business failed. He failed in his attempt to recover it from her on the grounds that she held on resulting trust for him. In the Court of Appeal, Lord Denning MR said:

'as against his wife he wants to say that it belongs to him. As against his creditors that it belongs to her. That simply will not do. The presumption is that it was conveyed to her for her own use, and he does not rebut the presumption by saying that he only did it to defeat his creditors'.

Chapter 8
Constructive trusts

THE NATURE OF A CONSTRUCTIVE TRUST

Constructive trusts, like resulting trusts, are implied by equity. As Cardozo J said in an American case, *Beatty v Guggenheim Exploration Co* (1919), 'a constructive trust is the formula through which the conscience of equity finds expression'. When the owner of property has acquired it, or retains it, contrary to the rules of equity, he is not entitled to the benefit of it but instead holds it on constructive trust for those who are.

Consider a simple example. As we shall see in Chapter 11, it is a rule of equity that a trustee may not profit from his position. So much for the rule; but what is to happen if a trustee does profit from his position? Suppose that, like the defendants in *Boardman v Phipps* (1967), a trustee, acting honestly and in the best interests of the trust, incidentally and unavoidably makes a profit for himself. Equity cannot say he does not own the profit: he clearly does. He is not like a thief, who possesses rather than owns what he has stolen. But equity can and does construe a trust from the fact that the profit the trustee owns has been made contrary to the rules of equity. He must hold his profit not for himself but on constructive trust for the beneficiaries of the trust from whose trusteeship he made his profit. The conscience of equity has thus operated to deprive him of the benefit of property which he owns, but ought not to own.

The role of the court. The trustee may not be prepared to admit that he holds his profit on constructive trust. He may take the view that as he made it, it is his to deal with as he wishes. In such a case it will be necessary to commence proceedings against the trustee, and in due course the court will declare that the profit is held on constructive trust. We must not, however, be misled into thinking that the court creates the trust. It does not. It merely recognises

The nature of a constructive trust

the circumstances which give rise to a constructive trust and declares authoritatively that one exists. A constructive trust is a set of rights and duties recognised and enforced by the court; it is not a remedy granted by the court. The beneficiaries of a constructive trust, like the beneficiaries of a disputed express trust, have their rights even before they go to court: their task is to convince the judge that the trust exists, not to persuade him to create it. The argument that a constructive trust is a remedy was decisively rejected in *Re Sharpe* (1980), where Browne-Wilkinson J said that this would be 'a novel concept in English law'. Later in the same case he pointed out that 'it cannot be that the interest in property arises for the first time when the court declares it to exist. The right must have arisen at the time of the transaction in order for the plaintiff to have any right the breach of which can be remedied'. It should be noticed that in America the constructive trust is regarded as a remedy. So although we began this chapter with a quotation from an American case, we can obtain no further help from American law on this subject.

SITUATIONS IN WHICH A CONSTRUCTIVE TRUST ARISES

Undue profit. A trustee's profit from his trust is held on constructive trust; so too is a profit made by any other fiduciary. In *Industrial Development Consultants Ltd v Cooley* (1972) the defendant owed fiduciary duties to the plaintiff company as its director and manager. He tried on behalf of the company to obtain a contract with the Gas Board, but was unsuccessful. He pretended he was ill, resigned from the company, and obtained a similar contract for himself. The profits from that contract were held by him on constructive trust for the company.

The same principle applies to some (but not all) other cases where a person makes an undue profit. If a sum of money is accidentally paid twice, the payee apparently holds the second payment on constructive trust for the payer: *Chase Manhattan Bank NA v Israel-British Bank Ltd* (1979). And a criminal may not profit from his crime. If David murders Elizabeth, and Elizabeth's will leaves property to David, he holds that property on constructive trust for those who would be entitled to it if he had predeceased her: *Re Crippen's Estate* (1911). If the killing is otherwise than by murder (manslaughter, perhaps, or causing death by reckless driving) the court has power under the Forfeiture Act 1982 to modify the rule that the criminal may not profit from his crime if 'the justice of the case requires'.

Sale of land. After the vendor and purchaser of land have exchanged contracts, there is usually a substantial period of time before the land is transferred to the purchaser. But it *ought* to be transferred; and, if, after the due date for completion, the vendor refuses, the purchaser may obtain a grant of specific performance obliging him to transfer in exchange for the purchase price. As the property ought to be transferred, the vendor ought not to retain it, so, while he does, he holds it on constructive trust for the purchaser. This is another way of saying 'equity looks on that as done which ought to be done', a maxim we met in Chapter 5. Until the property is actually transferred, it is regarded as having already been transferred in equity, for a constructive trust has arisen under which the purchaser is the beneficial owner. The vendor of land subject to a contract of sale is, however, trustee of it only 'in a modified sense', because he still has an interest of his own in the property. So he is entitled to the rents and profits until completion, and (subject to any contrary term in the contract) he is entitled to retain any incidental profit, for example compensation on derequisition after the war: *Re Hamilton-Snowball's Conveyance* (1959). A mortgagee who forecloses and sells the property is by statute trustee of the surplus proceeds (Law of Property Act 1925, s 105).

Statute not to be used as instrument of fraud. A person who obtains property by taking advantage of another's failure to comply with a statutory formality holds that property on constructive trust. The classic examples are secret trusts and mutual wills, discussed in the next chapter.

Shared homes. If husband and wife share a house, their property rights in it are of somewhat academic interest. While they live together, they are probably not worried about their entitlement, and if they separate or become divorced the court has jurisdiction under the Matrimonial Causes Act 1973, s 24 to make a just redistribution of their assets whatever the previous position might have been. If, on the other hand, two people who are not man and wife share a house, their property rights in it may be crucial. For if the relationship breaks up, the court can only enforce existing rights; it cannot give a beneficial interest to one who did not have it already. The House of Lords has made it clear in *Pettitt v Pettitt*

Situations in which a constructive trust arises 81

(1970) and *Gissing v Gissing* (1971) that there is no special regime applying to matrimonial and quasi-matrimonial homes: the matter is governed by the law of trusts. And in looking to see what are the parties' beneficial interests in the house, the court cannot consider what arrangements they would have made if they had known their relationship would not last; it can only examine and interpret the arrangements they actually did make (*Gissing v Gissing*). If, therefore, a house has been bought in the name of the man alone, (which is assumed to be the case in the following discussion, though the same principles apply between any unmarried housesharers) the woman may have some difficulty in showing that she is entitled to an interest in it.

It may be that there was an express agreement between the parties, or a declaration of trust, which gave the woman a beneficial interest in the property. If so, it will be enforced, provided that it fulfills the requirements for an express trust of an interest in land: it must be evidenced in writing (Law of Property Act 1925, s 25(1)(b)). If there is no writing, however genuine the agreement the woman will not be able to enforce it as such. On the other hand, it may be that the woman has contributed money to the purchase of the house. If so, there will be a presumed resulting trust: the man will be presumed to hold on trust for himself and the woman in proportion to their contributions. The woman's contributions may be found in payment of the deposit, or some or all of the mortgage repayments. It is possibly enough that she contributed indirectly by working and paying household expenses, so that the man could make the mortgage repayments more easily. But for the resulting trust to be presumed, there must be some financial contribution, because there is no presumption of advancement between a man and his mistress. If there is no enforceable express trust, and no presumed resulting trust, it may well be that the woman has no interest in the house, in which case she cannot be given one by the court. An example is *Burns v Burns* (1984).

The Court of Appeal has recently shown, however, in *Grant v Edwards* (1986) that there is a third line of argument open to her. If there was an agreement that both parties should have beneficial interest in the house, and, though it was not evidenced in writing, she acted upon that agreement to her detriment, equity will infer a trust. When the parties in *Grant v Edwards* set up house together, the man refused to have the woman's name registered with his as owner, giving the excuse that it would complicate the matrimonial proceedings in which she was then involved. The court took this as

82   Constructive trusts

evidence of an agreement that both were to share in the beneficial interest in the house, because, but for the matrimonial proceedings, it seems that they would have been registered as joint owners. The man's income alone was not enough to keep him alive and make the mortgage repayments, so the woman made abnormally large contributions to the household expenses. The court concluded that she acted in this way, keeping him so that he could pay the mortgage, because she thought she had an interest in the house, and that she would have behaved differently if she had thought the beneficial interest in the house belonged to the man alone. In these circumstances, and in view of the evidence of the oral agreement between the parties, the court declared that the man held the house on trust for himself and the woman in equal shares. The trust is called constructive by Browne-Wilkinson V-C, but he pointed out that a similar result could have been achieved by applying the principles of proprietary estoppel, which, as we have seen, is one of the exceptions to the rule that a trust must be constituted. Alternatively, the case may be regarded as an application of the principle that a statute may not be used as an instrument of fraud. The man, having taken the benefit of the woman's contribution to housekeeping expenses, could not rely on the Law of Property Act, s 53(1)(b) to release him from the oral agreement. In any event, *Grant v Edwards* is an interesting illustration of the truth that the rules of equity are a seamless web of principles and cannot be neatly divided into chapters in a textbook.

Justice and good conscience.   During the 1970s the Court of Appeal several times showed its frustration that conveyancing practice and property law had not adapted to changing notions of morality and women's role as income-earners. Instead of applying established law to disputes about the ownership of matrimonial homes, Lord Denning MR, in particular, developed what he called in *Eves v Eves* (1975) 'a constructive trust of a new model'.

In *Hussey v Palmer* (1972) he said:

'It is a trust imposed by law whenever justice and good conscience require it. It is a liberal process, founded upon large principles of equity, to be applied where the legal owner cannot conscientiously keep the property for himself alone, but ought to allow another to have the property or the benefit of it or a share in it'.

In short, the idea was that the court would attempt to do justice between the parties by constructing and declaring property rights on the basis of conscience alone.

There are a number of objections to this policy. First, it runs didrectly counter to the decisions of the House of Lords in *Pettitt v Pettitt* and *Gissing v Gissing*, which are binding on all other courts. Secondly, a system of palm tree justice between the parties before the court may well wreak grave injustice upon others. A declaration, on no strictly legal grounds, that the woman is entitled to a half-share in the house may severely prejudice a mortgagee who lent to the man after justifiably concluding that he was solely entitled. Thirdly, when judgment purports to operate on the basis of the defendant's conscience, in fact it is likely to vary too much according to the judge's views. The resulting uncertainty is intolerable in property matters.

In a case in the Supreme Court of New Zealand, *Carly v Farrelly* (1975), Mahon J said that the idea that a constructive trust arose from principles of justice and good conscience alone is

'a supposed rule of equity which is not only vague in its outline but which must disqualify itself from acceptance as a valid principle of jurisprudence by its total uncertainty of application and result. It cannot be sufficient to say that wide and varying notions of fairness and conscience shall be the legal determinant. No stable system of jurisprudence could permit a litigant's claim to justice to be consigned to the formless void of individual moral opinion'.

In England, the Court of Appeal has gone some way towards ridding itself of the burden of the 'new model' constructive trust in *Burns v Burns* and has begun to establish a viable alternative to it in *Grant v Edwards*. It is greatly to be hoped that we shall soon hear the last of it.

Third parties. A third party to a trust or other fiduciary relationship may become liable as a constructive trustee if he receives, handles or assists in the disposal of property when he knows or ought to know that a breach of fiduciary duty is being committed. In *Nelson v Larholt* (1948) the executor of an estate drew eight cheques on the estate's bank account in favour of *L*, who cashed them for him in good faith without inquiring why he did not go to a bank. Denning J held that the circumstances put *L* on notice that the executor might be acting in breach of trust. Since in fact the executor was defrauding the estate, *L* became a constructive trustee of the proceeds of the cheques for the estate.

If the third party no longer has (or never had) the property he cannot be a trustee of it but is nevertheless obliged to account to the beneficiaries for the loss of it, because of his breach of trust. But if he acquires the property and only discovers (or ought to have discovered) the breach of duty later, he is not liable for events during his innocence. If he has already disposed of the property in good faith, he is therefore not liable to account.

An agent of a trustee or fiduciary may be liable as a constructive trustee, but in this case constructive notice is not sufficient. He will not be liable if he *ought* to have known something was afoot, but only if he himself is guilty of some 'want of probity' because he either knew of the breach of duty or recklessly disregarded it. This rule, and the reason for it, was given in 1874 by Lord Selborne LC in *Barnes v Addy*.

'Strangers are not to be made constructive trustees merely because they act as the agents of trustees, unless those agents receive and become chargeable with some part of the trust property or unless they assist with some knowledge in a fraudulent design on the part of the trustees. If those principles were disregarded, I know not how anyone could safely discharge the office of solicitor, of banker, or of agent of any sort to trustees'.

Although there was some authority that an agent might be made a constructive trustee if he had constructive notice of the breach, the Court of Appeal has now endorsed the traditional view: *Belmont Finance Corp Ltd v Williams Furniture Ltd (No 1)* (1979).

Chapter 9
Secret trusts and mutual wills

SECRET TRUSTS

A testator's wishes as to the disposition of his property will be enforced after his death, provided he fulfils the law's stringent requirements. His will must be in writing and signed, and the signature must be witnessed by two witnesses (Wills Act 1837, s 9, as substituted by Administration of Justice Act 1982, s 17). Neither of the witnesses nor their spouses can take beneficially a gift under the will (Wills Act 1837, s 15). As a practical matter, because the law on the interpretation of wills is so complex, the will should be drafted by a lawyer. And after the testator's death the will must be deposited in the proper probate registry, and is open to public inspection (Supreme Court Act 1981, s 124).

These provisions may cause the intending testator some difficulty. He may not want the world to know who are the objects of his posthumous benevolence: perhaps he has a secret mistress, or an alliance with an unpopular political party. Or he may feel that he will not be able to make a final decision as to the disposal of his property until just before his death, when there may not be enough time to comply with the formalities. Or he may want to change his mind so often that he fears his estate will be consumed by the lawyers' fees on each redrafting.

In order to avoid these problems, testators sometimes make use of the device known as a 'secret trust'. The word 'secret' in this context indicates nothing more than that, although the trust is to take effect on death, some part of its details do not appear in a will. The trust property is given to the trustee by the will, thus completely constituting the trust, but the details, and sometimes the very existence, of the trust are agreed separately between the deceased and the trustee. The matters not contained in the will are, naturally, not subject to the law relating to wills, and so the secret trust is said to operate 'dehors' (outside) the will.

Secret trusts may be either 'fully secret' or 'half secret'. In the case of a fully-secret trust, even the fact that a trust is intended does not appear in the will: the gift will look, on the face of the will, like an absolute gift to the person who has agreed to hold it on trust. In a half-secret trust the existence of a trust does appear on the face of the will, but the beneficiaries do not. So the gift may be 'to Fred upon the trusts I have communicated to him', for example. The advantage of a half-secret over a fully-secret trust is that, because the trustee is named *as trustee* in the will, he cannot deny the existence of the trust; nor can he claim that he was intended to be one of the beneficiaries of the trust, because that would be contrary to the terms of the will, which names him only as trustee: *Re Rees' WT* (1950). The advantage of a fully-secret trust over a half-secret trust is explained below.

Secret trusts are enforced in equity provided that the gift complies with certain conditions. First, there must be a valid transfer of the trust property to the intended trustee. Normally the transfer will be by will, but a person may create a secret trust on his intestacy by arranging a trust with a person who will inherit his estate or part of it: *Stickland v Aldridge* (1802). If the transfer is by will, its validity will be judged solely by the law relating to wills. It follows that a gift on *fully-secret* trust to one of the witnesses of the will (or his spouse) is void, because as far as appears from the will the gift is of a beneficial interest, which is made void by the Wills Act 1837, s 15. But a gift on *half-secret* trust to an attesting witness is valid because on the face of the will he does not take beneficially but as trustee (*Cresswell v Cresswell* (1868)). The beneficiary of a secret trust may witness the will with impunity, because *by the will* he takes nothing at all (*Re Young* (1951)). The doctrine of lapse likewise applies to fully-secret trusts: if the intended trustee predeceases the testator the trust fails as the gift, being absolute on the face of the will, lapses: *Re Maddock* (1902). On the other hand, if an intended trustee under a half-secret trust predeceases the testator the trust does not fail, for 'equity will not allow a trust to fail for want of a trustee', and on the face of the will it is clear that the person in question was to take as trustee.

The second condition for the validity of a secret trust is that the testator should have communicated with the intended trustee, telling him that he is to be left some property on the former's death, and asking him to hold it on trust for certain named persons or charitable purposes. No formality is required, and the communication may be written or oral. For a half-secret trust to be valid this communication must have taken place, at the latest, by the time the will itself is executed (*Blackwell v Blackwell* (1929)). But in the case of a fully-secret trust the communication may be after the will is executed, so long as it is before the testator's death. If the donee does not discover that he was intended to be a trustee, or does not discover the details of the trust, until after the testator's death, the secret trust fails: *Re Boyes* (1884). It is allowed, however, for the testator to communicate with either a fully-secret or a half-secret trustee by giving him (within the required time) a sealed envelope, not to be opened until after the testator's death, provided that the trustee knows it contains the details of the trust. For, as Lord Wright MR remarked in *Re Keen* (1937) 'a ship which sails under sealed orders is sailing under orders though the exact terms are not ascertained by the captain until later'. It is clear from the rules about the time of communication that half-secret trusts are substantially less flexible than fully-secret trusts. The advantage of a fully-secret trust is that a fickle or wavering testator (or, more usually, testatrix) may leave his estate or part of it by will absolutely to a person he trusts, and from time to time, up to the moment of his death, give that person binding instructions as to how he is to deal with the property. The stricter rule for half-secret trusts has often been criticised as illogical, but it is well-established and the loss of flexibility may be seen as a fair exchange for the safety, which is the half-secret trust's particular advantage.

Because of the difference in the latest time of communication it is, of course, necessary to determine whether any secret trust is fully-secret or half-secret, and this is another matter which depends purely on the construction of the will. (A secret trust arising on intestacy must be fully-secret: there is no will for the donee to be trustee on the face of.) So if 'precatory words' are used in the will, they must first be construed, and if it is decided that they are not adequate to impose a trust, then there is no trust on the face of the will and the secret trust, if there is one, is fully-secret. If, on the other hand, the words in the will are held to create a trust, the secret trust, if there is one, must be half-secret; and, if it is to be valid, the communication of its terms must have taken place before, or on the date of, the execution of the will. If the words in the will are to the effect of 'to Fred upon the trusts I *shall* declare', the (half-) secret trust is bound to fail for two reasons. For if the communication was after the execution of the will it was too late for a half-secret trust to be valid; and evidence of communication which was not after the execution of the will will not be allowed as that would conflict with the terms of the will: *Re Keen*.

It is necessary not only to communicate with the intended secret trustee: if the trust is to be valid, the trustee must accept the obligation. Contrary to the rule in ordinary contracts, however, acceptance will be presumed in the absence of a contrary indication (*Moss v Cooper* (1861)). But a person will not be presumed to have accepted an obligation to deal in a particular way with a sum of money, merely because he previously accepted a similar obligation in respect of a smaller sum of money. So if a testator creates a secret trust, properly communicated, of £5,000 but later increases the sum left to the trustees to £10,000, without telling them, the trust fails as regards the increase, and only the first £5,000 is held on the secret trusts: *Re Cooper* (1939). That case concerned a half-secret trust; the same rule applies to fully-secret trusts. If there are intended to be two (or more) trustees but the testator fails to communicate with, and obtain acceptances from, all of them, then the position appears to be that those with whom there was no communication are bound if and only if the gift to them in the will was induced by their co-donees' acceptances (*Re Stead* (1900)). Notice that there is no requirement to communicate the terms of the trust to anybody except the trustee: however, it may be wise for the testator to leave a written notice of the trusts with either a beneficiary or some disinterested person. Otherwise, if the trustee turns out to be less trustworthy than the testator thought, he may keep the trust rather more secret than the testator intended.

Lastly, just as the transfer of property must be valid by the law of succession, so the trust must itself be valid. Secret trusts are, like any other trusts, prone to fail for lack of a beneficiary, or for perpetuity, or for many other reasons.

If any of the conditions are not fulfilled, the secret trust will fail and in that case the beneficial interest passes as appropriate, according to the usual rules, unmodified by the law of secret trusts. So if an intended fully-secret trustee is not told before the testator's death even that he is to be a trustee, he is not bound by any trust and so takes absolutely, according to the terms of the will. If, however, a fully-secret trustee is notified that he is to take as trustee, but is not notified of the beneficiaries until after the testator's death, he holds an automatic resulting trust for the residuary legatees or the person entitled on intestacy, as appropriate: *Re Boyes*. The same applies if a half-secret trustee is not notified of the beneficiaries until after the execution of the will. One may be tempted to ask whether it matters that the secret trust is not formally valid, if the legatee is prepared to regard himself as bound by the testator's wishes? The answer is that it does not matter, provided that the failure is such that the legatee takes absolutely. If, on the other hand, the failure is such that the legatee takes on an automatic resulting trust he is in breach of that trust if he purports instead to carry out the terms of an invalid secret trust.

Half-secret trusts should not be confused with either of two other superficially similar institutions. The first is the doctrine of *incorporation by reference*. If a will refers to and sufficiently describes a document existing at the date of the execution of the will, that document is considered to be part of the will: *Habergham v Vincent* (1793). No question of a secret trust arises, therefore, if a testator refers in specific terms to a particular pre-existing document; the doctrine of incorporation by reference takes effect to make the contents of the document part of the will, rather than secret. This principle will not apply where the will refers to beneficiaries 'whose names my trustee well knows' or 'whose names I have communicated to my trustee by letter'; but it will apply to a reference to beneficiaries 'whose names are set out in a letter from me to my trustee dated 15 October 1978'. So a testator intending to create a half-secret trust should ensure that, if he communicates the terms of the trust by letter, he does not refer too precisely to the letter in his will. If he does, it will be incorporated, and he will lose his secrecy. Secondly, the distinction should be drawn between a gift on trust for 'the persons whose names I have given to my solicitor' (half-secret trust) or 'the persons whose names I shall give to my solicitor' (invalid attempt to create a half-secret trust) on the one hand, and a gift on trust for 'those with whom I may be in partnership at my death' (for example) on the other. The last example is a valid trust, not an invalid half-secret trust, although the beneficiaries' names are not mentioned in the will. The reason for the difference is that in the last case the beneficiaries are defined by reference to facts of *independent legal significance* – independent, that is, of the intention that they should benefit under the trust. Where beneficiaries, or, indeed, trust property, is defined in a will by reference to facts of independent legal significance, evidence will be admitted to show who is entitled and the will is then read as if those persons had been named on its face. There is again no question of secrecy.

MUTUAL WILLS

H and *W* have been married for many years and have a daughter, *D*. As their fortunes have been linked during their life, so they want to make joint provision for their estates after their deaths. They could each leave a life interest to the other with remainder to D, so that after the death of the first to die, his estate would devolve upon the other for life and thereafter upon D absolutely. But the trouble with this arrangement is that the survivor of H and W has no access to the capital of the other's estate, but only to income. They therefore decide that each should leave his estate to the other absolutely, with a gift over to D if the other is already dead. So if H dies first, his estate will pass under *his* will to W, and at her death her estate will pass under *her* will to D (H being already dead). There is, however, a problem. A will cannot be made irrevocable: *Vynior*'s Case (1609). So what is to stop W, having inherited all H's wealth, from marrying $H2$ and leaving her estate to him instead of to D? Nothing can prevent it, but if the wills of H and W are so closely connected that equity regards them as mutual wills, equity will enforce the gift in favour of D. Although $H2$ may obtain W's estate under her will, he is bound to hold it on trust for D.

Wills are mutual when they are made by two parties – they need not be husband and wife – in substantially similar terms; and are so made because the parties have agreed both to make similar wills and not to revoke them. It is not enough that the wills are similar: there must be the agreement, by which each promises not to revoke, in consideration of the other's doing the same (*Dufour v Pereira* (1769)). Relying on that agreement, H goes to his death knowing that his property will pass to W and her whole estate to D. It would be inequitable for W, after his death, to try to go back on the agreement. If W does leave her will unrevoked, all is well, but if she makes a new will, whoever takes under it will hold on trust for D: thus equity enforces a lifetime agreement by imposing a trust on the apparent beneficiary under a will, in the same way as where there is a fully-secret trust.

The one remaining difficulty is the nature of W's interest in the property after H's death. We saw that she was given an absolute interest so that she had access to capital, so she is not to be prevented from using it; but on the other hand she has an equitable duty of some sort towards the eventual beneficiary, D, so she cannot be allowed to give it all away during her life, so that D receives nothing by the will. A solution was suggested by Dixon J in the Australian case, *Birmingham v Renfrew* (1937), and was adopted by Nourse J in *Re Cleaver* (1981). It is that after H's death, W's property is subject to a 'floating equity'. During her life she is entitled to deal with it in any way which is consistent with the agreement. But if she tries (for example by gifts to $H2$) to defeat the intention of the agreement, the equity will 'crystallise' and descend on the property in the form of a binding trust, as it will in any event upon her death. Equity is thus able to allow her to use the property but to prevent her from abusing it.

THEORETICAL BASIS

Secret trusts and trusts arising from mutual wills are gifts taking effect on death but not contained in a valid will. Why, then, are they enforced, rather than being rendered void by s 9 of the Wills Act 1837? The answer which has been given since the early cases (e g *Thynn v Thynn* (1684)) is that a person who tries to rely on a statutory requirement of formality in order to escape an obligation imposed upon him by the testator is committing a fraud, and 'equity will not allow a statute to be used as an instrument of fraud'. The secret trust is therefore recognised and enforced in equity, because, if it were not, the intended trustee would be able to commit a fraud by pleading the Wills Act. If the trust is half-secret, we have seen that the trustee himself cannot take beneficially; but the potential fraud in all these cases is said to be not the trustee's securing a benefit for himself, but the trustee's failing to carry out his obligations to the testator. Of course, asserting the existence of a secret trust does not necessarily mean that anybody is being accused of fraud: as Megarry V-C pointed out in *Re Snowden* (1979), in some cases there is an attempt to commit a fraud; in others the possibility of fraud still forms the background to the rules. Perhaps it is better to avoid using the word and instead say, with Nourse J in *Re Cleaver*:

'A court of equity will not permit a person to whom property is transferred by way of a gift, but on the faith of an agreement or clear understanding that it is to be dealt with in a particular way for the benefit of a third person, to deal with that property inconsistently with that agreement or understanding. If he attempts to do so after having received the benefit of the gift equity will intervene by imposing a constructive trust on the property which is the subject of the agreement or understanding.'

The final question about secret trusts and mutual wills to be discussed is their nature: are they express trusts or constructive trusts? Nourse J in the passage quoted above describes them as constructive, but this classification has sometimes been doubted. It may be felt that secret trusts *must* be express, seeing that they are formed by express communication between settlor and trustee and that the trust as enforced reflects the settlor's intentions. The question is of practical importance when the subject matter of the trust is land, because, as we have seen, the creation of an *express* trust of land must be evidenced in writing: Law of Property Act 1925, s 53(1)(b). In *Ottaway v Norman* (1972) a fully-secret trust of land was held valid despite the absence of any writing, which would suggest that fully-secret trusts are constructive trusts; but in the 1886 case *Re Baillie* it was suggested obiter that a half-secret trust of land would be invalid for lack of writing. The position probably is that both fully-secret and half-secret trusts are constructive trusts; although the relationship between settlor and trustee is entered into expressly, the trust is enforced by the equitable principle for the avoidance of fraud, and the avoidance of fraud is the principal basis for the creation of constructive trusts.

Mutual wills, though enforced on the same principle, probably do not give rise to a trust at all while the survivor is alive, but merely impose some fiduciary duties. After the survivor's death, if her will is not in accordance with the agreement, the trust under which the property is held is probably constructive, for the same reason as in the case of secret trusts: the existence of the trust prevents a fraud taking place.

Part II
The administration of trusts

Chapter 10
The trustee

WHO CAN BE A TRUSTEE?

The basic rule, to which there is only one exception, is that any person legally capable of holding property may be a trustee of that property. 'Person' includes corporation; some companies are set up primarily in order to be trustees of charitable or private trusts. The special type of trustee called a 'trust corporation' is discussed below.

The exception to the rule is that a person under 18 may not be appointed as a trustee (Law of Property Act 1925, s 20) and so cannot be a trustee of an express trust. We have seen, however, that a minor may find that he holds personalty on a presumed resulting trust (*Re Vinogradoff* (1935) p 75 above) and there seems to be no reason in principle why a minor should not be a constructive trustee of personalty. Under no circumstances can a minor be a trustee of a legal estate in land, for s 1(6) of the Law of Property Act 1925 provides that a legal estate in land cannot be held by a minor.

Some special kinds of trustee

The Public Trustee. The office of Public Trustee was established by the Public Trustee Act 1906. He may act either as sole trustee or jointly with others and is appointed in the same way, and by the same persons, as any other trustee. He may not refuse to act solely because of the small value of the trust property. He is, however, entitled to refuse appointment for any other reason, and he is prohibited from accepting appointment as trustee of any trust for the benefit of creditors, any trust made solely by way of security for money, or any trust exclusively for religious or charitable purposes. He is greatly limited in his power to accept appointment to a trust involving the management or carrying on of a business. There is a standard scale of charges for his services (Public Trustee

(Fees) Act 1957 and orders made thereunder). The Public Trustee is a corporation sole with perpetual succession, so one of the advantages of appointing him is that the trust need have no fear of losing all its trustees by death; and the costs of administering the trust are reduced because he never needs to be replaced. Another advantage is that the state guarantees beneficiaries that it will make good any losses caused by breach of trust by the Public Trustee (including losses caused by the acts and defaults of his officers) for which an ordinary trustee would be liable (Public Trustee Act 1906, s 7(1)). The Public Trustee undoubtedly served a useful purpose in 1906 and continues to do so today; but the tendency nowadays is for a settlor who wishes to appoint a secure, corporate trustee to choose a bank's trustee department rather than the Public Trustee.

Custodian trustees. Custodian trustees are a creation of the Public Trustee Act 1906, s 4. A custodian trustee may be regarded as a treasurer. The idea is that all the property is vested in him as if he were sole trustee; but the other trustees, the 'managing trustees', retain all the powers and duties relating to the administration of the trust. So, for example, in a discretionary trust the trust property may be vested in a custodian trustee who will make payments as directed by the managing trustees. As a custodian trustee is always a corporation the trust is saved the trouble and expense of vesting the property in new trustees on their appointment and gains the security that a corporate trustee offers, without losing the advantages of having the management of the trust in the hands of individuals. The same corporation may not be both custodian and managing trustee (*Forster v Williams Deacon's Bank Ltd* (1935)). The question who may be appointed a custodian trustee is answered by the Act and by the rules made under it, and those capable of so acting include the Public Trustee, the Treasury Solicitor, local authorities in relation to certain trusts for their areas and, most important, certain trading companies. The conditions for such a company to be a custodian trustee are that it is constituted under the law of any part of the EEC; that it has one or more places of business in the United Kingdom; that it is empowered under its constitution to undertake trust business; and that it is (a) incorporated by Special Act of Parliament or Royal Charter; or (b) registered under the companies legislation of some part of the EEC and has an issued capital of at least £250,000, of which at least £100,000 is paid up in cash; or (c) an unlimited company registered in some state of the EEC and has as one of its members a company within (a) or (b). Most corporations likely to be appointed custodian trustees, such as the trust departments of banks and insurance companies, qualify under (b).

Trust corporations. The law gives gentle encouragement to the appointment of a trust corporation as trustee, for a trust corporation can act alone in cases where two individuals would be required by statute. For example s 27(2) of the Law of Property Act 1925 provides that a person buying land from trustees who hold it on trust for sale shall not pay the purchase money to fewer than two persons as trustees for sale, except where the trustee is a trust corporation. The principal advantage, however, of appointing trust corporations is that most of them are professional trustees and so will bring to the administration of the trust experience and expertise which few individuals would be able to offer. A disadvantage – and this applies to all corporate trustees – is that they tend to be very cautious. Of course the settlor will wish the trust to be properly administered; but a professional trustee can never afford to take, and can never be persuaded to take, any action which involves the slightest risk of a breach of trust, whereas individual trustees may well be prepared to take such a risk if there is a clear benefit to all the beneficiaries.

Any corporation may be a trustee, but not every corporate trustee is a trust corporation. The list of trust corporations is a long one, but for practical purposes it is sufficient to state that any corporation capable of being appointed a custodian trustee is also a trust corporation.

Judicial trustees. Sometimes it happens that the administration of a trust begins to break down, normally because a trustee is inefficient or incompetent without being actually fraudulent. The traditional solution was for the court to undertake the administration, and order that no step be taken without the court's direction. The expense of this procedure in effect prevented it from being used unless it was really necessary and the trust property was of substantial value. A cheaper form of control by the court was therefore introduced by the Judicial Trustees Act 1896, and a judicial trustee may be appointed under the provisions of that Act and the rules made under it; but it appears that these advantageous provisions are, in practice, rarely used. A judicial trustee is normally required, upon his appointment, to give security for his conduct, and to furnish the court with a statement of the trust assets and income. He must have the trust accounts audited under the court's supervision each year. He is at all times subject to the supervision of the court, and may seek directions from it; but nevertheless he acts in all other respects as a private trustee and does not have to obtain the court's approval for all his acts.

Any person may be appointed as a judicial trustee, on the application of a trustee or a beneficiary or an intending settlor. A judicial trustee may be appointed sole trustee or jointly with others, and may be appointed to replace all the existing trustees. But whether a judicial trustee is appointed, and who is appointed, is a matter entirely within the court's discretion, so nobody has a right to have a judicial trustee or to choose who shall hold that office. If the court does not approve of the person nominated for appointment it may instead appoint some other person or an official of the court. On the appointment of a judicial trustee the court may order that he be allowed remuneration. A judicial trustee may retire from his office with the sanction of the court or be removed or suspended by the court.

Trustee de son tort. A trustee de son tort, or 'trustee of his own wrong', is a person who, without any authority to do so, 'takes upon himself to intermeddle with trust matters or to do acts characteristic of the office of trustee' (*Mara v Browne* (1896) per A L Smith LJ). Any trust property he receives is held by him as constructive trustee. For instance, in *Lyell v Kennedy* (1889), the defendant, who had been the deceased landowner's manager, continued to collect rents after his employer's death and put them in a separate bank account. When the heir appeared, 22 years later, he obtained a declaration that the defendant was trustee de son tort and so held the money on constructive trust for him. This type of trustee differs from other constructive trustees in that he does not act for himself but purports to act for the beneficiaries. It is therefore perhaps better simply to regard him as a special kind of trustee, a person who 'of his own wrong' has appointed himself trustee and therefore bears a trustee's duties in respect of the property he holds.

APPOINTMENT, RETIREMENT AND REMOVAL OF TRUSTEES

THE CHOICE OF TRUSTEES

The settlor is completely unfettered in his choice of an eligible person to be the first trustee. When it becomes necessary to appoint new trustees, how they are chosen will depend on whether they are to be appointed by individuals or the court. Individuals with a power to appoint new trustees must merely ensure that the appointee is not being put into a position where he will have a conflict of interest. Subject to that, it is quite in order to appoint a beneficiary, or a relative of a beneficiary, or a professional person who has previously been retained by somebody connected with the trust. Individuals exercising the statutory power to appoint trustees may normally appoint themselves if they wish. Where the court makes the appointment, it makes its choice subject to more stringent rules, which were set out by Turner LJ in *Re Tempest* (1866). The court will bear in mind that the interests of all the beneficiaries must be protected and hence will avoid appointing a person who is connected professionally or by family to only some of them. The trust must be administered efficiently, and so the court will not appoint someone outside the jurisdiction unless for some reason it is desirable to have an overseas trustee. Finally, the court will bear in mind the wishes of the settlor, if there is evidence of what those wishes are or would have been.

THE FIRST TRUSTEES

We have seen that when a settlor creates a lifetime trust he must completely constitute it, either by declaring himself a trustee or by transferring the property to the trustees. The first trustees of an inter vivos trust are therefore selected by the settlor, and if he fails to transfer the property to the trustees the trust will be incompletely constituted and will fail. A trust created on the settlor's death, however, can never be incompletely constituted, because the settlor has at least managed to part with the trust property. If he names in his will those who are to be the trustees, and they are able and willing to act, no problem arises; but if he does not name trustees, or if those named are unwilling or unable (perhaps because they have predeceased the testator) to act, the trust will still be valid, for it is completely constituted and 'equity will not allow a trust to fail for want of a trustee'. A trustee will be appointed in exactly the same way as if in replacement of one who had died after the creation of the trust; for which, see below.

Disclaimer. Nobody can be compelled to be a trustee of an express trust. A person who finds he has been appointed to be a trustee of a new trust, and who does not wish to accept appointment, must disclaim all interest, preferably by deed of disclaimer, before doing any act of administration of the trust. (Such an act would normally be deemed acceptance of the trusteeship and one cannot disclaim after acceptance.) The effect of the disclaimer is that as far as the person disclaiming is concerned, it is as if he was never appointed. But even if he was to be the sole trustee, so that his disclaimer revests the property in the settlor, the trust is regarded as completely constituted, and the settlor is the trustee. The trust is completely constituted because the settlor did all he could to transfer the property to the trustee, and the one factor lacking, the trustee's acceptance, was outside the settlor's control. The settlor holds the property on the trusts that he declared previously and cannot behave as though he were still beneficial owner: *Mallot v Wilson* (1903).

NEW TRUSTEES

After the trust is constituted, new trustees may be appointed by a person exercising an express power in the trust instrument; or, if there is no express power, by a person exercising the statutory power given by the Trustee Act 1925, s 36; or, if for some reason the s 36 power cannot be used, by the court, normally under s 41 of the same Act. It is not usual for the trust instrument to contain an express power to appoint new trustees, as the statutory power is wide and specifically envisages that the settlor will have nominated somebody to exercise it. Notice that the settlor himself cannot appoint new trustees, unless he has reserved a power to do so; nor can the beneficiaries, even if they are all sui juris: *Re Brockbank* (1948) p 54 above.

Trustee Act 1925, s 36

Section 36 gives power to appoint new trustees either to replace existing or former trustees, or to augment the number of trustees. A new trustee or trustees may be appointed in any of seven different circumstances which are set out in the section; these are as follows:

(1) Where a trustee is dead. This includes the case of a trustee nominated in a will but predeceasing the testator (s 36(8)), and is deemed to include the case of an individual trustee who has been removed under a power contained in the instrument creating the trust: s 36(2).
(2) Where a trustee remains out of the UK for a continuous period of more than 12 months.

(3) Where a trustee desires to be discharged from all or any of the trusts or powers reposed in or conferred upon him. Thus a trustee can retire and a new trustee can be appointed in his place, or partly retire and a new trustee can be appointed with him. If a *corporate* trustee has been removed under a power contained in the instrument creating the trust it is deemed to desire to be discharged.
(4) Where a trustee refuses to act.
(5) Where a trustee is unfit to act. This circumstance would include the case where a trustee is convicted of an offence involving dishonesty. It is not clear whether bankruptcy by itself makes a trustee 'unfit to act', but in *Re Wheeler and De Rochow* (1896) it was held that a bankrupt trustee who absconded certainly came within this provision.
(6) Where a trustee is incapable of acting. In the case of an individual trustee, this includes both mental and physical incapacity, and in the case of a corporate trustee, its dissolution (s 36(3)).
(7) Where the trustee is an infant. We have seen that it is only in the case of a resulting or constructive trust of personalty that an infant can be a trustee; even then he can be replaced purely on the grounds of his infancy.

An appointment of a new trustee or trustees under s 36 is to be made by (1) the person or persons nominated to appoint new trustees in the instrument, if any, creating the trust; or, if there is no such person, (2) the surviving and continuing trustees or trustee; or, if the trustees are all dead, (3) the personal representatives of the last trustee. There is a small difference between the powers of 'the person or persons nominated' and the others. The former can appoint in any of the seven circumstances set out above; the latter need the permission of the relevant authority (normally the Court of Protection) before replacing a trustee who has become unfit to act by reason of mental disorder within the meaning of the Mental Health Act 1983, if that trustee is also entitled to a beneficial interest in possession under the trust.

Because the facility of appointing new trustees is a power, it must, like any power, be exercised jointly by all those entitled to exercise it. So if there are three trustees, and one dies, the power to replace him is vested in the two survivors and can only be exercised by them both together. But where a trustee is to be replaced under s 36 because he refuses to act or because he desires to be discharged, it is specifically provided by s 36(8) that he may take part in the appointment of his successor, but need not do so.

Appointment by the court

The court has power to appoint new trustees as part of its general jurisdiction to supervise trusts; but it is seldom necessary to use the inherent power, since s 36 is supplemented by s 41 which gives the court a statutory power to appoint a new trustee or trustees whenever it is expedient to do so and it is found inexpedient, difficult or impracticable to do so without the court's assistance. The new trustee or trustees may be appointed in addition to, or in substitution for, existing trustees. There are many occasions upon which it may be necessary to call upon the court to exercise its power under s 41. The most common are probably those where, for one reason or another, one of the persons who have to act jointly to appoint a new trustee is unable to do so, for example if he is abroad, or is a mental patient. In *Re Somerset* (1887) the court made an appointment because the persons with power to appoint new trustees were a husband and wife who were judicially separated, and the husband lived in Australia. The power to appoint new trustees may become exercisable jointly by a number of people who cannot agree: here too the court will help. In addition to the powers under s 41 the court may, as we have seen, appoint a judicial trustee in certain circumstances; and there are various statutory powers connected with the administration of trusts where a mental patient is a trustee.

The effect of appointment: the trust property

Section 36 demands that the appointment made under that section be in writing, but in practice it should be made not merely in writing but by deed. The reason is that one of the trustee's tasks is usually to be owner or joint owner of the legal title to the property, and appointing a person to be trustee does not of itself give him the property. Section 40 of the Trustee Act 1925 provides, however, that if a trustee is appointed by deed, the deed also vests the appropriate title to the property in him. Certain types of property are excluded, of which much the most important is 'any share, stock, annuity or other property which is only transferable in books kept by a company or other body' (s 40(4)). Such property does not pass by virtue of the deed, and must be transferred to the new trustee in the usual way. When the court appoints a new trustee it has power to vest in the trustees any land or interest in land which is part of the trust property (s 44); and, in relation to stock and shares and other things in action, it may make an order vesting in the trustees 'the right to transfer or call for a transfer of stock, or to receive the dividends or income thereof, or to sue for or recover the thing in action' (s 51). But, in any event, the effect of an appointment under s 36 or by the court is that, even before the trust property is vested in him, the new trustee 'shall have the same powers, authorities and discretions, and may in all respects act as if he had originally been appointed a trustee by the instrument, if any, creating the trust' (ss 36(7), 43); and, on the appointment of a trustee, anything requisite for vesting the trust property in the trustees 'shall be done' (s 37(1)(d)).

THE NUMBER OF TRUSTEES

On the creation of a trust of pure personalty, the settlor may appoint any number of trustees, though he should be aware that it may be dangerous to leave everything in the hands of one person, and that it may be difficult to administer the trust if there are too many trustees. If the trust property is, or includes, land there are statutory restrictions on the number. There may not be more than four trustees of land at any time (Trustee Act 1925, s 34); and, if there is only one individual trustee it will not be possible to sell the land because of the rule that capital money must be paid to two trustees or a trust corporation as sole trustee: Law of Property Act 1925, s 27(2); Settled Land Act 1925, ss 18(1), 94.

There is no duty to keep the number of trustees at that chosen by the settlor. By the use of the powers to appoint new trustees the number may be kept the same; or it may be reduced or increased.

Reduction in number

Trustees hold the trust property, as well as their powers, as joint tenants, with the result that when a trustee dies, the trust estate automatically goes to the surviving trustees. A dead trustee may be replaced under s 36 of the Trustee Act 1925, but he need not be, so the number of trustees may be gradually reduced by death. When the last trustee dies the trust estate goes to his personal representatives who thus have the power of appointing new trustees, or they may choose to accept the trusts themselves. The number of trustees may also be reduced if a trustee retires. Section 36 gives him a power to retire from office and be replaced; but under s 39 he may retire without being replaced. The section provides that a trustee who desires to be discharged from the trust may retire provided that (1) after his retirement there will remain at least two trustees or a trust corporation; and (2) the other trustees and any other person with the power of appointing new trustees consent to his retirement. Both the retirement and the consents must be by deed: there will therefore normally be one deed, executed by the retiring trustee and the continuing trustees. On the appointment of new trustees, either under s 36 or by the court, the number may be reduced simply by appointing fewer than would be needed to maintain the number; but the court will not usually appoint a sole trustee (except a trust corporation). It is not normally possible to remove a trustee against his will without appointing another in his place.

Increase in number

The court may appoint a new trustee in addition to the existing trustees. The persons with power to appoint new trustees under s 36 also have power under s 36(6) to appoint an additional trustee although no trustee needs to be replaced, provided that none of the existing trustees is a trust corporation. The power cannot be used to increase the number of trustees above four. In this case, the restriction to four trustees applies to all trusts, not only those involving land; and the appointers may not appoint themselves. As with reducing the number of trustees, the number may be increased on an appointment under s 36 or by the court, by appointing more than would be necessary, as long as the statutory maximum for trustees of land is not exceeded (s 37(1)(a)).

Chapter 11
General duties and powers of trustees

The office of trustee has many varied duties. It is, 'if faithfully discharged, attended with no small degree of trouble and anxiety' and 'it is an act of great kindness in any one to accept it' (*Knight v Earl of Plymouth* (1747) per Lord Hardwicke LC). The trustees' primary duties are to obey the terms of the trust, and, subject thereto, to act for the benefit of the beneficiaries. In order to carry out their duties, they have various powers or discretions, which are also to be used for the benefit of the beneficiaries. In this chapter we consider the standard of care imposed upon trustees; and then, after a glance at the derivation of many of the trustees' powers, we discuss the duty to be active, the power to delegate and the duty to act without remuneration. Duties and powers relating particularly to the trust property are dealt with in Chapter 12, and the powers of maintenance and advancement in Chapter 13. These three chapters cover all the principal duties and the powers of trustees.

STANDARD OF CARE

The standard of care required of trustees in the performance of their duties is perfection. If they stray at all from the terms of the trust or fail in any other way to carry out their duties they are answerable for their breach of trust. Nothing will excuse them, but the court, under s 61 of the Trustee Act 1925, may relieve them from liability.

The standard of care required of trustees in the exercise of their powers and discretions is somewhat lower. They must at all times act honestly, and with the interests of the trust at heart. An unpaid trustee must 'conduct the business of the trust in the same manner that an ordinary prudent man of business would conduct his own' (*Re Speight* (1883) per Jessel MR). But the standard is higher for a paid trustee. In *Bartlett v Barclays Bank Trust Co Ltd (No 1)* (1980) Brightman J said:

'A trust corporation holds itself out in its advertising literature as being above ordinary mortals. I think that a professional corporate trustee is liable for breach of trust if loss is caused to the trust fund because it neglects to exercise the special care and skill which it professes to have'.

A discretion is a very personal thing, and cannot be exercised by anyone except those to whom it is given under the terms of the trust. If a discretion is coupled with a duty to exercise it (for example, the discretion to choose the beneficiaries in a discretionary trust) the court will compel its exercise or, if necessary, replace a trustee who refuses or neglects to exercise it. But if the person with a discretion has no duty to exercise it, or if he has exercised it, that is normally the end of the matter. The position was set out as follows by Lord Truro LC in *Re Beloved Wilkes's Charity* (1851). The court's duty in supervising a discretion is limited to inquiring into honesty, integrity and fairness. The trustees are not obliged to give the reasons for a particular decision, and if they choose merely to say that they have met and considered and come to a conclusion, the court has no means of questioning the correctness of their conclusion. So unless a disappointed beneficiary can show bad motive, he cannot upset the trustees' decision.

TRUSTEE ACT 1925, s 69(2)

The Trustee Act 1925 confers many powers on trustees. It consolidates previous legislation, and incorporates a number of powers which previously needed to be inserted individually into each trust instrument. The result is that, generally, the administrative powers exercisable by the trustees of any trust nowadays are derived not from the trust instrument but from the Act. The word 'generally' in the previous sentence is important. For s 69(2) of the Act reads as follows:

'The powers conferred by this Act on trustees are in addition to the powers conferred by the instrument, if any, creating the trust, but those powers [ie the powers conferred by the Act], unless otherwise stated, apply if and so far only as a contrary intention is not expressed in the instrument, if any, creating the trust, and have effect subject to the terms of that instrument'.

So if we want to know the powers of the trustees in relation to a particular trust, we should always look at the trust instrument first, for the powers conferred by the Act may be modified or excluded by it. It is for the settlor to decide what powers he gives to his trustees: the Act merely gives him a model, which he can accept (by saying nothing) or reject as he pleases. It is true, however, that s 69(2) does include the words 'unless otherwise stated'. The powers given to trustees despite anything in the trust instrument are those under s 14 (power of trustees to give receipts), s 16 (power to raise money by sale, mortgage, etc) and s 27 (protection by means of advertisements). In the case of all other powers of trustees, the settlor's wishes expressed in the trust instrument take precedence over the Act.

THE DUTY TO BE ACTIVE

Equity does not recognise the concept of a passive trustee. Trustees act jointly, and it is the duty of every trustee (except a custodian trustee) to take an active part in the management of the trust. A trustee cannot obtain exemption from liability for breach of his duties on the basis that he was a 'sleeping partner'; and any purported exercise of a discretion is a nullity if it has not in fact had the considered approval of each trustee. An interesting illustration of this principle is *Turner v Turner* (1983). In 1967 the settlor created a trust, under which the trustees had a discretionary power to distribute capital or income among the beneficiaries. The trustees appointed were relatives and friends of the settlor. In 1967, 1971 and 1976 they executed deeds by which they purported to exercise the discretion conferred on them by the trust instrument. Subsequent investigation, however, showed that none of the trustees had any conception of the duties of trusteeship: they appear to have thought being a trustee was rather like being a godfather. On each occasion the deed of appointment had been prepared on the instructions of the settlor (who was not a trustee or even a beneficiary) and the trustees had executed it without making any inquiry about what they were being asked to do. One of them said that he thought that his signatures were required as a formality and that he had no business to look into the settlor's affairs. Mervyn Davies J held that the trustees were in breach of their duties, the purported appointments were of no effect, and the discretion had not, in reality, yet been exercised at all.

THE POWER TO DELEGATE

Although trustees are required to be active, they are not required to do all the work themselves. They may 'instead of acting personally, employ and pay an agent, whether a solicitor, banker, stockbroker or other person, to transact any business or do any act': Trustee Act 1925, s 23(1). More particular powers to delegate are granted by s 23(2), (3); and s 25 allows a trustee to delegate by power of attorney any or all his duties, powers and discretions for a period not exceeding 12 months. So, according to Maugham J in *Re Vickery* (1931), a trustee does not have to do anything himself: he can employ an agent whether there is necessity for it or not. There are, however, two restrictions. He should only employ a person qualified for the particular business – a solicitor for legal work, an accountant for financial work, and so on. And he cannot, except by power of attorney under s 25, delegate his discretions, for they are personal to him. Where a choice is to be made, the trustee must make it himself. He can take advice, but the decision must be his.

The trustee's liability when an agent is employed

Suppose an agent is employed and, by fraud or incompetence, he mismanages the trust business, so that the trust suffers a loss. Is the trustee liable? There are two different reasons why he might be. It might be that he is personally required to ensure that the trust is properly conducted at all times, so that if there is a loss he is personally liable for *his own* breach of duty ('primary liability'). Or it might be that, when he employs an agent, he becomes responsible for the *agent's* defaults ('vicarious liability'). It is not clear that this distinction was fully appreciated in *Re Vickery*, which is one of the leading cases in this area. The position appears to be as follows. As regards *vicarious* liability, s 23(1) provides that the trustee 'shall not be responsible for the default of any such agent if employed in good faith'. So if a trustee employs an agent in good faith, which means giving proper consideration to choosing him, and employing him only to do work for which he appears to be qualified, the trustee does not become liable *simply* because the agent does wrong: he is not vicariously liable for his agent's defaults. As regards the trustee's *primary* liability, however, the governing statutory provision is not s 23(1), but s 30(1):

'A trustee shall be chargeable only for money and securities actually received by him notwithstanding his signing any receipt for the sake of conformity, and shall be answerable and accountable only for his own acts, receipts, neglects or defaults, and not for those of any other person with whom any trust money or securities may be deposited, nor for any other loss, unless the same happens through his own wilful default'.

The trustee remains liable for loss occurring 'through his own wilful default'. So, although he is not liable simply because the agent does wrong, he is liable if the agent was able to default because the trustee did not supervise him properly or ignored signs that he was not acting in the trust's best interests. The trustee is not vicariously liable, but he retains his duty to be active. If he is in breach of that duty, he must make good any resulting loss.

A TRUSTEE MAY NOT PROFIT FROM HIS TRUST

The rule that a trustee may not profit from the trust has three aspects. He is not paid for his work; he may not traffic in the trust property; and, as a fiduciary, he may not make an incidental profit from his position.

THE DUTY TO ACT WITHOUT REMUNERATION

Trusteeship is gratuitous. Many trustees are, in fact, paid for their work, but in principle the office is one which is performed without payment. If you employ a plumber or an accountant you expect to pay him unless there has been an agreement that he will work for nothing; but a trustee works for nothing unless he is authorised to receive payment. Such authorisation may be derived from any of the following sources.

1 *The trust instrument.* The trust instrument may contain a clause entitling trustees to receive payment for their trouble. Any well-drafted settlement will contain a clause allowing any professional person who is appointed a trustee to make his usual charges for work done about the trust. The reason is that those who make a profession of trusteeship will not accept appointment if they are not allowed to charge; and though the intention may be to have 'family friends' as trustees initially, it is as well to leave open the option of appointing a solicitor or accountant or trust corporation at a later date.

2 *The Treasury.* The Public Trustee's charges are fixed from time to time by the Treasury with the sanction of the Lord Chancellor, and fees of the same amount may be charged by any custodian trustee (Public Trustee Act 1906, ss 4(3), 9; Public Trustee (Fees) Act 1957).

3 *The court.* The court has inherent power to authorise remuneration from the trust fund for a new or existing trustee, or to increase the amount of any remuneration granted by the trust instrument. The power is part of the court's general jurisdiction to secure the efficient administration of trusts, so it will only be exercised when to grant or to increase remuneration would be in the interests of all the beneficiaries, for example if it is important to have the services of a particular trustee, or if nobody can be found who will take the office without payment: *Re Duke of Norfolk's ST* (1981). Remuneration may be authorised in retrospect, where the trustee's duties have been more than ordinarily burdensome or have involved more than ordinary skill and where the beneficiaries have received more than ordinary benefit. It was on this ground that the defendants in *Boardman v Phipps* (1967) (see p 112 below) were allowed to retain some of the profit they had made.

There is statutory power to authorise 'such remuneration as the court may think fit' when the court appoints a corporation as trustee either solely or jointly with another person (Trustee Act 1925, s 42).

4 *The rule in* Cradock v Piper. A solicitor-trustee cannot (without authorisation) charge costs which will give him a profit, but where work is done in *litigation*, not on behalf only of the trustee who is a solicitor, but on behalf of himself and another trustee, the solicitor may charge his usual costs provided that the expense is the same as if he had appeared for the other trustee alone: *Cradock v Piper* (1850).

It should be emphasised that, for one reason or another, a very large proportion of trustees are in fact paid, so that the rule that trusteeship is gratuitous is perhaps apparent more in its exceptions than its substance. Further, the rule does not apply at all to the trustee's expenses, which he can always reclaim from the trust fund (Trustee Act 1925, s 30(2)).

A TRUSTEE MAY NOT TRAFFIC IN THE TRUST PROPERTY

1 *Trustee buying trust property.* A sale of any of the trust property to the trustee is liable to be set aside. As the trustee was both buyer and seller the matter does not admit of proper investigation, so any beneficiary can have the sale transaction cancelled by his mere assertion that he is not satisfied with it. The beneficiary's right is quite general, and does not depend on his showing that the trustee made a profit or the trust made a loss: *Ex p Lacey* (1802). This 'self-dealing rule' is part of the general principle that a man must not be in a position where his interests and his duties conflict; so in the very rare case where the purchaser has no fiduciary duties to the beneficiaries, the sale may be allowed to stand. Such a case was *Holder v Holder* (1968), where a person who was only technically a trustee and to whom the beneficiaries did not look for protection of their interests, bought, at public auction, a farm for a much higher price than anyone else would have given. A majority in the Court of Appeal held that the court had discretion to refuse the beneficiary's claim to set the sale aside. But normally the rule will be applied with full vigour, and, in the most recent case, *Re Thompson's ST* (1985), it was again pointed out that the beneficiaries are entitled to require the trustees to give consideration to the business of the trust without in any way being clouded by motives of self-interest.

2 *Trustee selling property to trust.* There is no English authority, but the principle is precisely the same as in the preceding case. In *Bentley v Craven* (1853) a sugar-dealer, who was also a partner in a partnership of sugar-refiners, sold some sugar for a fair price to the partnership and made an honest profit thereby. It was held that he was constructive trustee of the profit for the partnership. He had fiduciary duties to his partners, and should have acted at all times for the benefit of the partnership. There is no reason to suppose that the rule would be less strict if the fiduciary relationship were that between trustee and beneficiary.

3 *Trustee buying equitable interest from beneficiary.* If a trustee buys an equitable interest, there is nothing inherently wrong, because here he is not both buyer and seller. But the contract will be most closely examined, because of the possibility of undue influence. The trustee has the task of showing 'that he has taken no advantage of his position, and has made full disclosure to the beneficiary, and that the transaction is fair and honest' (*Tito v Waddell* (No 2) (1977) per Megarry V-C).

A FIDUCIARY MAY NOT MAKE AN INCIDENTAL PROFIT

Any benefit which a trustee receives, or gains an opportunity to receive, by his position as trustee, is held on constructive trust. To take a simple example, it sometimes happens that a trust's shareholdings are used (for the best of motives) to elect trustees to the board of a company. They must account to the trust for their directors' fees: *Re Keeler's ST* (1981). The rule is strict and is applied inexorably. The reason can be seen from the judgment of Lord King LC in the classic case *Keech v Sandford* (1726). A trustee held a lease of the profits of Romford market on trust for an infant. As the lease was about to expire, the trustee sought a renewal on behalf of the trust. The lessor refused, because this particular type of lease was rather difficult to enforce against an infant. The trustee then took a renewal of the lease for himself. The beneficiary claimed that the trustee held the renewed lease on the same trusts as the old lease. This appears entirely unjust, because the trustee acted perfectly honestly, and the beneficiary was seeking to obtain indirectly what the lessor had refused to grant directly. Yet the beneficiary's claim was successful. Lord King LC said, rather cynically:

'I very well see, if a trustee, on the refusal to renew, might have a lease to himself, few trust estates would be renewed [for the beneficiary]. . . . He should rather have let it run out, than to have had the lease to himself. This may seem hard, that the trustee is the only person of all mankind who might not have the lease; but it is very proper that rule should be strictly pursued, and not in the least relaxed'.

However honest the trustee might have been, he must disgorge his benefit for the same reason as in the self-dealing rule: he must not be in a position where self-interest might conflict with his duties to his beneficiary. If any fiduciary in such a position has received a benefit, he cannot possibly show that he was motivated not at all by self-interest, so he holds the benefit on constructive trust for the other party to the fiduciary relationship.

A contemporary example of the rule's being 'strictly pursued' is *Boardman v Phipps*. The defendants were the solicitor to a family trust and one of its beneficiaries. Realising that the trust property was in danger, they appealed to the trustees for them to remedy the situation by increasing their holdings of shares in the family company, so as to obtain control of it. The trustees refused. The defendants therefore bought shares themselves, took over the management of the company, and reversed its fortunes, making it very profitable. The value of the trust's shareholding increased – but so, of course, did the value of the shares the defendants had bought on their own account. Another of the beneficiaries claimed that all the defendants' profits were held on constructive trust for the beneficiaries of the principal trust. They were fiduciaries (one was the solicitor and the other had become subject to fiduciary duties for various reasons during the negotiations); they had been enabled to gain a benefit by their position; they must disgorge it. A strong minority in the House of Lords felt that as the trustees had refused to invest further in the company, there was no conflict of interest; but the majority applied the rule in *Keech v Sandford*. They did, however, allow the defendants generous remuneration for the work they had done on behalf of the trust.

The reasoning is the same when the fiduciary relationship arises without any trust. In *Regal (Hastings) Ltd v Gulliver* (1942) the plaintiff company, which owned a cinema, resolved to form a subsidiary in order to acquire two further cinemas and sell the group of three as a going concern. The share capital required was £5,000. The plaintiff could only afford £2,000, so its directors subscribed for the remaining 3,000 £1 shares. The scheme was successful, and there was a profit of £2 16s 1d per share. The House of Lords decided that the directors held the profits they had made on constructive trust for the plaintiffs. Lord Porter saw that there was an element of unfairness in the situation, but he adhered to the rule, and his words may serve as a summary of it:

'the principle that a person occupying a fiduciary relationship shall not make a profit by reason thereof is of such vital importance that the possible consequence in the present case is in fact as it is in law an immaterial consideration'.

Chapter 12
Duties and powers in relation to trust property

Sometimes a settlor indicates that his beneficiaries are to enjoy the benefit of the very property he settles upon them – a collection of pictures, for example, or a house, or the family business. But more frequently the principal item of property in a trust is a sum of money represented from time to time by various investments. In either event the trustees have a duty to keep the property safe. In the latter case they have, in addition, a power to invest the trust property and to change the way it is invested, and a duty to select investment which will benefit the beneficiaries as a whole. We shall consider first the trustees' duties as regards the property, and then their powers, and shall conclude by summarising some recent proposals for reform.

TRUSTEES' DUTIES IN RELATION TO THE TRUST PROPERTY

On appointment. As soon as possible after accepting his appointment, a trustee should make a full inquiry into the state of the trust property. He should make sure that the title is vested in him and his co-trustees, see if any of the property is affected by mortgages or other incumbrances, and check that any rights which need to be protected by notice are so protected. To enable him to perform these duties a new trustee can compel his predecessors in office to show him minutes of meetings of trustees, records, diaries and similar documents. If any of the trust property seems to have been lost, he must attempt to discover the circumstances, and assess the probability of recovering it, perhaps by suing his predecessor. In carrying out these duties, as always, his loyalty must be to the trust and its beneficiaries. He must not allow himself to be deterred from action to protect the trust property simply because he is unwilling to take proceedings against a close friend or relative. To fail to take all necessary steps would be a breach of trust on his part: *Re Brogden* (1888).

Bearer securities must be deposited with a bank for safe custody and collection of income, unless they are held by a trust corporation: Trustee Act 1925, s 7. Other valuable trust documents, including non-negotiable securities and documents of title, may be deposited with a bank (Trustee Act 1925, s 21), but it is no breach of trust to leave them in the custody of one of the trustees. Trustees should not remain in possession of any substantial sum of money: it should be banked or invested. If it is kept as cash for an unreasonably long time and, as a result, lost, the trustee responsible will be liable to make good the loss: *Moyle v Moyle* (1831). As regards other property, it is perhaps surprising that the trustees have no general duty to insure. They do not even have a general power to insure except as given by s 19(1) of the Trustee Act 1925. That section, which does not apply to bare trusts, allows a trustee to insure trust property, against loss or damage by fire (only), to an amount not exceeding three-quarters of its value. The premiums are payable out of trust income. Of course it is open to a settlor to give his trustees an express power to insure.

Accounts. During the whole of the period of his office, a trustee must keep clear, accurate and up-to-date accounts. He must, according to Plumer MR in *Pearse v Green* (1819), be 'constantly ready' with them. If an action of any sort is brought by a beneficiary against a trustee, and the costs are increased because of a trustee's neglect to keep proper accounts, the trustee will be personally liable for the extra costs even if the action is unsuccessful. It is no excuse that the trustee was unable to prepare accounts: in that case he should have employed a qualified person to prepare them for him, using his general power under s 23(1) of the Trustee Act 1925 to employ and pay agents. Trustees are also given power by s 22(4) of the Act to have their accounts audited by an independent accountant, not more than once every three years unless a more frequent audit is reasonable in view of the nature of the trust or any special dealings with the trust property. Further, any trustee or beneficiary may apply to the Public Trustee for an audit of the accounts of the trust, provided it is more than one year since the last audit. The applicant may be ordered to pay the costs of the Public Trustee's audit if it appears that it was unnecessary (Public Trustee Act 1906, s 13; *Re Utley* (1912)).

The right of a beneficiary to inspect documents relating to the trust property and its administration was reviewed in the Court of

Appeal in 1964 in *Re Londonderry's Settlement*. Any beneficiary (and this perhaps includes a potential beneficiary of a discretionary trust, as has been held in Eire: *Chaine-Nickson v Bank of Ireland* (1976)) is entitled to see the trust accounts and to have information about the trust property and about his own beneficial interest. He may inspect other documents concerning the property such as title deeds, vouchers or counsel's opinions. His right in relation to these documents and the information they contain is a proprietary right: they belong to the trust of which he is a beneficiary. In addition to the duties thus imposed upon trustees to respond to a beneficiary's request for information, a trustee of an express trust with an infant beneficiary is bound to inform him of his interest upon his attaining majority: *Hawksley v May* (1955).

In *Re Londonderry's Settlement*, however, the Court of Appeal also held that a beneficiary is not, in the general run of things, entitled to have any information which would reveal to him the reasons behind a decision of the trustees to exercise a discretion in a particular way. Provided that the decision was made in good faith, the trustees are under no duty to disclose their reasons. Any other rule would be likely to cause bad feeling among disappointed beneficiaries, and make the trustees' task impossible. But if a beneficiary wishes to allege that the trustees exercised their discretion in bad faith he may bring an action against them and may obtain an order for discovery of documents which contain such information.

Distribution. On the distribution of any trust property, whether income or capital, trustees have a duty to pay it only to those entitled to it. The duty is absolute as regards documents or facts of which the trustees have notice. They will be liable to make good any moneys paid out as a result of wrongly construing the trust deed, or of accepting a forged document as genuine. But where some event has happened of which the trustees neither have, nor ought to have, knowledge, they are not liable if they pay on the faith of the apparently trustworthy information which they have. So if the trust contains a power to appoint capital, and the trustees have a document, executed by the donee of the power, appointing capital to *B*, the trustees can safely pay *B* if they have no reason to suspect there was anything wrong with the exercise of the power. If it later appears that *B* was not in fact entitled, as the power had previously been completely exhausted by being exercised in favour of *A*, the trustees will not have to pay again. *A* can only attempt to recover from *B*. Likewise, statute absolves trustees from being deemed to know of the existence of illegitimate or adopted children; though they must use their actual knowledge, if any: Family Law Reform Act 1969, ss 14–17; Legitimacy Act 1976, s 7; Adoption Act 1976, s 45.

If trustees are in any doubt as to who is entitled, they may seek the directions of the court; but if their doubt is purely a matter of determining which or how many beneficiaries or potential beneficiaries are alive and entitled, they should use the power to advertise, granted by s 27 of the Trustee Act 1925, which applies despite any contrary provision in the trust instrument. The section provides that trustees may place advertisements in the *London Gazette*, a newspaper circulating in the area in which any trust land is situated, and elsewhere, announcing that persons, including beneficiaries, who have a claim against the trust should give notice of their claim to the trustees within a period, fixed in the advertisement, and not shorter than two months. After the expiry of the period, the trustees may distribute the property having regard only to the claims, whether formal or not, of which they have notice and are not liable to any person of whose claim they had no notice.

DUTIES IN CHOOSING INVESTMENTS

The trustee's normal standard of care, that of an ordinary prudent man of business, is subject to some modification as regards the choice of investments. For prudent businessmen might well decide that a proportion of capital should be placed in high-risk investments, where the hope of large returns compensates for the risk of loss. Such investments are not open to trustees, unless a power expressed in the plainest terms is inserted in the trust instrument. As Lord Watson said in *Learoyd v Whiteley* (1887):

'[the trustee] is not allowed the same discretion in investing the moneys of the trust as if he were a person dealing with his own estates. It is the duty of a trustee to confine himself to the class of investments which are permitted by the trust, and likewise to avoid all investments of that class which are attended with hazard'.

Lindley LJ had pointed out in the same case in the Court of Appeal that the trustee is to act not like a businessman investing for his own benefit alone. If the trust has both present and future beneficiaries, both must be considered, for the trustee is to invest for the benefit of the trust as a whole:

'The duty of a trustee is not to take such care only as a prudent man would take if he had only himself to consider; the duty rather is to take such care as an ordinary prudent man would take if he were minded to make an investment for the benefit of other people for whom he felt morally bound to provide'.

Two important aspects of the trustee's duty to invest for the benefit of the trust are the duty to choose investments for the financial benefit of the beneficiaries, and the duty to choose investments so as not to favour some beneficiaries against others.

Financial benefit

Where the purpose of the trust is to provide financial benefits for the beneficiaries (as is usual), the trustees may not select investments by reference to non-financial consideration, if to do so would reduce the financial benefits available to the beneficiaries. The trustees' duty is to obtain the best possible benefits, and they are not to be hindered by their own moral or political feelings. To take a simple example, it was held in *Buttle v Saunders* (1950) that where trustees had orally accepted an offer from a third-party purchaser, but had not legally bound themselves to accept it, and a better offer emerged, they had a duty to prefer the latter. Their instincts as honourable men must take second place to their duty to obtain the highest possible price for the beneficiaries. The most important treatment of this area of the law was by Megarry V-C in *Cowan v Scargill* (1984). The trust involved was a mineworkers' pension scheme, with a fund of about £3,000m. Some of the trustees wanted to follow an investment policy which would have avoided investing in foreign countries or in concerns which were in competition with coal as a fuel. The Vice-Chancellor admitted that in some rare cases, where the beneficiaries were all ascertained adults who were known to have decided views on a particular topic such as tobacco or alcohol, it might be proper on non-financial grounds to exclude some type of investment from consideration. But when a trust was established purely to provide financial benefits for present and future beneficiaries there could only be one investment programme. The trustees should, without regard for their personal views or moral reservations, make those investments which would provide the best return for the trust. To do otherwise would be a breach of trust, and, in the future, there might well be some beneficiary who felt that sound ideology was a poor substitute for spending-money.

Holding the balance between the beneficiaries

It is probably safe to say that no low-risk investment provides both good capital growth and high income. Where a trust is established for persons in succession, normally as life tenant and remainderman, the trustees must be careful to spread their investments properly. The more they invest in long-dated, fixed-interest securities, the more they favour the life tenant, who is getting a high income while the remainderman's capital is eroded by inflation. They may redress the balance by buying short-dated stock, which combines a miserly income with certain capital appreciation; or they may decide to invest as much as possible in equities, which roughly maintain the balance between income and capital growth. Overall, the fund must be invested so as to favour neither those entitled to income, nor those eventually entitled to capital, at the expense of the others. The duty of the trustees is to maintain the balance between classes of beneficiaries, and it applies whenever they make a new investment of any of the trust fund.

When a new trust is created, the settlor may state expressly that his trustees are not subject to this duty. Alternatively, he may be taken to have implied that the duty be excluded by settling property in a form which clearly does favour some beneficiaries. So, in a lifetime trust, in which the property must be specific, the trustees are entitled to honour the settlor's implied wishes and retain it in the form in which they received it (except that money must be invested, and will be invested so as to keep the balance between the beneficiaries). The same applies when either land or specific personalty is left on trust by will.

The duty to convert. Where, however, a testator settles his residuary personalty on persons in succession, there is a presumption, seeing that the property was not named specifically, that it is to be treated as a fund. Hence the trustees have an immediate duty to render it into a form which will not particularly favour either life tenant or remainderman. This duty is known as 'the duty to convert under the rule in *Howe v Lord Dartmouth* (1802)'. It applies only to bequests of residuary personalty to persons in succession, and the duty is to convert only those types of property which are extremely unbalanced, that is to say wasting assets, such as copyrights and mines, which provide high income while the capital depreciates to zero, hazardous investments, which provide high income at great risk to the capital, and reversionary interests, which provide no income at all, but an injection of capital at some time in the future. Property of any of these types must be sold and the proceeds re-invested; that is to say, the property must be 'converted' into permanent, balanced investments. Apart from the rule in *Howe v Lord Dartmouth*, the trustees have a duty to convert any property if it is an express term of the trust that they do so: it is common for will trusts to require that the trustee sell the property and stand possessed of the proceeds of sale on trust for the beneficiaries.

The duty to apportion. Whenever there is a duty to convert, it exists from the moment that the property comes into the trustee's hands, unless there is an express power to postpone conversion. In practice, it may be some time before the property is actually sold, during which time it will be either producing income (to the unjustifiable advantage of the life tenant) or not doing so (to his detriment). But equity looks on that as done which ought to be done, so in equity the property to be converted is regarded as having been converted as soon as the duty to convert arose. Therefore, when the property remains in the trustee's hands for some time before it is sold, it is necessary to divide the total of the price received on sale and the income (if any) received before sale in a way that reflects that it belongs (not necessarily in the proportion of income to capital in which it exists at present), partly to those who would have obtained the capital if the sale had taken place immediately, and partly to those who would have received the income on that capital if it had been invested immediately. The requisite division is called 'apportionment', and the calculations are based on the assumption that the life tenant is entitled to interest at 4%: the figure was fixed in 1924 in *Re Baker* and has not been altered since. Therefore, if the trustees have wasting assets or hazardous investments which are to be converted, the tenant for life is entitled to be credited with income at 4% of the value of the property from the time when the duty to convert arose up to the time when the property was sold, and re-invested, and no more. The excess of income over 4% belongs to the capital. If the trustees have a reversionary interest which is to be converted, the apportionment is made under the rule in *Re Earl of Chesterfield's Trusts* (1883). It is necessary to discover what sum, if invested at 4%, compounded yearly, from the time when the duty to convert arose to the time when the property was sold, would, after deduction of income tax, have produced the amount realised by the sale. That sum is treated as capital, and the rest of the sale price counts as income for the life tenant.

A duty to apportion arises in a number of other circumstances, which need not be treated in detail here. In each case the object is simply to ensure that income and capital are credited to those entitled to receive them. But although, where there is a duty to apportion, the rules are strict and may require complex calculation, there are many circumstances where there is no such duty. For example, a cash bonus paid on shares belongs in its entirety to the life tenant: the remainderman receives only capital distributions. And it is provided by statute that, in the absence of an express direction in the trust instrument, where land is held on trust for sale the income pending sale is not to be apportioned (Law of Property Act 1925, s 28(2)). It is often felt that, as there are common situations such as these when there need be no apportionment, it is pointless to enter into the complex calculations involved when there is duty to apportion. Settlors therefore frequently exclude the rule in *Howe v Lord Dartmouth*, or the duty to apportion, or both, by an express clause.

THE POWER TO INVEST

In connection with the trustees' duty to invest property so as to produce the best financial benefit for the trust and to hold the balance between classes of beneficiaries, they need a power to invest: that is, a power to make and to vary investments. Such power is given expressly upon the creation of the trust, or by statute, or, much more rarely, by the court.

Express powers of investment

Many settlors have felt that the powers of investment provided by statute from time to time were inadequate, and so most well-drafted settlements include an investment clause. A common type authorises the trustees to invest in such property of whatsoever nature and wheresoever situate as they shall from time to time in their absolute discretion think fit. A settlor may grant a wide power of this sort over the whole of the trust property, or, if that seems too risky, over a lesser portion. A different type of investment clause is one which authorises the trustees to purchase or to retain investments of some specified class, for example, shares in the family business. When there is no express investment clause, or when the clause does not apply to the whole of the trust property, the trustees must rely on their statutory powers.

Statutory powers of investment

The statutory powers of investment are contained principally in the Trustee Investments Act 1961. The Act applies to all trusts coming into effect before it was passed, but may be modified or excluded in a trust made afterwards. The powers given by the Act are in addition to any other powers to make or retain investments that the trustees may have. We consider first the situation of trustees who have the statutory powers only.

The Act includes a list of authorised investments in Schedule 1, which is divided into three parts. Part I, entitled 'narrower-range investments not requiring advice' contains investments whose capital value cannot fluctuate, such as National Savings Certificates, Defence Bonds, and bank deposits. Part II is entitled 'narrower-range investments requiring advice'. It consists of a long list of authorised investments, most of which have a fixed interest rate but whose capital value may rise or fall. Among the most important are gilt-edged securities, mortgages on freehold property or leasehold property with not less than 60 years to run, building society loans and deposits (not share accounts) and company debentures. Part III, 'wider-range investments', contains company shares, building society shares, and units in approved unit trusts. In the case of company debentures and company shares, the company must be registered in the United Kingdom, have an issued and paid-up share capital of not less than a million pounds, and have paid a dividend in each of the last five years on all shares which ranked for a dividend in those years; and the securities must be securities issued and registered in the United Kingdom.

Thus Schedule 1 divides authorised investments in two ways. They are narrower-range (Parts I and II) or wider-range (Part III); and they may be made without advice (Part I) or only with advice (Parts II and III).

Any part of the trust fund may at any time be invested in narrower-range securities. But before making or retaining any wider-range investment the trustees must value the fund and divide it into two equal parts. For this purpose it is provided by s 5 that a valuation obtained in writing by a trustee from a person reasonably believed by him to be qualified to make it shall be conclusive in determining whether the division has been duly made. The two parts of the trust fund so produced are called 'the narrower-range part' and 'the wider-range part'. The wider-range part may contain both wider-range and narrower-range investments, and may at any time consist wholly of investments in either range. But the narrower-range part must comprise only narrower-range investments: s 2(1),(2). Once the division has been made, it is never made again, even though the parts, having been originally equal in value, may in the course of time become very unequal, particularly because if any property needs to be taken out of the trust fund, it may be taken from either part: s 2(4). When any new property (including dividends or interest) accrues to the trust fund, it is to be evenly split between the two parts; but when property other than dividends or interest accrues to a trustee as owner or former owner of property comprised in either part of the fund, the new property is to be treated as belonging to that part of the fund (s 2(3); this would apply to a bonus issue of shares). The purchase of new property, however, even at a reduced consideration, counts as an investment. So a trustee will be able to take up a rights issue of shares only if he can find capital in the wider-range part to pay for them.

Before making any investment of the sort contained in Part II or Part III of Schedule 1, a trustee must obtain advice from a person reasonably believed by him to be qualified by his ability in, and practical experience of, financial matters. The advice must be in writing or confirmed in writing; and it is specifically provided that, if one of several trustees is qualified to do so, he may provide the advice on which the others may rely: s 6(2),(4),(5),(6). While the trust fund contains any investments within Part II or Part III, the trustees must from time to time obtain and consider advice on whether those investments should be retained or sold: s 6(3).

Relationship between the Act and other powers of investment. When the trustees have a power to invest other than that contained in the Trustee Investments Act 1961, s 3 and Schedule 2 of the Act govern the relationship between the various powers. Any property held by the trustees which (a) is authorised other than by the Act (including investments authorised both by the Act and by the additional or 'special' power), and (b) is not narrower-range property, is called 'special-range property'. Special-range property is put in a part of the fund by itself, and powers given by the Act then refer not to the whole fund but to so much of it as does not consist of special-range property. As a result, when there is an express power in general terms exercisable over the whole fund, the Act has no practical effect. When the special power is of limited ambit, the Act applies to the rest of the fund, so that the trustees really do have the powers given by the Act in addition to those given by the settlor.

Choice of investments within the ranges. Section 6(1) is declaratory of the existing law. It sets out the duty of a trustee when choosing investments under the Act or a special power as follows:

'In the exercise of his powers of investment a trustee shall have regard –
  (a) to the need for diversification of investments of the trust, in so far as is appropriate to the circumstances of the trust;
  (b) to the suitability to the trust of investments of the description of investment proposed and of the investment proposed as an investment of that description'.

Some particular forms of investment

1 *Mortgages.* Mortgages, that is to say money lent on the security of land, are within Part II of the Act. It is not clear exactly what types of mortgage are authorised, and, in particular, it seems that a second mortgage is probably not an authorised investment.

If a trustee proposes to lend money on a mortgage, he should employ an independent surveyor or valuer to make a report on the value of the property to be mortgaged. He should follow that person's advice, and, in any case, should not lend more than two-thirds of the value of the property stated in the report. If he follows this procedure he will not be liable to the trust if it turns out that, in fact, the amount of the loan was disproportionate to the value of the property: Trustee Act 1925, s 8(1).

2 *Land.* There is no power under the Trustee Investments Act 1961 to buy land, nor will the court imply such a power where a trust of personalty does not expressly contain it. If there is an express power to invest in land it will be strictly construed. In *Re Power* (1947) it was held that a power to invest in freehold land did not authorise the trustees to buy a house for the beneficiaries to occupy as their home: such use of the funds could not be considered an 'investment'.

If, however, the trust was, upon its creation, a trust of land, whether settled land or land held upon trust for sale, capital money may be used to purchase land in England or Wales. The land may be either freehold or leasehold with at least 60 years unexpired: Settled Land Act 1925, s 73; Law of Property Act 1925, s 28. Notice that if land is purchased under these powers it will be a special-range investment for the purposes of the Trustee Investments Act 1961, for it is authorised apart from the provisions of *that* Act.

3 *Personal security.* Trustees may not lend money on the so-called security of a promise to repay it, or on the security of personal property, unless they have express power to do so. This principle 'ought to be rung into the ears of everyone who acts in the character of trustee': *Holmes v Dring* (1788) per Lord Kenyon.

4 *A controlling interest in a company.* When the trust has (under an express power, or because they were the original trust property) enough shares to give it control of a company, the trustees' duties are especially severe. They must exercise their powers as shareholders in such a way as to benefit the beneficiaries. In *Bartlett v Barclays Bank Trust Co Ltd* (1980) Brightman J said that the trustees must ensure that they are kept fully informed about the conduct of the company. They must conduct the trust in the usual cautious way; and that may mean that they have to intervene in the management of the company, if necessary by using their voting power to remove the directors. The duty is of constant supervision; it is not enough simply to satisfy themselves that the directors are competent.

Variation of powers of investment

If the trustees find that their powers of investment, whether express or statutory, are inadequate, they may make an application to the court for variation of the trusts, under the Variation of Trusts Act 1958. The application will be considered in the same way as, and is subject to the same conditions as, any other application under that Act (see Chapter 14). Many applications for variation of investment powers were granted between 1958 and 1961; but immediately after the passing of the Trustee Investments Act 1961 it was held (in *Re Kolb's WT* (1961)) that the powers given thereby should be regarded as sufficient. Now, however, the 1961 Act has become outdated because of the impact of inflation, and trustees who have to rely on the powers it gives them may find that the trust capital is wasting away. So in *Trustees of the British Museum v A-G* (1984) Megarry V-C held that it has become appropriate once more to grant applications under the Variation of Trusts Act 1958 for the variation of investment powers. If the statutory provisions are changed by Parliament so as to be in line with present-day conditions, for example by adopting the proposals of the Law Reform Committee outlined below, the *Re Kolb's WT* rule will apply again.

If the trustees require power to invest in some specific type of property on one occasion, they may apply to the court for authorisation under s 57 of the Trustee Act 1925, which is also discussed in Chapter 14.

PROPOSALS FOR REFORM

The Law Reform Committee, in its 23rd Report, *The Powers and Duties of Trustees* (1982 Cmnd 8733), has recommended several changes in the law discussed in this chapter. The Report suggests that the power to apply to the Public Trustee for an audit, which is seldom used, should be removed by the repeal of s 13 of the Public Trustee Act 1906. The duty to convert and the duty to apportion 'should be subsumed in a new statutory duty to hold a fair balance between the beneficiaries, in particular those entitled to capital and those entitled to income'. The most important suggestion is that the Trustee Investment Act 1961 should be repealed, and replaced by new legislation which would give the trustees increased powers. They should be allowed to invest any amount of the trust fund in what are now known as narrower-range investments, or in unit trusts, without taking advice; and they should be allowed, after taking professional advice, to invest any amount of the trust fund in freehold or leasehold land, or in investments quoted on The Stock Exchange. But the duty to have regard to the need to diversify investments (s 6(1)(a) of the 1961 Act) should be retained. The decision in *Re Power*, it suggests, should be reversed.

No legislation has yet been introduced to implement these proposals.

Chapter 13
Maintenance and advancement of beneficiaries

One of the commonest functions of private trusts is to give the benefit of property to children while allowing it to be managed by adults. But a gift to a child poses special problems for the settlor, because he is providing for someone whose needs and character may change dramatically after the trust is created. Besides, the settlor may want the children to take only after the death of their parents, and he may not wish to enrich the estate of a child who dies before his parents, or before he reaches the age of majority: perhaps he feels the money could be spent better elsewhere.

So it happens that, where an infant is to be one of the beneficiaries of a trust, his interest is often *deferred* to some future event which must happen ('to A after the death of B' or 'to A one year after my death') or made *contingent* upon some future event which may or may not happen. The latter device may be used to prevent trust capital passing into the estate of a person who dies young ('to A if he shall attain the age of 18 years' or 'to such of my children as shall survive both their parents') or to cause a person to conform his life to a plan prepared by his benefactor ('to A if he shall become a chartered accountant'). Making a gift deferred or contingent may satisfy the settlor and, in the long run, it may be best for the beneficiaries. But the trouble is that until the date to which a gift is deferred, or until conditions of a contingent gift have been met, the beneficiary has nothing. Perhaps he will acquire a fortune if he remains alive for another year, but in the meantime he is in rags. He will become rich if he passes the Chartered Accountants' Professional Examinations, but he cannot afford the examination fees. He will inherit if he attains the age of 25, but his parents are dead and he urgently needs capital to buy somewhere to live. In all these cases, and many others that can be imagined, the state of affairs is unsatisfactory for two reasons: first, the trust property is being preserved and is accumulating income uselessly, while a person who may become entitled to it,

128 Maintenance and advancement of beneficiaries

and who was selected by the settlor as an object of his bounty, goes wanting. Secondly, a person who may, by the passage of time or by the fulfilment of certain conditions, become wealthy, is unable to obtain access to funds to prepare him for his future station in life. On the other hand, the settlor may be content to give the infant a vested interest. Here again there are likely to be difficulties as regards both income and capital. The capital will probably be directed to be held on trust until the beneficiary is 18, so he cannot demand it until then. The income poses a different problem, for although he may be entitled to it as it arises, it is unlikely to be in his best interests to pay it all to him, with no thought as to how it will be used.

The trustees are therefore given statutory powers to pay income and capital to, or for the benefit of, persons not yet entitled to it. Sections 31 and 32 of the Trustee Act 1925, which contain these powers, should be seen as the two halves of a complete scheme. Section 31 deals with income, and provides that it may be paid out for a person with an interest under the trust during his minority, and shall be paid to him after he attains the age of 18. Section 32 concerns capital, and gives a limited power to pay capital for the benefit of a person with an interest under the trust, whatever his age.

THE POWER TO MAINTAIN OR ACCUMULATE

Where property is held on trust for any person for any interest, vested or contingent, s 31 gives the trustees power to apply the income for his maintenance up to the age of 18, and imposes on them a duty to pay him the income after he reaches the age of 18 even if his interest is still a contingent interest. The power and the duty both depend on a condition: if the gift is deferred or contingent, it must be one which 'carries the intermediate income'. We must consider the meaning of this phrase before examining the statutory power in detail.

Gifts carrying the intermediate income

Suppose property is held on trust for a beneficiary, but he is not to become entitled to it until some time in the future. The gift may be deferred or it may be contingent. Suppose further that time passes or the conditions are fulfilled, so that the beneficiary is now entitled to the property. He is entitled to the capital; but what about past income? Does he obtain the income which has arisen, since the date of the gift, on the capital to which he is now entitled? If he does, the gift of capital is said to carry the intermediate income: the income of that part of the capital belonged, as it arose, to the capital. If, on the other hand, the income belongs to somebody else until the beneficiary becomes entitled to the capital, the gift of capital is said not to carry the intermediate income. The question whether a gift carries the intermediate income is answered in some cases by statute; in others it is a matter of construing the terms of the gift.

Gifts by will. Where the gift is by will, the rules are complex and not entirely coherent. The effect of the cases and the statutory provisions, including the Law of Property Act 1925, s 175 and the Trustee Act 1925, s 31(3), is that any deferred or contingent gift in a will carries the intermediate income unless it is a contingent general or pecuniary legacy. If it is a contingent general or pecuniary legacy it carries the intermediate income, for these purposes, only if it is a gift by a parent to a child or by a person to someone to whom he was in loco parentis, or if the capital of the gift is directed to be set aside so as to be immediately available when the contingency is fulfilled. All these rules yield to a contrary intention expressed by the settlor.

Lifetime gifts. Where the gift is not by will, the terms of the trust must be carefully construed. The gift will carry the intermediate income provided that there is no gift of that income to someone else, unless the settlor has been so silent on the matter that there is an automatic resulting trust of it.

Assuming that the gift does carry the intermediate income, the income is available for purposes of maintenance. It should be emphasised that the power to maintain a beneficiary out of income is available even though he has only a contingent interest and so may never be entitled to the capital.

Maintenance and accumulation

While a beneficiary is under 18 years of age, and provided he still has an interest in the trust fund, the trustees are empowered to pay any of the income of the property in which he has an interest to his parent or guardian or otherwise apply it towards his 'maintenance, education or benefit' (s 31(1)(i)). Any income not paid out is accumulated and added to the capital, even if the infant has a vested interest. But the trustees may use accumulated income from former years for maintenance as if it were income arising in the current year (s 31(2)). The trustees make maintenance payments 'at their sole discretion' and s 31 specifically entitles them to pay out even if there is another fund available for the purpose or another person who is bound by law to provide for the beneficiary's maintenance or education (for example, his father). They must exercise their discretion, however, not pay automatically, as the trustees did in *Wilson v Turner* (1883): the Court of Appeal held that this was not proper exercise of the power of maintenance. They are required in particular to have regard to 'the age of the infant and his requirements and generally to the circumstances of the case, and in particular to what other income is available for the same purposes'; and the amount to be paid out is 'the whole or such part, if any, of the income as may, in all circumstances, be reasonable'. Where several funds are available for the maintenance of one infant, the payments are to come proportionately from each fund (s 31(1)). In the exercise of their duty to have regard to the circumstances of the case, it is especially important to review the position a little time before the infant's 18th birthday, to see whether accumulations of interest from previous years should be paid for his 'maintenance, education or benefit': for as soon as he attains the age of majority the accumulations remaining, if any, are irretrievably converted into capital (s 31(2)).

When the beneficiary attains the age of 18 years, if he does not have a vested interest in the income but still has some interest in the trust property, the trustees are directed by s 31(1)(ii) to pay to him the income arising on the capital and the income arising on any accumulations of income from the years of his infancy. The accumulations themselves are normally added to the capital and treated as one fund with the capital for all purposes: s 31(2). If, however, the beneficiary had a vested interest in the income during his minority, or if the trust is such that he becomes entitled to the capital upon his attaining the age of 18 or marrying under that age, then, when he fulfils the contingency, the accumulations are held for him absolutely.

General points

1 *Older trusts.* Eighteen years was substituted for 21 as the age of majority by the Family Law Reform Act 1969, which came into force on 1 January 1970. If the beneficiary's interest arises under an instrument *made* before that date (for instance, a will made in 1968, even though the testator did not die until 1980) s 31 is to be read as if the references were to the age of 21 instead of the age of 18.

The power to maintain or accumulate 131

2 *Contrary intention.* Section 31 applies to any trust only insofar as a contrary intention is not expressed by the settlor. He may show that the power of maintenance is not to be available by requiring all the income to be accumulated pending the fulfilment of the contingencies. Even if the direction to accumulate is itself illegal, it will serve to exclude the operation of s 31 because it demonstrates clearly the settlor's intention that the income was not to be available to the beneficiary: *Re Ransome* (1957). Section 31 may be completely excluded by the settlor, even though its provisions about what is to happen after the beneficiary attains the age of majority are in mandatory terms: *Re Delamere's ST* (1984). It is also open to a settlor to modify or enlarge the powers given by the section. Two common modifications which appear in many professionally-drafted trust instruments direct that it shall be read (a) as if the power was to pay such amount 'as the trustees shall in their absolute discretion think fit' instead of such amount 'as may, in all the circumstances, be reasonable'; and (b) as if the Family Law Reform Act 1969 had not been enacted.

THE POWER OF ADVANCEMENT

Section 32 of the Trustee Act 1925 gives the trustees power –

'at any time or times to pay or apply any capital money subject to a trust, for the advancement or benefit, in such manner as they may, in their absolute discretion, think fit, of any person entitled to the capital of the trust property or any share thereof'.

The beneficiary's interest

The power of advancement exists not only when the beneficiary's interest is vested in possession, but also when it is a remainder or reversionary interest, or a contingent interest, or when it is subject to termination ('to my widow until her remarriage'). Thus capital may be advanced to a person whose final entitlement under the terms of the trust is very doubtful. If the beneficiary never becomes entitled, or if his interest ceases, the capital advanced is not repayable. But if he becomes absolutely and indefeasibly entitled, the advancement has to be brought into account: that is to say, his entitlement is calculated on the basis that he has already had some of his capital and is due to be paid only the rest of it: s 32, proviso (b). When an advancement of capital is made, the amount of the income of the fund will diminish. Proviso (c) to s 32 therefore lays down that no advancement may be made which prejudices any person entitled to any prior or life interest in the capital, unless that person is in existence and of full age and consents in writing to the advancement.

The amount of the advancement is not to exceed one-half of the beneficiary's vested or presumptive share of the trust fund: s 32, proviso (a). A person's presumptive share is the share in which he at present appears to be going to attain an interest, although future events may increase or decrease his actual entitlement.

An example may help to clarify the effect of the three provisos. Suppose property is held on trust for A for life, with remainder to such of A's children as attain the age of 25. A is alive and has two children, B and C, neither of whom is 25. There is no power to make an advancement to A, because his interest, being a life interest, is in income, not capital. B and C have only contingent interests in the remainder, but it is nevertheless permissible to make advancements to them. The presumptive share of each of them is one-half, even though the share of either may be increased (by the death under 25 of the other) or reduced (by the birth of more children to A). An advancement of up to one-quarter (i e one-half of one-half) may be made to either B or C or both: proviso (a). Because A's income will be reduced by such advancements, his consent must be obtained in writing; if he were under 18 it would not be possible to make any advancement: proviso (c). Suppose an advancement of £20,000 is made to B. A has another child, D; and B, C and D attain the age of 25. Then A dies. The trust fund is now worth £100,000. B, C and D are entitled to one-third of the capital each, but B must bring his advancement into account (proviso (b)). The result is that C and D receive £40,000 each and B takes £20,000, so bringing his capital receipts up to £40,000 as well.

The meaning of 'advancement or benefit'

The phrase 'advancement or benefit' includes, as Lord Radcliffe said in the House of Lords in *Pilkington v IRC* (1964), 'any use of the money which will improve the material situation of the beneficiary'. He went on to hold that, provided that the proposed advancement is for the benefit of the beneficiary, 'it is no objection to the exercise of the power [of advancement] that other persons benefit incidentally'. Clearly there are countless ways in which an advancement of capital may improve the material situation of a beneficiary. Traditionally the power was used in order to enable a beneficiary to buy a house, or a business, or a commission in the army. More recently, it was held in *Re Clore's ST* (1966) that where a wealthy beneficiary felt a moral duty to contribute to charity, an advancement to the charity could be made on his behalf. He would be relieved of the moral obligation, and could spend his own money on other projects. Similarly, advancements whose purpose was to reduce the incidence of tax on the beneficiary's estate have been upheld by the courts.

Creation of a new settlement. One question which has arisen on a number of occasions is whether the power of advancement can be used to create a new trust by paying capital to trustees instead of to the beneficiary. In *Pilkington v IRC* the House of Lords held that, in principle, this would be a valid exercise on the power of advancement, provided the programme was for the benefit of the beneficiary. Two particular problems remain. The first relates to delegation. Trustees cannot usually delegate a discretion to select beneficiaries of a trust. It therefore appears that the new trust could not be a discretionary or protective trust, because the trustees of the principal trust could not grant the necessary discretionary powers to the trustees of the new trust. The second problem is that of perpetuity. For perpetuity purposes the effective terms of the new trust are read into the instrument creating the principal trust and tested for validity. If the advancement on new trusts turns out to be largely void for perpetuity or inalienability, so that the benefit conferred on the beneficiary is entirely different from what was intended, the whole advancement will probably be held to be invalid: the perpetuity problem shows that the trustees did not properly consider the implications of the advancement before making it (*Re Abrahams' WT* (1969)). On the other hand, where only subsidiary parts of the new trust fail, leaving the beneficiary to receive his intended benefit, the advancement will be valid (*Re Hastings-Bass* (1975)). The Perpetuities and Accumulations Act 1964 applies to new trusts created by a power of advancement only where the principal trust came into existence after 15 July 1964, so there is still a substantial possibility of the new trust being void for perpetuity.

The trustees' discretion

The advancement is to be made to benefit the beneficiary in such manner as the trustees in their absolute discretion think fit. The trustees must exercise their discretion properly, and in particular they should ensure that the proposed use of the capital really is for the benefit of the beneficiary. It is quite improper to advance capital to a beneficiary so that she can use it to pay a debt owed by her father to one of the trustees, as happened in *Molyneux v Fletcher* (1898). If the trustees make an advancement for a particular purpose, they may pay it directly to the person for whose benefit it is made if they reasonably believe that he can be trusted to carry out the purpose. In *Re Pauling's ST* (1964), however, the trustees, Coutts Bank, made a number of advancements, nominally for the benefit of persons entitled (subject to a prior life interest) to capital. In reality the sums advanced were used, as everyone concerned knew that they would be, for general family purposes, including, in particular, the reduction of the life tenant's overdraft. It was held in the Court of Appeal that several of the advancements were improper. In the circumstances outlined, the Bank was in breach of trust. As it knew that the beneficiaries could not be trusted to carry out the purposes for which they had sought the advancement, it should have applied the money itself instead of paying it in cash.

Application

Section 32 applies to all trusts except settlements of land, but it may be excluded, modified or enlarged by the settlor. One common form of modification is to allow the whole, instead of one-half, of the beneficiary's vested or presumptive share to be advanced.

Chapter 14
Variation of trusts

The trustees have one primary duty, which must colour everything they do. It is to obey the terms of the trust. If they deviate at all from those terms, even with the best of intentions, they are in breach of trust. It follows that, unless the settlor has specifically given them power to do so, they cannot alter the terms of the trust. It is, however, sometimes desirable that a trust should be changed after it has been set up, because circumstances have changed from what the settlor envisaged, or because a different distribution of the trust property would benefit everyone concerned. A variation of the trust may be made by all the beneficiaries and all the trustees acting together. When such unity of purpose cannot be achieved (often because not all the beneficiaries are in a position to consent) then application will be made to the court, which may authorise a variation.

INFORMAL VARIATION

We saw in Chapter 5 that the beneficiaries own the beneficial interest in the trust property, and that therefore if all the beneficiaries are ascertained and not under disability, they may together terminate the trust by requiring the trustees to give them the trust property (the rule in *Saunders v Vautier* (1841)). We saw, on the other hand, that the beneficiaries' rights as owners do not give them any right to control or direct the trustees while the trust continues (*Re Brockbank* (1948)). So the beneficiaries cannot vary the trust any more than the trustees can – except by terminating it altogether. But if a scheme is put forward to which all the trustees *and* all the beneficiaries agree, then it will take effect as a variation. In effect the trustees carry out the scheme in breach of trust; but there is nobody to object, because the beneficiaries want them to behave in this way. The trustees are absolutely safe,

135

because a beneficiary who has consented to a breach of trust cannot sue the trustee for it: *Fletcher v Collis* (1905). If one (or more) of the beneficiaries does not or cannot consent to the scheme, it can still be implemented if it leaves that beneficiary's entitlement unchanged or if it confers an extra benefit on him. But a scheme of this nature cannot take anything from a non-consenting beneficiary, even by giving him something much better in exchange. Despite having, on the whole, gained from the deal, he would be entitled to sue the trustees for his entitlement under the trust. This is a risk the trustees would not be prepared to take. So, unless all the possible beneficiaries of the trust are in existence, ascertained, over 18 and of sound mind, the scope for an informal variation of this kind is severely restricted. And unless all the trustees consent to the proposed course of action it cannot go ahead at all, because nobody can compel the dissenters to commit a breach of trust.

VARIATION BY AUTHORITY OF THE COURT

INHERENT POWER

The court has a general jurisdiction to supervise trustees, inherent in which is power to authorise variations of trusts. But, since the trustees' primary duty is to obey the terms of the trust, there are few occasions when the court will exercise its inherent power to authorise deviations from those terms. The cases fall under two heads.

1 *Emergency and salvage jurisdiction.* The court may allow the trustees to deviate from the terms of the trust when the alternative is loss of, or major damage to, the trust property which could not have been foreseen by the settlor. So they may be allowed (contrary to directions in the trust instrument) to mortgage a house, if that is the only way to raise money for its repair. In *Re New* (1901) the trust assets were affected by a company reconstruction under which the trust's shares were to be exchanged for shares of another class, in which the trust was not authorised to invest. The trustees could have refused to approve the reconstruction, but in that case it would still have gone ahead, and they would have been bought out at a disadvantageous price. It perhaps seems obvious that the trust should be authorised to invest in the new shares, but the Court of Appeal allowed it unwillingly, and only for a trial period.

Variation by authority of the court 137

Re New was referred to in Re Tollemache (1903) as 'the high-water mark' of the exercise of the emergency jurisdiction, which thus demonstrates how very narrow the jurisdiction is. It still exists, although it has effectively been superseded by s 57 of the Trustee Act 1925, which is much wider (see p 138 below).

2 *Compromise jurisdiction.* Some of the beneficiaries may think they are entitled to more than the trustees are giving them; or there may be some other dispute between beneficiaries and trustees about the meaning of the trust instrument. If it cannot be settled amicably, one side or the other will commence litigation. And then, as in any other civil case, the parties may come to an agreement or 'compromise' before judgment is given. To be binding, the compromise must be approved by the court. Now it is clear that an agreement which is concluded at such a late stage of the dispute must involve give and take on both sides. The trustees, on behalf of all the beneficiaries except those opposing them, must have agreed to give up some claims in exchange for their opponents' doing the same. So when the court approves the compromise, it is authorising a variation of the trust. The compromise jurisdiction is, however, limited to cases where there was a real dispute. It is not open to the trustees and the adult beneficiaries to commence litigation purely so that the court can authorise a variation in this way: *Chapman v Chapman* (1954).

STATUTORY POWERS

In the ever-changing conditions of modern life, there is no longer a strong feeling that a settlor should be able to tie capital up in the family for as long as possible. Events in an active economy may make his restrictions on investments obsolete. The vagaries of the tax system overshadow all settlements: at one blow a tax-saving trust may become a tax disaster requiring immediate modification. In short, trusts need to be altered on many more occasions than the inherent power allows. The trustees should be able to obtain authority to depart from the terms of their trust not only when there is an emergency or a dispute but whenever it would be for the benefit of the trust as a whole to do so. Accordingly, Parliament has by statute granted the court a number of powers to authorise variations. The most important are contained in s 57 of the Trustee Act 1925 and s 1 of the Variation of Trusts Act 1958. After discussing these two provisions in some detail, we shall refer briefly to the remaining statutory powers.

138 Variation of trusts

Trustee Act 1925, s 57

Under the Trustee Act 1925, s 57, the court may authorise the trustees to make any disposition or enter into any transaction 'in the management or administration of any property vested in trustees' if the proposed disposition or transaction is expedient for the trust as a whole and if the trustees do not otherwise have the necessary power. The words in inverted commas are crucial as showing that the section is not concerned with altering the beneficial interests, which are not 'property vested in trustees'. It can authorise only administrative deviations from the trust. 'The object of s 57 was . . . to authorise specific dealings with the property. . . . It was no part of the legislative aim to disturb the rule that the court will not rewrite a trust': *Re Downshire Settled Estates* (1953) per Lord Evershed MR.

The section has thus been used to allow the trustees to invest in shares which were not an investment authorised by the settlement (*Re Brassey* (1955); cf *Re New* p 136 above), to allow the trustees of two identical charitable trusts to amalgamate the funds (*Re Harvey* (1941)), and to sanction the sale of land where the power of sale conferred by the trust instrument could not be exercised because it was subject to a consent which had been refused (*Re Beale's ST* (1932)). With reference to the last situation, s 57(3) specifically provides that application to the court may be made by 'the trustees, or any of them, or by any person beneficially interested under the trust'. So it is not necessary that everybody involved with the trust agree that the proposed course of action is expedient. All that is necessary is that the applicant persuade the court that it is expedient.

Variation of Trusts Act 1958, s 1

Section 1 of the Variation of Trusts Act 1958 is set out at p 143 below. It allows the court to 'approve on behalf of' certain classes of persons an arrangement altering their beneficial interests or enlarging the powers of the trustees. The classes of persons on whose behalf the court may act in this way are broadly speaking beneficiaries unable to consent for themselves and potential beneficiaries. In nearly every case the court is required to find a 'benefit' in the arrangement for every person on whose behalf it gives approval. As Megarry J explained in *Re Holt's Settlement* (1968), the design of the Act is to extend the principle of *Saunders v Vautier*. If all the possible beneficiaries of the trust consent, then with the agreement of the trustees, the trusts can be varied informally. But if even one beneficiary or possible beneficiary is under 18, or insane, or not yet born, or unascertained, an informal variation is usually impossible. 'All that Parliament has done is to empower the court to provide the binding approval which the infants themselves could not give'. The jurisdiction granted by the Act is an implied exception to s 53(1)(c) of the Law of Property Act 1925 (which requires a disposition of an equitable interest to be in writing signed by the disponer: see Chapter 6).

There are three general points to be made before we discuss the Act's provisions in detail. First, the jurisdiction is to approve 'an arrangement varying or revoking all or any of the [existing] trusts', not a complete resettlement of the trust property. The proposal in *Re T's ST* (1964) failed for this reason. Wilberforce J said of it that 'though presented as a "variation" it is in truth a complete new resettlement. The former trust funds were to be got in from the former trustees and held on completely new trusts. I do not think the court can approve this'. In *Re Ball's ST* (1968) Megarry J elaborated and refined this theme:

'If an arrangement changes the whole substratum of the trust then it may well be that it cannot be regarded as merely varying the trust. But if an arrangement, while leaving the substratum, effectuates the purpose of the trust by other means, it may still be possible to regard that arrangement as merely varying the original trusts, even though the means employed are wholly different and even though the form is completely changed'.

Secondly, the words of the Act are used in their technical sense as legal terms of art and will be interpreted strictly. Section 1(1) lists the classes of person on whose behalf the court can approve an arrangement. Any beneficiary or potential beneficiary not listed there must himself actually consent to the variation. The court simply does not have jurisdiction to give its approval on behalf of anyone not on the list as strictly construed: *Knocker v Youle* (1986).

Thirdly, the court's power of approval is discretionary, to be exercised 'if it thinks fit'. This aspect of the Act is seen most clearly in the discussions of whether those on whose behalf the court is asked to give approval will receive a 'benefit' from the variation. We need, therefore, to consider two questions. On whose behalf can the court approve a variation? And what is a 'benefit'?

1 *On whose behalf?* Four categories of beneficiary and potential beneficiary are listed in s 1(1). Paragraph (a) consists of *actual*

beneficiaries (those 'having an interest') who are under 18 years old or are mental patients.

Paragraph (b) contains only potential beneficiaries ('who *may* become entitled to an interest'). Anybody who actually has an interest, however remote, is not in this category: *Knocker v Youle*. The potential beneficiaries in question are those who are, or may be, members of a class subject to a power of appointment, and members of a class of persons of a description which has not yet crystallised, like 'those with whom Dick is in partnership at the date of his death', when Dick is alive. Obviously it is not possible to say who will be in the class until Dick dies.

However, not all potential beneficiaries are within (b). Some people are a great deal nearer to being in the class (or of the description) than others. It was felt that the court should not be able to give approval on behalf of people who had fulfilled all the requirements of being in the class except that of waiting for a particular date or event – for example, Dick's death. Such people are 'to hand' and should give approval for themselves. Hence they are excluded by the 'proviso' of paragraph (b), its second half, beginning with the words 'so however'.

So in our example, although while Dick is alive we do not know who will be in the class, Dick's present partners are excluded from (b) by its proviso (because if Dick had died, they would be in the class). Employees of the firm, who hope to become partners before Dick dies, are within (b). They are not excluded by the proviso, because if Dick's death had happened, they would not be in the class; they need to become partners as well.

Likewise, if the gift is to Ernest's widow, the court can approve on her behalf if Ernest is not married, even if he is engaged; but if he is married, his present wife is excluded from (b) by the proviso, because if he had already died, she would be his widow. His wife is *one* contingency away – she has to survive him – so she is *not* in (b). His fiancée is *two* contingencies away – she has to marry him and survive him – so she *is* in (b). This 'double contingency' rule is derived from the interpretation of paragraph (b) in two judgments of Buckley J: *Re Suffert's Settlement* (1961) and *Re Moncrieff's ST* (1962). It is not easy to grasp at first reading, and the section itself will repay careful study.

Paragraph (c) contains all potential beneficiaries who are not yet born.

Paragraph (d) refers to protective trusts. If the principal beneficiary loses his life interest, the discretionary trust comes into effect, with a class of potential beneficiaries. That class is the subject of category (d). It is only when giving approval on behalf of persons in this category that the court does not have to find a 'benefit'.

Variation by authority of the court

2 *Benefit.* Before it can approve an arrangement on behalf of beneficiaries or potential beneficiaries in categories (a), (b) or (c) the court must be satisfied that the arrangement would be for the benefit of each of them. They must all be better off as a result of the variation. Usually, the benefit is financial, and although before the Act in *Chapman v Chapman* Lord Morton of Henryton lamented the possibility of 'a most undignified game of chess between the Chancery Division and the legislature', the Act has in fact most frequently been used to adjust the rights of beneficiaries so as to reduce liability to tax. An arrangement under which the gross amount due to a beneficiary decreases may be to his benefit because the net amount after tax is greater; and an actuarial calculation can be made of the benefit of having an interest in capital rather than a continuing right to income. In the same way a beneficiary or potential beneficiary whose interest is contingent and very remote may receive a benefit by exchanging it for even a small sum in cash (£100 or £500). The advent of capital transfer tax diminished the possibility of saving tax by splitting the capital between life tenant and remainderman, but many settlements have been varied so as to consist entirely of interests in possession and specially favoured accumulation and maintenance trusts. This type of variation will continue to be worthwhile because the Exchequer's discrimination against discretionary trusts survives the abolition of capital transfer tax.

In some cases the alleged benefit is not financial, or not wholly financial. The court must always undertake 'a practical and businesslike consideration of the arrangement, including the total amounts of the advantages which the various parties obtain, and their bargaining strength' (*Re Van Gruisen's WT* (1964) per Ungoed-Thomas J). But it is not easy to consider 'the total amounts of the advantages' when financial loss has to be measured against gain in family harmony, or financial gain against loss of some social or moral asset. In *Re CL* (1969) one of the beneficiaries was a mental patient of advanced years, who had a comfortable income apart from her protected life interest under the trust. The arrangement proposed that she should lose her interest and receive nothing in exchange. Cross J approved it on her behalf. The loss to her in financial terms was small, and it was greatly to her benefit to use the Act to do what she would certainly have wished to do herself if she had been of full capacity. *Re Remnant's ST* (1970) is much more difficult to justify. The trust had a religion-bar excluding from its benefits anyone who was, or was married to, a Roman Catholic. At the time of application to the court, one-half of the family was Roman Catholic. Pennycuick J approved an arrangement removing the religion-bar, on the basis that, although the financial position of the protestant members of the family was greatly diminished, there was a great benefit in the promotion of family unity. But can it really be said that the infant Protestant beneficiaries would have agreed to forgo their larger shares if they had been old enough to consent on their own behalf? Russell J would have thought not. In *Re Tinker's Settlement* (1960) the proposed arrangement would have rectified a drafting error in the original trust. He refused to approve it on behalf of those whose financial position would be made worse, however much family antagonism the unaltered trust might cause. The beneficiaries, he said, could not be benefited by having property given away to others which might have come to them.

Perhaps the most famous case in this area is *Re Weston's Settlement* (1969). A variation was sought under which the trustees would be discharged and the property would be resettled in Jersey with a great saving of tax. The Court of Appeal refused to approve it. Lord Denning MR said:

'There are many things in life more worthwhile than money. One of those things is to be brought up in this our England, which is still "the envy of less happier lands". I do not believe it is for the benefit of children to be uprooted from England and transported to another country simply to avoid tax'.

It is probably true to say that where the benefits and disadvantages are not purely financial, much depends on the outlook of the individual judge.

Other statutory powers

In many trusts, the trustees have powers of maintenance and advancement (normally under ss 31 and 32 of the Trustee Act 1925) which are in effect statutory powers to vary the trust in a limited way: see Chapter 13. Under s 53 of the same Act, whenever a person under 18 is (already) beneficially entitled to any property, the court may make any order enabling it to be used, as to capital or income, for his maintenance, education or benefit. The court has power to vary a settlement under s 24(1)(c),(d) of the Matrimonial Causes Act 1973 in divorce and similar proceedings and under s 2(1)(f) of the Inheritance (Provision for Family and Dependants) Act 1975 in proceedings under that Act: see Chapter 4. Lastly, the Settled Land Act 1925, s 64, allows the court to sanction any transaction affecting or concerning any land 'which in the opinion of the court would be for the benefit of the settled land, or any part thereof, or the persons interested under the settlement'. Section 57 of the Trustee Act 1925 (see p 138 above) does not apply to settled land, but s 64 of the Settled Land Act 1925 applies to both settled land and land held on trust for sale. Unlike s 57, s 64 enables the court to sanction a variation not only in the administration of the trust, but also in the beneficial interests in the land: *Re Downshire's Settled Estates* (1953).

VARIATION OF TRUSTS ACT 1958, s 1(1)

Where property, whether real or personal, is held on trusts arising, whether before or after the passing of this Act, under any will, settlement or other disposition, the court may if it thinks fit by order approve on behalf of

(a) any person having, directly or indirectly, an interest, whether vested or contingent, under the trusts who by reason of infancy or other incapacity is incapable of assenting, or
(b) any person (whether ascertained or not) who may become entitled, directly or indirectly, to an interest under the trusts as being at a future date or on the happening of a future event a person of any specified description or a member of any specified class of persons, so however that this paragraph shall not include any person who would be of that description, or a member of that class, as the case may be, if the said date had fallen or the said event had happened at the date of the application to the court, or
(c) any person unborn, or
(d) any person in respect of any discretionary interest of his under protective trusts where the interest of the principal beneficiary has not failed or determined,

any arrangement (by whomsoever proposed, and whether or not there is any other person beneficially interested who is capable of assenting thereto) varying all or any of the trusts, or enlarging the powers of the trustees of managing or administering any of the property subject to the trusts:

Provided that except by virtue of paragraph (d) of this subsection the court shall not approve an arrangement on behalf of any person unless the carrying out thereof would be for the benefit of that person.

Chapter 15
Remedies for breach of trust

In the event of a breach of trust, a beneficiary may sue the trustee for the value of any loss suffered by the trust. But the trustee may be insolvent or bankrupt, or he may have absconded, in which case the right to sue him will be worthless. But the beneficiary has a relationship not only with the trustee, who owes him fiduciary duties, but also with the trust property, of which he is beneficial owner. There is, therefore, another course of action open to him. If he can identify the trust property, he can recover it from anybody except one who purchased it for value in good faith and without notice of the trust. With such a choice of personal and proprietary remedies, he is in a better position than the victim of any other civil wrong. If both types of action are open to him, he has an unrestricted choice of which to commence, and may bring both, but he is not allowed to recover altogether more than the trust's loss. The remedies discussed in this chapter are available whether the trust is express or resulting or constructive; for the function of trusts implied by equity is to make the legal owner of property subject to the duties of a trustee of it, and those duties are enforced by legal proceedings exactly as if the trust were express.

THE PERSONAL LIABILITY OF TRUSTEES

Each and every trustee is in principle liable to make good the loss caused by any breach of trust to which he was a party. The beneficiary has only to prove that there was a breach of the trustee's duties and that loss to the trust followed therefrom. It is irrelevant that the trustee had a good motive and was acting for the best interests of the trust; it is even irrelevant whether he was purely ignorant or negligent or downright fraudulent. Interest at a proper rate will be added to the judgment against him: and, since his liability is to the trust, not specifically to the beneficiaries, he cannot claim a reduction in the sum adjudged on the basis that it will be subject to tax in the hands of the beneficiaries.

A trustee who has not concurred or joined in a breach of trust by his colleagues is not liable. This is an old rule, developed in the cases and given statutory force by s 30(1) of the Trustee Act 1925 which (in part) provides that 'a trustee shall be answerable and accountable only for his own acts, receipts, neglects or defaults, and not for those of any other trustee, unless the same happens through his own wilful default'. It should be remembered, however, that a trustee may be in breach of trust by being passive, so that inaction may be regarded as 'wilful default'. If there is loss which he could have prevented and did not, he will be chargeable for it: *Re Lucking's WT* (1967).

Statute does give a possibility of relief to the honest trustee, even if he has technically defaulted in his duties. By s 61 of the Trustee Act 1925, if a trustee 'has acted honestly and reasonably, and ought fairly to be excused for the breach of trust, then the court may relieve him either wholly or partly from personal liability for the same'. The power is discretionary ('*may* relieve') and in considering whether to exercise its discretion the court must bear in mind the need to act 'fairly', not only to the trustee, but to the beneficiaries as well. It is clear that a trustee will not obtain relief under this section if he has acted with less care than a prudent man (*Ward-Smith v Jebb* (1964)), and a professional trustee is very unlikely to be able to persuade the court that he ought fairly to be excused: *Re Pauling's ST* (1964). The trust is entitled to the high standard of trusteeship for which it has paid.

A profit may accrue from a breach of trust, for example if trust money is expended on a sound but unauthorised investment. The profit itself will normally be held on constructive trust and so will become part of the trust fund, but unless all the beneficiaries can and do approve the trustee's action he remains liable for it. The investment is his, not the trust's: as well as disgorging his profit he must reimburse the trust fund for the money he spent to acquire it. This is a situation in which the court might well be minded to grant relief under s 61.

Defences

A beneficiary who, with full knowledge of the facts, either agrees in advance to the trustee's breach of trust or ratifies it afterwards, cannot sue the trustee for it: *Fletcher v Collis* (1905). It is therefore always a defence for the trustee to show that the plaintiff beneficiary concurred in the breach. But the agreement of one beneficiary does not bind the others, so the trustee may still be liable. The court may then, in its inherent power or under s 62 of the Trustee Act 1925, impound the equitable interest of a concurring beneficiary towards the discharge of the trustee's liability. An order of this sort is most likely to be made if the beneficiary in question actively induced the breach; its result is that the loss falls on the beneficiary, up to the amount of his interest in the trust, rather than on the trustee. An application of the same principle is the rule that a trustee who is also a beneficiary cannot take any benefit from the trust until he has made good his liability to the trust (*Re Rhodesia Goldfields Ltd* (1910)), and must make his beneficial interest available to his co-trustees towards discharging any liability he has incurred jointly with them (*Chillingworth v Chambers* (1896)).

An action for breach of trust which is commenced a long time after the breach, may be met by a defence based on the Limitation Acts, or on the equitable doctrine of laches. The Limitation Act 1980 prescribes in s 21(3) a limitation period of six years (calculated from the date of the breach, or if later, the date when the plaintiff's interest fell into possession) for actions for breach of trust, and in s 22 a limitation period of 12 years (calculated from the date when the plaintiff became entitled to the property) for actions in respect of claims to the personal estate of a deceased person. Outside the limitation period no action may be brought: it is too late. In fact, however, the position of a beneficiary who wishes to sue on account of a serious breach of trust in the past is much more favourable than a bare recital of the limitation periods would suggest. For in the first place, if the action is based on the defendant's fraud, or if the facts giving rise to the action have been concealed by the defendant, time does not begin to run until the plaintiff discovers, or could with reasonable diligence have discovered, the fraud or concealment (s 32). Secondly, and more important, the limitation periods do not apply at all to an action by a beneficiary '(a) in respect of any fraud or fraudulent breach of trust to which the trustee was a party or privy, or (b) to recover from the trustee trust property or the proceeds of trust property in the possession of the trustee, or previously received by the trustee and converted to his own use' (s 21(1)). 'Fraud' in s 32, and presumably also in s 21(1), 'is used in the equitable sense to denote conduct by the defendant or his agent such that it would be against conscience for him to avail himself of the lapse of time' (*Tito v Waddell (No 2)* (1977) per Megarry V-C). And as Kekewich J said in *Re Timmis* (1902), the limitation periods are not intended to protect a trustee who has done something 'morally wrong or dishonest' or who, if he pleaded the statute, 'would come off with something he ought not to have'.

If the proposed action is not subject to any limitation period it may nevertheless be barred by laches (pronounced 'lay-cheese'), which is the practical application of the maxim 'delay defeats equity'. It is difficult to lay down any general rules as to when this defence is available, because it lies in the discretion of the court. In general there must be such a substantial lapse of time, that it may be said either that the plaintiff's neglect to pursue his claim amounts to a waiver of it, or that it would now be inequitable to allow him to pursue it, bearing in mind the position of the defendant and any interested parties. As we have seen, in *Allcard v Skinner* (1887) (p 30 above) a delay of about five or six years was sufficient to raise the defence.

The doctrine of laches has no application when a limitation period is laid down by statute. The plaintiff is entitled to the full six or twelve years, as the case may be: *Re Pauling's ST* (1962), per Wilberforce J at the first instance.

Criminal liability for breach of trust

Breach of trust is sometimes a crime as well as a civil wrong. It is theft if it amounts to dishonest appropriation of property belonging to another with the intention of permanently depriving the other of it (Theft Act 1968, s 1); it may, if dishonest, constitute some other office under the Theft Act, like false accounting or the suppression of documents (ss 17, 20); it may be insider dealing contrary to the Company Securities (Insider Dealing) Act 1985. Further, an agreement between two or more trustees to act so as to deprive the beneficiaries of their entitlement may be at common law a criminal conspiracy to defraud. The criminal courts do have power to make compensation orders and restitution orders against persons found guilty of crime. This jurisdiction, however, is intended only for simple cases, where there is no room for dispute about the ownership of the property (*R v Kneeshaw* (1975)) and is unlikely to be exercised in favour of the beneficiaries of a trust. They will need to proceed against the miscreant trustee in the civil courts, a task which may well be easier after his conviction.

Liability of the trustees among themselves

Where two or more people are liable in respect of the same breach of trust, any of them may seek contribution from the others under the

Civil Liability (Contribution) Act 1978. The amount he recovers will be 'such as may be found by the court to be just and equitable having regard to [the others'] responsibility for the damage in question' and may be any sum from nothing to a complete indemnity (s 2). The liability of the trustees among themselves is, however, no concern of the plaintiff beneficiaries. Liability for breach of trust is joint and several, so a beneficiary may recover the whole loss by suing any of the defaulters, and, if he obtains judgment, he may recover the whole sum from any defendant – though this rule does not, of course, entitle him to recover more altogether than the amount of the judgment.

PROPRIETARY REMEDIES

When a beneficiary on behalf of the trust seeks a proprietary remedy, he is claiming not that the trust is *owed* some sum of money on account of a breach of trust, but that it *owns* some property in the hands of the defendant. Two important consequences follow. First, the defendant in a proprietary action need not be the trustee: the action lies against anybody who is holding property which in equity belongs to the trust, even if he has no other duties to the plaintiff. Secondly, if the defendant is bankrupt, the plaintiff will recover what belongs to him before the assets are divided up to satisfy mere creditors, for what belongs in equity to the plaintiff does not form part of the bankrupt's estate: Insolvency Act 1986, s 283(3).

The common law developed a method of obtaining a proprietary remedy called 'following'. If the defendant still had the plaintiff's asset, or if he had sold it and kept the proceeds separate from his other funds, the plaintiff could recover it from him or obtain damages of its full value. Unfortunately, defendants seldom behave in this obliging way. They take money from several sources and mix it with their own money; they buy assets with part of the mixed fund, and dissipate another part. In these cases, the common law was powerless. It could not investigate a mixed fund because it had no apparatus to declare that part only of an asset belonged to the plaintiff. Equity, however, recognises the notion of a 'charge'. A charge is a type of equitable security. If property in A's hands is subject to a charge of (say) £5,000 in favour of B, A has an equitable duty to pay that sum to B, and B has an equitable right to be paid it. If A pays, he becomes beneficial owner of the property. If he does not pay, B's remedy is to apply to the court for an order that the property be sold and that he be paid out of the proceeds. So equity is able to treat the property as belonging to *A*, but also as representing in part property which belongs to *B*, with the result that *B* can 'trace' his property into a mixed fund or an asset bought with a mixed fund. The limitations of the common law process of following are seen particularly in bank accounts, and it is here that tracing in equity has proved most useful. As was said in *Banque Belge Pour L'Etranger v Hambrouck* (1921), 'the common law halted outside the bankers' door; equity had the courage to lift the latch, walk in, and examine the books'.

Tracing

Tracing in equity has its own particular limitations, and is not available in all circumstances when one party has gained at the expense of another: English law has no general remedy for unjust enrichment. Four conditions have to be fulfilled if tracing is to be allowed. There must be an initial fiduciary relationship; the property must be identifiable; tracing must not produce an inequitable result; and the right to trace must not have been lost.

1 *Initial fiduciary relationship.* The plaintiff must be able to point to some fiduciary relationship from which his claim arises. If there is no fiduciary relationship there can be no tracing. If a thief steals £500 from you and mixes it with his own money, you cannot trace into the mixed fund, for there is no fiduciary relationship between a thief and his victim. Although it produces such an odd result, this requirement has the authority of the House of Lords in *Sinclair v Brougham* (1914) and more recently the Court of Appeal in *Re Diplock* (1948). The courts have, however, been very astute to discover a fiduciary relationship in order to allow a tracing claim. An example is *Chase Manhattan Bank NA v Israel-British Bank (London) Ltd* (1979). The plaintiff paid the defendant a sum of about $2m and then, by error, paid it agian. Clearly the defendant owed the second payment to the plaintiff; Goulding J went further and held that the defendant in these circumstances was bound not in law only, but in conscience to repay: he had a fiduciary duty to the plaintiff. The latter could therefore trace, which was important as the defendant was by now in compulsory liquidation.

The fiduciary relationship need not be between the plaintiff and the defendant in the instant case, as may be illustrated by *Re Diplock*. The deceased's will directed his executors to apply his residuary estate for 'charitable or benevolent objects'. Making an elementary mistake of trust law, the executors took the view that this was a valid charitable gift and distributed a total of over £200,000 to many charities. In fact the gift was void (see p 156 below) and the testator's next-of-kin were entitled to the residue which had been paid to the charities. The Court of Appeal held that the next-of-kin could, in principle, trace into the hands of the charities and recover the money. There was no fiduciary relationship between the next-of-kin and the charities, but it was sufficient that there was an initial fiduciary relationship between the executors and those entitled to the deceased's estate.

2 *The property must be identifiable.* If the property in question is still separate, there is no problem. If an asset has been bought with money belonging in equity entirely to the plaintiff, he may either adopt the purchase (so claiming the asset) or he may have a charge on the asset for the amount of his money expended on it. The difficulties arise when property or money has been mixed.

The first principle is that the defendant (or his predecessor in title) must be presumed as far as possible not to have been in breach of his fiduciary duties. So if a mixed account contains £1,500, of which £500 belongs to the trust, the defendant is presumed to be drawing out his own money until there is only £500 left in the account: this is the rule in *Re Hallett's Estate* (1880). When there is only £500 in the account, the next withdrawal must be trust money. But if he then pays some money into the account it is *not* to be regarded as restoring the trust property unless he specifically intended to do so. The reason is that the addition to the account is 'new' money, and the plaintiff has no right to be preferred to general creditors in relation to it (*James Roscoe (Bolton) Ltd v Winder* (1915)). So if, after the balance has been reduced to £300, the defendant pays in £400, the plaintiff has a charge for £300 (only) on the mixed fund of £700.

But suppose that the trustee with, as before, £1,500 in his account of which £500 belongs to the trust, draws out £1,000 and invests it wisely, then draws out the remaining £500 and spends it on a holiday. If the rule in *Re Hallett's Estate* were followed rigorously here, the trustee could claim that the £1,000 must be presumed to be his own, and that the £500 belonging to the beneficiaries had unfortunately now disappeared. The solution is, as Joyce J pointed out in *Re Oatway* (1903), that whenever an asset has been bought out of a mixed fund (in this case the £1,500) the plaintiff can have a charge on the asset for the amount of his

Proprietary remedies 151

money in the fund. There is a suggestion in *Re Tilley's WT* (1967) that, if the asset has risen in value, the plaintiff can in addition claim a proportion of the profit.

It may be that the plaintiff cannot identify anything that represents his property. One of the charities in *Re Diplock* had used the money to discharge a debt. There could be no tracing in this instance: neither the plaintiff's money nor the proceeds of it were identifiable.

Where the funds of two or more trusts are mixed together, or where trust money is mixed with the money of an innocent volunteer (like the charities in *Re Diplock*), the owners of the mixed fund share it rateably or may adopt any assets purchased with it. Theoretically there is a different rule if the mixture is in an active continuous current bank account: then *Clayton's* Case (1816) requires that money be regarded as withdrawn in the order in which it was paid in. But *Clayton's* Case leads to arbitrary and absurd results, and although it has often been asserted as correct in this situation, it was described as 'a mere rule of evidence and not an invariable rule of law', and not followed, in one of the few cases which would have demanded its use (*Re British Red Cross Balkan Fund* (1914)).

3 *It must not be inequitable to trace.* The plaintiff will not be allowed to trace if the result would be inequitable. One of the charities in *Re Diplock* had used the money to improve their buildings. Tracing against them was not allowed because if a charge was imposed, they might be compelled to sell their own land.

4 *The right to trace must not have been lost.* A purchaser of the legal estate for value and without notice of equitable interests takes free of them (*Bassett v Nosworthy* (1673)). There is therefore no possibility of tracing against him, because the plaintiff no longer has beneficial ownership of the property: his equitable interest has gone. Notice, however, that to achieve this protection the purchaser must take a legal estate in the property, not merely another equitable interest; he must take if for value, not as a volunteer (donee), for tracing is available against volunteers (like the charities in *Re Diplock*); and he must take without notice of the equitable interests, because if he has notice of them he will himself become at least a constructive trustee.

The right to trace is also subject to the doctrine of laches, which has been discussed above in connection with the trustee's personal liability.

OTHER REMEDIES

If after suing the trustees personally and tracing the property where they can do so, the beneficiaries have still not recovered all their loss, they may be able to recover from an innocent volunteer personally. This type of claim was allowed by the House of Lords in the last episode of the *Diplock* litigation (*Ministry of Health v Simpson* (1950)). A creditor, legatee or next-of-kin who has received less than his entitlement from the estate of a deceased person can bring an action directly against the persons to whom the estate has been wrongfully distributed. It is by no means clear that the same type of action can be brought on events other than wrongful distribution of a deceased's estate, for example on a breach of trust.

This chapter has dealt solely with the remedies which are more or less unique to actions for breach of trust. It must not be supposed that these are the only remedies available to the beneficiary of a trust. On the contrary, there is a wide range, of which the action for an account, by which a person may be obliged to show what property he holds or held on behalf of another, and the possibility of an injunction if a breach of trust is threatened, may be most useful. Details of general remedies are outside the scope of this book and of trusts examination syllabuses.

Part III
Trusts for charitable purposes

Chapter 16
Charity

THE ADVANTAGES OF CHARITY

It is good to help one's fellow men, and the law encourages philanthropy by affording special benefits to trusts for charitable purposes. Such trusts have, in the first place, substantial fiscal advantages. A charity is exempt from income tax on its income under Schedule C in respect of any interest, annuities, dividends or shares of annuities, under Schedule D in respect of any annual payment, and under Schedule F in respect of any distribution (Income and Corporation Taxes Act 1970, s 360(1)(c)). Thus it is able to recover from the Inland Revenue the tax paid or credited on income paid net of tax, and the tax paid by individuals on their contributions under four-year covenants (s 434(1A)). It is exempt from income tax under Schedules A, B and D in respect of income from land, and from all other income tax and all capital gains tax provided that the income or gain is applied only for charitable purposes (Income and Corporation Taxes Act 1970, s 360; Capital Gains Tax Act 1979, s 145). Charities are to a large extent exempt from stamp duty (Finance Act 1982, s 129); corporate charities do not pay corporation tax (Income and Corporation Taxes Act 1970, s 250(4)). Gifts to charities made by an individual or from a discretionary trust, and transfers by charities, are exempt from inheritance tax (Inheritance Tax Act 1984, ss 23, 58(1)(a), 76). Premises occupied by a charity and used wholly or mainly for charitable purposes are entitled to exemption from one-half of their rates, and, in the case of churches, church halls and similar premises used for religious purposes, the exemption extends to the whole of the rates (General Rate Act 1967, ss 39, 40). It is small wonder that the definition of charity has been largely developed in Inland Revenue cases.

Charitable trusts also enjoy what may be regarded as technical advantages, in that they will frequently be valid in circumstances which would cause private trusts to fail. Charities have purposes, not persons, as their objects, so the beneficiary principle does not apply to them: if it is necessary to bring an action to enforce a charitable trust, the action is brought not on behalf of any particular beneficiaries but on behalf of the public. Purposes may last for ever, and so once a fund has become applicable to charity it may continue to be bound by the same trusts without regard to the rule against inalienability. On the other hand, purposes may be fulfilled. If a fund held on trust for charitable purposes is no longer needed for the purposes originally intended it will be applied to some other similar purpose by a cy-près scheme instead of resulting to the original donor. Or the donor himself may provide that upon the occurrence of certain events the property should pass from one charity to another: the rule against remoteness of vesting does not apply to transfers between charities. Finally, a charitable trust will not fail for uncertainty of objects: if it is clear that the donor intended a gift to wholly charitable purposes, a scheme will be drawn up for the application of the gift.

For these reasons, the administration of charitable trusts is very different from that of private trusts. Most charitable trusts are under the general supervision of the Charity Commissioners, whose powers, together with other administrative matters, are set out in the next chapter.

THE DEFINITION OF CHARITY

It must not be supposed that every trust for a purpose which might be regarded, even by a well-educated layman, as 'charitable' is entitled to the advantages of charity. They are only enjoyed by trusts for purposes which the *law* regards as charitable – and not merely charitable but wholly charitable. If any of the trust property may under the terms of the trust be applied for purposes which are not, in law, charitable, the trust as a whole will fail to achieve charitable status. In the leading case, *Morice v Bishop of Durham* (1805), the testatrix left the residue of her estate to the defendant upon trust 'to dispose of the ultimate residue to such objects of benevolence and liberality as the Bishop of Durham in his own discretion shall most approve of'. Sir William Grant MR held that, although some 'objects of benevolence and liberality' are charitable, some are not. As the gift was not restricted to the former, it was not wholly charitable and so not entitled to any of the benefits of charity. It therefore failed, because it contravened the Rule against Perpetuities.

The definition of charity 157

To be regarded as charitable in law, a purpose must fulfil two requirements. (1) It must be a purpose of a charitable nature; and (2) it must be such as to benefit the public.

The purposes which the law considers to be of a charitable nature are those mentioned in the preamble to the Charitable Uses Act 1601, and those which, though not mentioned there, may by analogy be regarded as within its 'spirit and intendment'. They are commonly divided into four classes or 'heads' on the basis of an analysis suggested in argument in *Morice v Bishop of Durham* and given judicial approval in *CIT v Pemsel* (1891) where Lord Macnaghten said in the House of Lords: '"Charity" in its legal sense comprises four principal divisions: trusts for the relief of poverty; trusts for the advancement of education; trusts for the advancement of religion; and trusts for other purposes beneficial to the community'. It will be convenient to take the four heads in turn. Under each head will be discussed the kinds of purposes which are included under that head, and how each of them fulfils the requirement of benefit to the public.

1 *The relief of poverty*

A trust for the relief of poverty, or, as the 1601 preamble has it, 'aged, impotent and poor People' may be charitable. 'Poverty' may mean destitution, but it need not: trusts have been held charitable under this head where their purposes has been to help those 'who have to "go short" in the ordinary acceptance of that term' (*Re Coulthurst* (1951) per Evershed MR). But it is essential that what is provided by the trust is not merely benefit, but relief. As Peter Gibson J said in *Joseph Rowntree Memorial Trust Housing Association Ltd v A-G* (1983), 'The word "relief" implies that the persons in question have a need attributable to their condition as aged, impotent or poor persons which requires alleviating, and which those persons could not alleviate, or would find difficulty in alleviating, themselves from their own resources'. Even if the purpose of the trust is to provide benefits of the sort normally provided for the relief of poor people, it will not be charitable under this head if its terms are such that the benefits may also be enjoyed by those not in need of them. So in *Re Gwyon* (1930) a trust to provide free trousers for boys at Farnham was held to be not for the relief of poverty (or, which comes to the same thing, not exclusively for the relief of poverty) because there was no term restricting the benefits of the gift to poor boys.

It is sometimes said that there is no public benefit requirement in trusts for the relief of poverty. The better view is perhaps that all such trusts benefit the public. The poor are always with us, and if relief is provided by individual benefactions, the burden on the social services is reduced and rates and taxes may be correspondingly smaller. A trust for the relief of poverty among a group of people will be charitable however small the group and however defined: for example, the employees of a company (*Dingle v Turner* (1972)) or the relatives of a named person. However, a trust for the relief of named individuals who are poor is not charitable, because in such a case the public benefit is nearly nil. It is for this reason that *Re Abbott Fund Trusts* (1900) fell to be discussed in the chapter on resulting trusts and not here.

2 *The advancement of education*

The preamble refers to 'Schools of Learning, Free Schools, and Scholars in Universities', but the category of trusts which are charitable as being for the advancement of education is by no means limited to those concerned with the provision of formal schooling. 'A ride on an elephant may be educational' as Farwell J said in *Re Lopes* (1930). Charitable trusts under this head have included those for the support of museums and learned societies, for the study of the works of the composer Delius, for the production of the Law Reports, for sporting facilities connected with educational institutions, and for a chess contest for young men in Portsmouth. But there are limits. Sporting facilities generally are not charitable unless they come within the scope of the Recreational Charities Act 1958. And not every endeavour to accumulate or publish facts is educational. *Re Pinion* (1964) concerned an attempt to found a museum consisting of the studio of an untalented artist, containing a selection of his works and a worthless collection of furniture and other objects. In giving judgment that the trust was not charitable, Harman LJ said 'I can conceive of no useful object to be served in foisting on the public this mass of junk. It has neither public utility nor educational value'.

The public benefit requirement is applied to educational charities much more strictly than to those for the relief of poverty. The courts have held that for this type of charity to pass the test of public benefit, the educational experience it provides must be able to be enjoyed by the public as a whole or, at least, a group which constitutes a section of the community. A group does not constitute a section of the community if its members share a common link or nexus with a named individual, for example, because they are all his relatives, or his employees, or relatives of his employees. This rule applies even if the class is very large and by any other test would clearly comprise a section of the community. In *Oppenheim v Tobacco Securities Trust Co Ltd* (1951) the trust was for the education of children of employees or former employees of the British-American Tobacco Company Limited or any of its subsidiary or allied companies. The number of employees of the company and its subsidiary and allied companies was over 110,000. The House of Lords held that the trust could not be charitable as there was no public benefit. There is public benefit in the support of an educational institution; but where the trust is for the education of a class of persons at large, 'it seems to me' said Lord Simonds LC, who gave the leading judgment, 'that it would be an extension [of the legal definition of charity], for which there is no justification in principle or authority, to regard common employment as a quality which constitutes those employed a section of the community'. A trust for the relief of poverty among one's relatives or employees may be charitable; a trust for their education cannot be.

3 The advancement of religion

A trust whose purpose is the advancement of religion, whether by the provision of repair of churches or by the support of clergy or missionaries, may be charitable; and the courts have been generous in their interpretation of what is a religion. Charitable status under this head is clearly not confined to trusts advancing the Christian religion, but will in addition cover those promoting any form of monotheistic theism. Philosophy, however, is not the same thing as religion, so a trust for the advancement of ethical or moral principles without reference to a deity, though desirable, is not charitable under this head. In *Re South Place Ethical Society* (1980) the Society's aims, which were 'the study and dissemination of ethical principles and the cultivation of a rational religious sentiment' were held by Dillon J not to be for the advancement of religion:

'Religion, as I see it, is concerned with man's relations with God, and ethics are concerned with man's relations with man. The two are not the same . . . If reason leads people not to accept Christianity or any known religion, but they do believe in the excellence of qualities such as truth, beauty and love, or believe in the Platonic concept of the ideal, their beliefs may be to them the equivalent of a religion, but viewed objectively they are not religion'.

160   *Charity*

As regards public benefit under this head, the courts have been very liberal and are generally prepared to consider that any trust which has as its purpose the advancement of religion is for the public benefit. There are only two exceptions. One is where the rules of the sect, whose religion it is the purpose of the trust to advance, prohibit its members from contact with the rest of the world. In *Gilmour v Coats* (1949) a gift to a cloistered community of nuns was held by the House of Lords to be lacking in public benefit, and in *Broxtowe BC v Birch* (1983) the Exclusive Brethren were refused rating relief in respect of premises to which only the brethren were admitted. The other exception is where the type of observance promoted by the gift is such as to confer benefits on individuals only and not on any section of the community, however small. It was partly for this reason that a gift to support ceremonies connected with the gratification of the spirits of the donor's ancestors was held non-charitable in *Yeap Cheah Neo v Ong Chen Neo* (1875) and a similar fate befell a gift to enable church bells to be rung half-muffled on the anniversary of the donor's death in *Re Arber* (1919). But these exceptions are of uncertain extent. A gift for the general purposes of the Exclusive Brethren was held charitable in *Holmes v A-G* (1981) and so was a trust for the saying of masses for the dead in *Re Caus* (1934). The court will apparently lean in favour of finding a public benefit in a religious trust if it is possible to do so.

4 *Other purposes*

When Lord Macnaghten gave 'other purposes beneficial to the community' as his fourth head of charity, he did not mean that all other purposes are charitable if they benefit the community, but merely that there are some purposes which are charitable, and which benefit the community other than by the relief of poverty or the advancement of religion or education. For a purpose to be within the fourth head it is not enough that it benefit the community: it must in addition be within the 'spirit and intendment' of the preamble to the Charitable Uses Act 1601. This means that either it, or something very like it, is mentioned in the preamble, or else that one can say as one reads the preamble that the line of thought of its author was such that, if he had thought of this purpose, he would have included it. When it considers this matter, a court should have regard to previous decisions on which purposes are charitable and which are not; as Lord Wilberforce said in *Brisbane City Council v A-G for Queensland* (1978), the way to determine whether a trust is charitable under this head is by 'precedent and analogy'. Working by analogy from the precedents he held that a trust of a piece of land to be used for a public park, recreational reserve, show ground, or other similar purposes by the city was charitable.

The list of what may be charitable under the fourth head is endless. All that can be done here is to give some examples, thus:

(1) Purposes specifically mentioned in the 1601 preamble, such as the maintenance of bridges and roads, and the relief of the sick. Trusts for the support or maintenance of hospitals come within the last category (*Re Smith's WT* (1962));
(2) The promotion of the health of animals generally, because this type of purpose has the effect of promoting the better feelings of humanity (*Re Wedgwood* (1915));
(3) Purposes which better the quality of life, for example by improving standards of design, or the efficiency of techniques of agriculture (*IRC v Yorkshire Agricultural Society* (1927));
(4) The relief of distress, for example to assist or improve the fire-fighting or the lifeboat services (*Thomas v Howell* (1874));
(5) The promotion of efficiency in the police and the armed forces (*Re Lord Stratheden and Campbell* (1894));
(6) Public utilities, if non-profit making (*Scottish Burial Reform and Cremation Society v Glasgow City Corp* (1967)).

It must be emphasised that this list is not complete, and a trust may be charitable although it is not within any of the six classes.

What about public benefit under this head? One might think that since all these trusts are, by definition, for purposes 'beneficial to the community', the public benefit requirement would have been satisfied already. That view would be wrong; for the list is of types of purpose, with no reference to the number or categories of possible beneficiaries. Some of these purposes, like those for the support of the police and the armed forces, clearly benefit us all, but a trust to maintain a hospital to be used only by retired Leeds cloth-workers of the Roman Catholic faith might need to be viewed rather differently. Lord Simonds LC suggested on several occasions that in his view the public benefit requirement was not satisfied if those to be benefited were defined as a 'class within a class'. So in *IRC v Baddeley* (1955) he said 'A trust cannot qualify as a charity within the fourth class in *Pemsel*'s Case if the beneficiaries are a class of persons not only confined to a particular area but selected from within it by reference to a particular creed'. It is not clear at present what the law on this topic is. On the one hand, it is clear that a mutual benefit society, providing relief only to its members, fails to fulfil the public benefit requirement. On the other hand, it is equally certain that, if the benefits of a trust are available to all, it does not matter that few are likely to want to or even to be able to take advantage of it. But between these two extremes it is perhaps better to avoid the dogma of Lord Simonds LC and say instead, with Lord Cross in *Dingle v Turner*, that public benefit is a matter of degree to be determined on a case-by-case basis with reference to the size of the class and the purpose of the trust.

GENERAL CONSIDERATIONS

1 *Which head?*

A trust is charitable if it fulfils the requirements of any head. Some trusts qualify under more than one head. Some trusts fail to qualify under the head which at first looks most suitable, but succeed under another head. So, although Dillon J held in *Re South Place Ethical Society* that the Society did not advance religion (see p 159 above) he nevertheless held it to be charitable under the second and fourth heads. A trust providing hospital benefits for poor members of a church bell-ringing society could not be charitable under the fourth head, but might qualify under the first and third; and so on.

2 *Sport and recreation*

Sporting and recreational purposes are not by themselves charitable. Many trusts for such purposes are charitable because the facilities they provide are such as to advance some other charitable purpose. Examples are a trust to promote the playing of association football and other games in schools and universities (second head: *IRC v McMullen* (1980)); a trust to provide a prize in a chess competition for young men (second head, because chess is an education game: *Re Duprèe's Deed Trusts* (1944)); a trust to promote fishing, cricket, football and polo in a named regiment (fourth head, because it promotes the physical efficiency of the army: *Re Gray* (1925)). There are, however, many other trusts for primarily recreational purposes, which run the risk of not qualifying under the fourth head, if those allowed to enjoy their benefits constitute 'a class within a class'. Obvious possible casualties are local associations, such as Womens' Institutes. The Recreational Charities Act 1958 was passed in order to clarify the status of such trusts. The Act provides that the provision of facilities for recreation or leisure-time occupation is charitable if:

(1) It is for the public benefit. This requirement must be read with the others, which essentially indicate what constitutes 'benefit' and what is 'a section of the community' in this context; and
(2) The facilities are provided in the interests of social welfare. This wording was probably chosen because it has been used in other statutes. If so, it seems fair to give it the same meaning as in those other statutes. Lord Denning MR, interpreting one of them in a rating case, *National Deposit Friendly Society v Skegness UDC* (1958), defined social welfare as 'doing good to others who are in need'; and
(3) The object is to improve the conditions of life of those for whom the facilities are primarily intended. Note the word 'primarily'. The trust will not fail to be charitable simply because a few people not in need of the facilities may also use them; and
(4) *Either* the facilities are primarily intended for a group of people who need them because of their youth, age, infirmity, disablement, poverty or social and economic circumstances, *or* the facilities are to be available to the members or female members of the public at large.

Notice that even after the Act many recreational trusts are not charitable. The trust in *Re Nottage* (1895) to provide a prize for a yacht race would still fail, not only because the prize was not provided in the interests of social welfare, but also because, although a prize promotes recreation, it is probably not 'facilities'.

3 Profit

Certainly a trust may be charitable even if those benefiting under it make some payment for their benefits: *Joseph Rowntree Memorial Trust Housing Association Ltd v A-G* (1983) (subsidised housing). But suppose those benefiting are required to pay the economic cost of their benefits, or more – or suppose that a charity runs a profitable activity. Do school fees, or charity gift shops, cause organisations to be non-charitable? Clearly not. The question is not whether the organisation makes a profit, but what it does with any profit. If the profits must, under the terms of the trust, be applied exclusively to charitable purposes, then the organisation's charitable status is not endangered. If, on the other hand, it conducts an enterprise for the profit of individuals, or if under its rules any profit might possibly be applied to non-charitable purposes, then, however desirable the enterprise, it cannot be charitable in law. Privately-owned preparatory schools are therefore not charitable under the second head, nor are security companies under the fourth.

4 *Gifts for uncertain purposes*

It is one of the advantages of charity that a charitable gift will not fail for uncertainty of object. If property is given to trustees to hold for charitable purposes, but those purposes are not adequately defined by the donor, a scheme for the application of the property will be drawn up either by the court or by the Charity Commissioners. But if, on the other hand, property is given to charity other than by way of trust, and it is not certain which charity was intended to benefit (for instance, if a testator leaves 'my entire residue to charity') the gift passes to the Crown, but will be applied to charitable purposes under the Royal Prerogative. In either case, those who have to work out the scheme will take into account such matters as what the donor's interests were, and where he lived, in order to decide how his gift should be used.

This doctrine has another aspect. When a gift is given to the holder of an office which may be regarded as generally charitable, it takes effect as a charitable gift for that person's charitable functions. So a gift to 'His Eminence the Archbishop of Westminster Cathedral for the time being to be used by him for such purposes as he shall in his absolute discretion think fit' was upheld in *Re Flinn* (1948). But a gift to a charitable office-holder will not be a charitable gift if the very words of the gift entitle the recipient to use it wholly or partly for non-charitable purposes. We have seen that the gift in *Morice v Bishop of Durham* failed for this reason. The courts' attitude to vague gifts of this type has on occasion been stretched to absurd lengths: in *Re Smith* (1932) a gift to 'my country England' was held to be valid and a scheme was drawn up for its application to charitable purposes.

5 *Politics*

The one type of purpose which can never be charitable is a political purpose. And, as the courts have taken a broad view of what constitutes education, or religion, or a purpose beneficial to the community, so too they have taken a broad view of what constitutes a political purpose. The veto applies not only to trusts in support of particular political parties, but to any trust which has as one of its principal purposes the promotion of a change in the law. The leading case is *National Anti-Vivisection Society v IRC* (1947) in which Lord Simonds LC cited with approval a passage from a leading textbook which states the problem precisely: 'However desirable the change may really be, the law could not stultify itself by holding that it was for the public benefit that the law should be changed. Each court in deciding on the validity of a gift must decide on the principle that the law is right as it stands'. The question, then, is one of public benefit: a change in the law may be of public benefit, but the court is incapable of determining that it is. So a trust to promote a change in the law cannot fulfil the public benefit requirement. A recent example of a trust which failed to prove charitable status for this reason was that set up by Amnesty International and considered in *McGovern v A-G* (1981). The trust included as its aims 'attempting to secure the release of Prisoners of Conscience' and 'procuring the abolition of torture or inhuman or degrading treatment or punishment'. The carrying out of these purposes would necessarily involve the promotion of political or legal change in foreign countries. Slade J held that the trust was not charitable:

'There would arise a substantial prima facie risk that such a trust, if enforced, could prejudice the relations of this country with the foreign country concerned. The court would have no satisfactory means of assessing the extent of such risk, which would not be capable of being readily dealt with by evidence and would be a matter more for political than for legal judgment'.

If the rationalisation of the law on a particular subject area is merely a subsidiary purpose of a trust, the political element will not necessarily jeopardise the trust's charitable status. The Charity Commissioners have issued guidelines which indicate that a charity is entitled to make comments on proposed changes in the law in response to a request from the government, and may brief members of either House of Parliament on a bill before them. It may help the government to reach a decision, but 'the emphasis must be on rational persuasion'. Charities which have educational purposes must be careful to avoid overstepping the line between education and propaganda; and all charities should avoid seeking to bring pressure on government to change its policy or to remedy poverty or injustice which has its origin in social, economic or political conditions.

A trust whose purposes are political in a way which is more than merely ancillary to its main purposes will be refused registration as a charity. After a charity is registered, its trustees must ensure that they do not apply any of the funds for political purposes. They must adhere to the Charity Commissioners' guidelines. Otherwise, they will be found to be in breach of trust in that they misapplied trust property. They will be personally liable to repay the money so expended, and the trust will run the risk of partially losing its tax exemptions. It is by no means infrequent for registered charities to engage in activities which are extremely close to the political line, and the Commissioners' annual reports contain detailed comments on such cases as have come to their notice.

A trust which has as its purpose the continuance of the legal status quo is not political and so may be charitable. A quaint example is *Re Pardoe*, where in 1906 a gift to the bell-ringers of Cirencester Church who should ring each year in celebration of the Restoration of Charles II to the throne, was held charitable under the third head. The 'happy thoughts' promoted by the bells 'necessarily connote a feeling of gratitude to the giver of all good gifts' per Kekewich J.

6 Discrimination

The provisions of the Race Relations Act 1976 and the Sex Discrimination Act 1975 have no effect on the legality of private trusts, and little on charitable trusts. The benefits of a charitable trust may be confined to members of one of the sexes, or of one or more races to the exclusion of others. Discrimination on grounds of colour is, however, not allowed, and the instrument creating the trust will be read as if the reference to colour were omitted (Race Relations Act 1976, s 34(1)).

Chapter 17
The administration of charitable trusts

(*All references in this chapter are to sections of the Charities Act 1960 unless the contrary appears*)

As charities are for the public benefit and receive a measure of public subsidy, it is appropriate that they should be subject to public supervision. The law relating to their administration was substantially modernised by the Charities Act 1960, which gave many new functions and powers to the Charity Commissioners, who constitute an independent department of the civil service. In the result, it is they, and not the courts, who determine nearly all questions of law relating to individual charities; but the rules they apply have been developed over hundreds of years in decisions of the courts, and this is one of the few areas of law in which many seventeenth- and eighteenth-century cases are still relevant.

THE CHARITY COMMISSIONERS

The three Commissioners are appointed by the Home Secretary, and they have a substantial staff. Their powers are derived in the main from the Charities Act 1960. They have the general function of 'promoting the effective use of charitable resources by encouraging the development of better methods of administration, by giving charity trustees information or advice on any matter affecting the charity and by investigating and checking abuses' (s 1(3)); and their general object is 'so to act in the case of any charity (unless it is a matter of altering its purposes) as best to promote and make effective the work of the charity in meeting the needs designated by its trusts' (s 1(4)). Any charity trustee may seek advice from them on the performance of his duties, and he is safe in acting upon it (s 24). The Commissioners do not, however, have power to act in the administration of a charity. They advise and supervise; they do not manage.

The Register of Charities. The Commissioners maintain a register of charities, and trustees of a charitable trust which is not excepted from registration are required to apply for it to be admitted to the register. When the Commissioners have examined the trust instrument they enter it on the register if they consider that the trust is in law charitable (s 4). There is provision for an appeal to the High Court against refusal to register (or, indeed, against registration) but it is rarely used: the Commissioners' decision is normally accepted as final. If registration of a new charity is refused, it may be possible to amend its objects so as to comply with the Commissioners' requirements, and then reapply. An institution on the register of charities is conclusively presumed to be a charity (s 5(1)).

Charities excepted from the duty to register include museums, universities and private schools, religious charities and charities which have neither an income of more than £15 per year, nor the use and occupation of any land (s 4 and Sch 2).

Charity property. Many charities have funds which are too small to be spread over a range of investments. Section 22 gives the Commissioners power to bring into effect 'common investment schemes' which would enable charities to pool their property, and become entitled to a proportionate share in the capital and income of the pool. The most important of the schemes is the Charities Official Investment Fund. It is, in effect, a unit trust open only to charities, and has a total value of well over £100 m. Another special problem in the administration of charities is that their trustees are prone to change very frequently, for example at each annual general meeting. Valuable resources can be wasted in vesting the property in the new trustees on each occasion. The ideal solution is the appointment of a custodian trustee. One of the Commissioners' staff acts as Official Custodian for Charities, a corporation sole with perpetual succession (s 3). Any charity may, if he consents, appoint him as custodian trustee, and the trustees of the charity may then transfer to him any property (other than an interest in land) while retaining to the full their powers of management. Alternatively, he may be appointed by the court as custodian trustee of any property (including land) held on charitable trusts (ss 16–17).

The Act imposes a few restrictions on the power of charity trustees to deal with the trust property. In particular, land which forms part of the permanent endowment of a charity, or which has at any time been occupied for the purposes of the charity, cannot be disposed of without the consent of either the Commissioners or the court (s 29). On the other hand, the Commissioners may sanction any action in the administration of a charity if it is expedient in the interests of the charity, even if it would not otherwise be within the power of the trustees (s 23). Hence it will not normally be necessary to apply to the court under s 57 of the Trustee Act 1925 to make a particular 'expedient' transaction.

Schemes. Variations of charitable trusts are effected not under the Variation of Trusts Act 1958 but by making and enforcing a scheme. The court has inherent power to establish schemes, but s 18 gives concurrent power to the Commissioners and most are in fact made by them. They may exercise their jurisdiction if either the matter is referred to them by the court or the charity makes an application to them. In the latter event, however, they are required not to act in difficult or contentious cases: such must be determined by the court. And they cannot use their scheme-making jurisdiction to try to settle disputes about the trusts, which again must be left for the court.

The Commissioners regard the task of making schemes as one of the most important of their activities, as it is the main way in which they perform the functions laid on them by s 1(3). Some schemes are comparatively simple, changing the name of a charity or setting up a new board of trustees or dealing with problems caused by trustees dying or disclaiming. Others are complicated, involving a change to the whole structure and perhaps also the objects of a trust. Very frequently (in the case of nearly 1,000 institutions per year) the Commissioners direct a scheme under which charities are grouped together or amalgamated, so that they can be run more efficiently. Where the original objects of a charity have become difficult to achieve, they will be replaced by cy-près objects under a scheme.

For purely administrative changes to a trust, it is not always necessary to draw up a scheme. Section 23 specifically provides that the Commissioners may use their power under that section not only to authorise a particular transaction, compromise or the like, or a particular application of property, but also 'so as to give a more general authority'. They may for example, 'authorise a charity to use common premises, or employ a common staff, or otherwise combine for any purpose of administration with any other charity'.

Inquiries and proceedings. The Commissioners' duty to investigate and check abuses imposes on them the task of receiving and investigating complaints. Under s 6 they can institute an inquiry into the affairs of a particular charity or class of charities, but the power has seldom been used because nearly all complaints and irregularities can be dealt with informally. If necessary the Commissioners can remove or replace a trustee, and, if there has been misconduct or mismanagement, they may restrict dealings with the trust property or require it to be transferred to the Official Custodian for Charities (s 20). If the Commissioners think that the trustees ought to have applied for a scheme but have unreasonably refused or neglected to do so, they may ask the Home Secretary to refer the case to them with a view to making a scheme.

Legal proceedings with reference to a charity may be taken by the charity itself, any of its trustees, any person interested in the charity, any two or more inhabitants of the relevant area if it is a local charity, or the Attorney General, but not by anybody else (s 28(1),(6)). The Attorney General, representing the public at large, may sue either on his own motion or by a 'relator' action (in which he gives permission for somebody else to sue in his name). His right of access to the courts is unrestricted; but nobody else may sue unless the Commissioners authorise the action, which they must not do if they have power to deal with the problem themselves. The effect is that it is quite rare for disputes about the administration of a charity to come before the courts.

THE TRUSTEES OF A CHARITY

Charity trustees have all the duties and liabilities of trustees of a private trust with some additions. The provisions of the Trustee Act 1925 and the Trustee Investments Act 1961 apply to them, as does much of the Settled Land Act 1925, for land belonging to a charity is deemed to be settled land (Settled Land Act 1925, s 29(1)). However, there is no restriction on the number of trustees, for s 34 of the Trustee Act 1925 does not apply to 'land vested in trustees for charitable, ecclesiastic or public purposes'. Charity trustees may be appointed, removed or replaced by the Commissioners, and may act by majority. They have a statutory duty to keep accounts and preserve them for seven years, and they should insure the trust property for its full value.

As regards schemes and other variations, the general duty of the trustees is to be watchful, so as to be able to make an application at the proper time. There are, however, two statutory provisions enabling them to act of their own motion contrary to the terms of the trust. Under s 12 they may (notwithstanding anything in the trusts of the charity) co-operate with the local authority in a review of charities, publish information about other charities, and make arrangements for co-ordinating their work with that of the local authority or another charity. Rather wider powers of variation are given by ss 2-3 of the Charities Act 1985. Section 2 applies to a local charity for the relief of poverty which is over 50 years old. The trustees may, by unanimous resolution, change the objects of such a charity if they think that the original objects are obsolete and that a change is necessary. Section 3 applies to any charity with an income of not more than £200 per year. The trustees may, by unanimous resolution, decide that the whole of the trust property be transferred to another charity with similar objects. In either case, the resolution is effective only after the Commissioners have given notice that they concur with it. Any other change to the objects of a charity will require a cy-près scheme, which is not made by the trustees.

CY-PRÈS

If it becomes impossible or impracticable to carry out the purpose for which property has been given to charity, there is not an automatic resulting trust as there would be if the gift was non-charitable. Instead, a cy-près scheme will be drawn up and the property will continue to be applicable to charity, for some purpose similar to that originally intended. 'Cy-près' is legal (i e approximate) French for 'as near as possible'. It is apparent from the first sentence of this paragraph that there are two conditions to be fulfilled before the cy-près jurisdiction is available: (1) it must be impossible or impracticable to carry out the purpose; and (2) property must have been given to charity.

Impossibility and impracticability

In the old cases there was a tendency for this requirement to be interpreted very strictly, and cy-près was confined to situations where it was completely impossible to carry out the original purpose, for example teaching Christianity to natives near Harvard (*A-G v City of London* (1790)). Since 1960, the question is likely to be answered entirely by reference to s 13, which provides that the purposes of a charitable gift may be altered to allow the property to be applied cy-près in the following circumstances:

(a) where the original purposes, in whole or in part, have been (as far as may be) fulfilled, or where they cannot be effectively carried out, or not according to the directions given;

(b) where the original purposes provide a use for only part of the property;
(c) where it would be more effective to use in conjunction property held on similar trusts;
(d) where the original purpose was defined by reference to an area which ceased to be an area for some other purpose, or by reference to an area or class of persons which has ceased to be suitable;
(e) where the original purposes have been adequately provided for by other means, or have ceased to be charitable, or have ceased in some other way to be a suitable and effective way of using the property.

When determining what is 'suitable' or 'effective', regard is to be paid to 'the spirit of the gift'.

It is difficult to think of any contingency which might properly be regarded as 'impossibility or impracticability' which is not covered by s 13. Notice, however, that, relaxed as the definition is, there are at least two matters which it does not cover. In (e) there is a reference to purposes which have *ceased* to be charitable. This would include, for example, private schools if their charitable status were removed by a future Labour government. It does not include purposes which were not charitable at the date of the gift, for example political purposes. Cy-près is a way of keeping a trust charitable. It cannot be used to turn a non-charitable gift into a charitable one: *Re Jenkins's WT* (1966). Secondly, in *Re J W Laing Trust* (1983), Peter Gibson J held that s 13 has no application to purely administrative directions in a trust, because they are not properly described as the 'original *purposes*' of the gift. In a proper case, directions as to administration of the charity may be given or changed by the court in the exercise of its inherent or statutory jurisdiction, but not as a cy-près scheme.

Section 13(5) reads as follows:

'It is hereby declared that a trust for charitable purposes places a trustee under a duty, where the case permits and requires the property or some part of it to be applied cy-près, to secure its effective use for charity by taking steps to enable it to be so applied'.

One of the tasks of the trustees of a charity is therefore to consider from time to time whether the funds under their control are being fully exploited for the purposes for which they were given. If it is felt that circumstances have arisen such as are described in s 13, so that the trust has become impossible or impracticable, the trustees must apply to the Commissioners or the court for a cy-près scheme to be established.

Has the property been given to charity?

Subsequent failure. If the original purposes become impossible or impracticable after property has vested in the charity, there is no problem. The property has clearly been given to charity and is now applicable cy-près. Unless the donor specifically provides otherwise, once the property has been dedicated to charitable purposes, it remains so dedicated for ever.

Initial failure. The situation is quite different where the purpose specified by the donor is already impossible or impracticable at the time the gift would take effect. It is then necessary to decide, by construing the words of the gift, whether there was only an attempt to give property for a *particular charitable purpose*, in which case, the purpose having already failed, there is an automatic resulting trust, or whether the property has been given to *charity* in some wider sense, in which case it is applicable cy-près. The classic statement of the distinction is that by Parker J in *Re Wilson* (1913).

'The authorities must be divided into two classes. First of all, we have a class of cases where, in form, the gift is given for a particular charitable purpose, but it is possible, taking the [instrument] as a whole, to say that, notwithstanding the form of the gift, the paramount intention is to give property in the first instance for a general charitable purpose rather than a particular charitable purpose, and to graft onto the general gift a direction as to the desires or intentions of the [donor] as to the manner in which the general gift is to be carried into effect. Then there is the second class of cases where, on the true construction of the [instrument], no such paramount general intention can be inferred, and where the gift being in form a particular gift – a gift for a particular purpose, and it being impossible to carry out that particular purpose, the whole gift is held to fail'.

If the case is within Parker J's first class, there will be a cy-près scheme; if within his second, a resulting trust. The more particular and precise are the donor's directions, the more difficult it will be to find that he had an intention to benefit charity in any wider sense. In *Re Wilson* itself, the testator left directions that his estate should pay part of the salary of a schoolmaster (whose duties were laid down), who would teach pupils (whose fees were laid down) in a school which, with the master's house, was to be erected by voluntary subscription in the parish of Aitken, Cumberland 'on a hill near to the gate that divided Biglands and Wampools Commons (now enclosed)'. There was no possibility of carrying out these instructions, and, bearing in mind the precision of the testator's language, it could not be said that he had a wider intention in favour of (say) education in Cumberland, onto which he had grafted his particular desires. The gift therefore failed.

If the donor's intention seems to have been to divide his estate among various charities, it may be possible to infer wider charitable intention from the gift's context. In *Re Satterthwaite's WT* (1966) there was evidence that the testatrix hated people. She left her entire estate to be divided between nine legatees: seven animal charities, the National Anti-Vivisection League (which she may have thought was charitable) and one body that could not be identified. It was held that the context showed a general intention to benefit animal charities, and the last portion could therefore be applied cy-près. Goff J applied the same principle in *Re Finger's WT* (1971) to gifts to charitable bodies which had ceased to exist. Wider charitable intention cannot, however, be inferred from the context when the disputed gifts form a small part of a series of gifts to family members and charitable and non-charitable objects. An interesting distinction was drawn in *Re Harwood* (1936). If a small gift is given to a particular charitable body, by name and with no reference to its purposes, and that body has ceased to exist, it will be very difficult to discover a wider charitable intention. But if the named donee is a body which has never existed, the gift must be construed as generally for the supposed purposes of that body, and, provided those purposes can still be fulfilled, the property will be applied cy-près. So one small gift to the Wisbech Peace Society, which had existed, failed; whereas another to the Peace Society of Belfast, which had never existed, took effect as a gift for the charitable purpose of promoting peace in Belfast.

In some circumstances s 14 may be used to find a wider charitable intention. It provides that such intention shall be presumed where the donor cannot be found or has executed a written disclaimer, and shall be conclusively presumed where the property is the proceeds of a cash collection or other money-raising activity. Further, the court may order that property be treated as given for charitable purposes generally, if it would be too expensive to trace the donors or it would be unreasonable for the donors to expect the money to be returned. Thus, if money is collected for the relief of a disaster which turns out not to have happened, or for a project which requires more funds than are obtained, it will normally be possible to apply the property cy-près.

To sum up: if a charitable purpose becomes impossible or impracticable, property already devoted to that purpose will be applied under a cy-près scheme. If a gift is made to a charitable purpose which is at the time of the gift impossible or impracticable, the gift is applicable cy-près if and only if the donor has shown a wider charitable intention.

Index

Accounts
  false accounting, as breach of trust, 147
  trust property, relating to, trustees' duties as to, 115–116
Accumulation of income
  rule against, 26–27
Administration of trusts
  charitable, 167–175. *See also* CHARITABLE TRUSTS
  maintenance and advancement of beneficiaries, 127–134. *See also* BENEFICIARIES
  remedies for breach of trust, 144–152. *See also* BREACH OF TRUST
  trustees, role of. *See* TRUSTEES
  variations of trusts, 135–143. *See also* VARIATION OF TRUSTS
Agent
  liability of trustee when agent is employed, 108–109
  trustee's power to employ, 108
Agriculture
  charitable trusts for improving techniques of, 161
Animals
  charitable trusts for promotion of health of, 161
  specific, trusts for the maintenance of, 40
Appointment
  power of. *See* POWER OF APPOINTMENT
Apportionment
  trustees' duties as to, 120–121, 126
Armed forces
  charitable trusts to promote efficiency of, 161

Bankruptcy
  court's general powers as to trusts in cases of, 33–34

Bankruptcy – *continued*
  defendant, of, remedy for breach of trust, 148
  voidable trusts in relation to, 32–33
Beneficiaries
  accumulation, power of. *See* maintenance and accumulation, power of, *below*
  advancement, power of –
    application, 134
    beneficiary's interest, 131–132
    creation of new settlement, 133
    discretion, trustees', 133–134
    meaning of 'advancement or benefit', 132–133
    need for legislation, 127–128
    statutory provision as to, 131
    trustees' role as to, 131–134
  also trustee –
    liability of, for breach of trust, 146
    possibility of, 5
  balance of investments between –
    apportion, duty to, 120–121, 126
    convert, duty to, 119–120, 126
    holding, generally, 119
  certainty of objects in relations to –
    fixed trusts, 47–48
    generally, 47
    personal power of appointment, where, 51
    power of appointment, where trustees have, 48–50
    series of gifts each subject to a condition, 51–52
    generally, 35
  maintenance and accumulation, power of –
    contrary intention, 131
    gifts carrying the intermediate income, 128–129
    need for legislation, 127–128
    older trusts, in relation to, 130

177

Beneficiaries – *continued*
  maintenance and accumulation, power of – *continued*
    statutory provisions as to, 129–130
    trustees' role as to, 128–131
  potential –
    categories of, 139, 143
    fixed trust, in, 48
    variation of trusts and, 139–141
    power of appointment and. *See* POWER OF APPOINTMENT
  principle –
    generally, 35, 36–37
    non-charitable unincorporated associations, 37–40
    trusts without a beneficiary, 40–41
  proprietary rights of, 52–54
  protective trusts, 46–47
  remedies of, for breach of trust –
    generally, 144, 152
    personal liability of trustees, 144–148
    proprietary remedies, 148–151
    recovery from innocent volunteer personally, 152
    See also BREACH OF TRUST
  several, distribution of trust property between, 41–42
  trustees buying equitable interest from, 111
  trusts without a beneficiary, 40–41
  variation of trust, powers as to, 135, 136. *See also* VARIATION OF TRUSTS
  who can be a beneficiary, 35–36

Breach of trust
  defences to actions for –
    beneficiary concurring in breach, 145–146
    concealment of facts, where, 146
    fraud, where, 146
    laches, scheme of, action barred by, 147
    limitation period, outside, 146–147
  liability of trustee –
    criminal liability, 147
    defences, 145–147 *See also* defences to actions for, *above*
    honest trustee, 145
    not concurred or joined in breach of trust, where, 145
    personal, remedies for, 144–148
    principle of, 144–145

Breach of trust – *continued*
  liability of trustee – *continued*
    profit accruing from breach of trust, 145
    trustees among themselves, of, 147–148
  protection of trust property, as to, 114–115
  remedies for –
    bankrupt, where defendant is, 148
    charge on beneficiary, 148–149
    'following', by, 148–149
    generally, 144, 152
    personal liability of trustees, 144–148. *See also* liability of trustee, *above*
    proprietary remedies, 148–151
    recovery from innocent volunteer personally, 152
    tracing, 149–151 *See also* TRACING

Bridges
  charitable trusts for maintenance of, 161

Charitable trusts. *See also* CHARITY
  administration of –
    Charity Commissioners, by, 167–170. *See also* CHARITY COMMISSIONERS
    cy-près, 171–175. *See also* CY-PRÈS SCHEME
    generally, 167
    trustees of a charity, 170–171
  advantages of charity, 155–156
  agriculture, for improving techniques of, 161
  animals, for promotion of the health of, 161
  armed forces, to promote efficiency of, 161
  beneficial to the community, which are, 160–162
  bridges, for maintenance of, 161
  Charity Commissioners. *See* CHARITY COMMISSIONERS
  classes of, 157–162
  cy-près scheme, 171–175. *See also* CY-PRÈS SCHEME
  definition of 'charity', 156–166
  design, for improving standards of, 161
  distress, for relief of, 161
  education, for the advancement of, 158–159

Index 179

Charitable trusts – *continued*
 fire-fighting, to assist or improve, 161
 gifts for uncertain purposes, 164
 hospitals, for support and maintenance of, 161
 inquiries and proceedings by Charity Commissioners, 169–170
 lifeboat services, to assist or improve, 161
 police, to promote efficiency of, 161
 politics and –
  Charity Commisssioners' guidelines as to, 165, 166
  political purposes, cannot be for, 164–165
  position of registered charities as to political activities, 165–166
 profit-making, 163–164
 public utilities, non-profit making, for, 161
 recreational purposes, for, 162–163
 relief of poverty, for, 157–158
 religion, for the advancement of, 159–160
 requirements for, 157–162
 roads, for maintenance of, 161
 schemes for variation of, 169
 sick, for relief of, 161
 sporting and recreational purposes, for, 162–163
 trustees of a, 170–171
Charities Official Investment Fund
 function of, 168
Charity. *See also* CHARITABLE TRUSTS
 Commissioners. *See* CHARITY COMMISSIONERS
 definition of, 156–166
 property, 168–169
 Register of Charities, 168
Charity Commissioners
 appointment of, 167
 charity property, role as to, 168–169
 inquiries and proceedings, duties as to, 169–170
 Official Custodian for Charities, 168
 political activities of charitable trusts, guidelines as to, 165, 166
 Register of Charities, 168
 role of, 164, 167
 schemes for variations of charitable trusts, 169
Chattels
 gift of, 58–59

Chose in action
 transfer of special types of, 58
Company
 controlling interest in, as investment, 125
 shares, gift of, 57–58
Constituting a trust
 completely constituted, meaning of, 55
 exceptions to rule that equity will not perfect imperfect gift – equitable exceptions, 68–69
 generally, 67
 statutory exceptions, 67
 incompletely constituted, meaning of, 55
 principles as to, 55–56
 requirement as to, 55
 summary, 69
 ways of making a gift. *See* GIFTS
Constructive trusts
 arises, situations where, 79–84
 breach of, remedies for, 144. *See also* BREACH OF TRUST
 justice and good conscience in relation to, 82–83
 nature of –
  generally, 78
  role of the court, 78–79
 sale of land, as to, 80
 secret trusts, whether express trusts or, 91–92·
 shared homes, in relation to, 80–82
 statute not to be used as instrument of fraud, 80
 third parties and, 83–84
 undue profit, due to, 79–80
Convert
 trustees' duties to, 119–120, 126
Court
 Chancery Division of the High Court, matters relating to trusts coming before, 6
 county court, matters relating to trusts coming before, 6
 remuneration from trust fund, powers to, 110
 trust set aside by the, under a statutory power –
  bankruptcy, 32–33
  circumstances generally, 30–31
  family provision, 31–32
  general powers, 33–34
  matrimonial proceedings, 31, 142

Index

Creation of a trust
beneficiary, 35–54. *See also*
BENEFICIARIES
constituting a trust, 55–69. *See also*
CONSTITUTING A TRUST
constructive trusts, 78–84. *See also*
CONSTRUCTIVE TRUSTS
formalities –
certainty of words, 9–11
generally, 9
statutory requirements, 11–13
generally, 3–8
intention, need to show, 9–11
mutual wills, 89–92
resulting trusts, 70–77. *See also*
RESULTING TRUSTS
secret trusts, 85–89, 91–92. *See also*
SECRET TRUSTS
trust property, 14–17. *See also*
TRUST PROPERTY
void and voidable trusts, 18–34. *See also* VOID TRUSTS; VOIDABLE TRUSTS
ways of, 9
Custodian trustees
appointment of, 96–97
charges of, 110
role of, 96
Cy-près scheme
given to charity, whether property has been, 173–175
impossibility and impracticability, requirement as to, 171–172
initial failure, 173
meaning of, 171
subsequent failure, 173

Design, improvement of
charitable trusts for, 161
Disclaimer
first trustee, by, 69, 99–100
Discretionary trusts
choose beneficiaries in, 106
power of appointment and, 45–46
protective trusts and, 47
Distress, relief of
charitable trusts for, 161
Distribution
trust property, of, trustee's duties as to, 116–117
Divorce
variation of trusts in relation to, 31, 142
void trusts in relation to, 27–28

Divorce – *continued*
voidable trusts in relation to, 31
Donatio mortis causa
equitable exception where an imperfect gift, 68

Education
charitable trusts for the advancement of, 158–159
Equitable interests
gift of, 57–58
Equity
secret trusts enforced in, 86. *See also* SECRET TRUSTS
sources of rules of, 4–5, 6
trusts –
implied by. *See* CONSTRUCTIVE TRUSTS; RESULTING TRUSTS
set aside by settlor on general equitable principles, 29–30
will not perfect imperfect gift, exceptions to rule, 67–69
Estoppel
proprietary, equitable exception where, 69
Expenses
trustees, of, 110
Express trust
breach of, remedies for, 144. *See also* BREACH OF TRUST
constituting. *See* CONSTITUTING A TRUST
creation of, 6
land, of, statutory requirements, 11
nature of, 6–7
secret trusts, whether constructive trusts or, 91–92
trusts implied by equity and, compared, 8
written, statutory requirements as to, 11–13

Family provision
variation of trusts and, 31–32, 142
voidable trusts in relation to, 31–32
Fire-fighting
charitable trusts to assist or improve, 161
Fixed trusts
certainty of objects, 47–48
power of appointment and, 45
protective trusts and, 46

Fraud
  action for breach of trust based on, 146
Gifts
  charitable, for uncertain purposes, 164
  complete, making –
    chattels, 58–59
    company shares, 58
    compared with other methods, 62–64
    equitable interests, 57–58
    generally, 57
    land, 57
  completely constituted trust of the benefit of a covenant, 66–67
  conveyance of land to an infant, 67
  disclaimer, equitable exception as to, 69
  donatio mortis causa, 68
  imperfect, exceptions to rule that equity will not perfect –
    equitable exceptions, 68–69
    generally, 67
    statutory exceptions, 67
  incomplete settlement of land, 67
  incomplete transfer –
    supported by consideration, 60–62, 62–64
    to trustees, supported by consideration, 64–66
  intermediate income, carrying, 128–129
  lifetime, 129
  proprietary estoppel, equitable exception where, 69
  Re Rose, rule in, 68
  series of, each subject to a condition, certainty where, 51–52
  Strong v Bird, rule in, 68
  unincorporated associations, non-charitable, to, 37–40
  ways of making –
    comparison, 62–64
    complete gift. *See* complete, making, *above*
    generally, 56–57
    incomplete transfer. *See* incomplete transfer, *above*
    property transferred to trustees by settlor, 60, 62–64
    settlor declares himself trustee, 59–60, 62–64
  will, by, 129

Homes
  shared, constructive trusts in relation to, 80–82
Hospitals
  charitable trusts for support and maintenance of, 161
Implied by equity
  trusts which are –
    express trusts and, compared, 8
    nature of, 7
Income
  accumulation of, rule against, 26–27
  inalienability of, rule against, 25
Infant *See* MINOR
Insider dealing
  breach of trust, as, 147
Insolvency. *See* BANKRUPTCY
Investments
  advice on, 123
  authorised, 122–123
  balance between beneficiaries –
    apportion, duty to, 120–121, 126
    convert, duty to, 119–120, 126
    holding, generally, 119
  Charities Official Investment Fund, 168
  choosing, trustees' duties in choosing, 117–121
  controlling interest in a company as, 125
  financial benefits, need to provide, 118
  land, 124
  mortgages, 124
  personal security, position as to, 125
  power to invest, trustees' –
    express powers, 121
    forms of investment, 124–125
    generally, 121
    proposal for reform, 126
    statutory powers. *See* statutory powers, *below*
    variation of, 125, 135. *See also* VARIATION OF TRUSTS
  securities, in, 122–123
  statutory powers as to –
    choice of investments within the ranges, 124
    generally, 122–123
    relationship between Act and other powers of investment, 123
    trustee's standard of care as to, 117–118

Judicial trustees
appointment of, 97–98

Laches, doctrine of
defence to action for breach of trust, as, 147
tracing subject to, 151

Land
constructive trust in relation to sale of, 80
conveyance of, to an infant, 67
express trusts of, 11
gift of, 57
incomplete settlement of, 67
investment, as form of, 124
legislation governing trusts of, 14–15
minor cannot be trustee of legal estate in, 95
settled, variation of trusts and, 142–143
strict settlement, 15–16
trust for sale, 15

Liability
agent employed, trustee's when, 108–109
trustee, of, for breach of trust. See BREACH OF TRUST

Lifeboat services
charitable trusts to assist or improve, 161

Limitation of actions
breach of trust, for, 146–147

Marriage
void trusts in relation to, 27–28

Matrimonial proceedings
variation of trusts in cases of, 31, 142
voidable trusts in relation to, 31

Minor
conveyance of land to, 67
maintenance and advancement of, trusts for –
advancement, power of, 131–134
generally, 127–128
maintain or accumulate, power to, 128–131
personalty on presumed resulting trust, holding, 75, 95
trustee, cannot be appointed a, 95

Mortgages
investment as form of, 124

Mutual wills
meaning of, 90
purpose of, 89–91
theoretical basis as to, 91–92
trusts arising from, 91–92

Perpetuities
rule against. See RULE AGAINST PERPETUITIES

Personal security
investment, as, 125

Police
charitable trusts to promote efficiency of, 161

Politics
charitable trusts and –
cannot be for political purposes, 164–165
Charity Commissioners' guidelines as to, 165, 166
position as to activities of registered charities, 165–166

Poverty
charitable trusts for the relief of, 157–158

Power of appointment
certainty of objects and, 48–51
discretionary trust, 45
donee's power of choice, 43–44
duties of acting responsibly imposed on donee, 44
exercised unanimously, 44
fixed trust, 45
granting, 43–45
meaning of, 42–43
personal, certainty of objects where, 51
trust instrument, bound to obey, 45–46
trustees having, certainty of objects where –
administratively workable, must be, 50–51
evidential certainty, 49–50
generally, 48
linguistic certainty, 49

Property
charity, 168–169
trust. See TRUST PROPERTY

Proprietary estoppel
equitable exception where, 69

Protective trusts
creation of, 46–47

Public trustee
charges of, 95–96, 110
office of, 95–96

Public utilities
charitable trusts for non-profit making, 161

Recreation
charitable trusts for, 162–163

Register of Charities
function of, 168
Religion
charitable trusts for the advancement of, 159–160
non-charitable religious trusts, 40
Remoteness of vesting
rule against, 20–24
Resulting trusts
automatic –
acceleration, 71–72
gift or trust, whether there is, 72–74
principle of, 70–71
breach of, remedies for, 144. *See also* BREACH OF TRUST
generally, 70
meaning of, 70
presumed –
advancement, presumption of, 76
rebutting the presumptions, 76–77
where arising, 74–75
Roads
charitable trusts for maintenance of, 161
Rule against perpetuities
accumulations of income, rule against, 26–27
history of, 19
inalienability of income, rule against, 25
infringement of, determination of, 19–20
legislation relating to, 19
need for, 18–19
remoteness of vesting, rule against, 20–24

Secret trusts
accept obligation, trustee must, 88
communication of testator with intended trustee, 86–87
constructive trusts, whether, 91–92
enforced in equity, 86
enforcement of, in equity, 91
express trusts, whether, 91–92
failure of, 88–89
fully-secret –
determination as to whether, 87
distinguished, 86
half-secret –
determination as to whether, 87
distinguished, 86, 89
reasons for having, 85
theoretical basis as to, 91–92

Secret trusts – *continued*
valid transfer of trust property to intended trustee, must be, 86
Securities
investment in, 122–123
safe custody of, 115
Security
personal, as investment, 125
trust property, 114–115
Settlor. *See also* GIFTS; MUTUAL WILLS
death of, trust taking effect on, 11–12
declares himself trustee, 59–60, 60–64
distribution of trust property between several beneficiaries, powers as to, 41–42
express powers of investment, giving, 121
sole trustee, as, 9
transfers property to trustees, 60, 62–64
trust set aside by, on general equitable principles, 29–30
Sick
charitable trusts for the relief of, 161
Sport and recreation
charitable trusts for, 162–163
Statutory trusts
nature of, 7–8

Testamentary dispositions
statutory requirements as to, 11
Tombs
trusts for the erection or maintenance of, 40
Tracing
conditions for –
inequitable to trace, must not be, 151
initial fiduciary relationship, 149–150
property must be identifiable, 150–151
right to trace must not have been lost, 151
doctrine of laches, subject to, 151
remedy for breach of trust, as, generally, 149
Trust property. *See also* LAND
alienation of interest in, 14
certainty of subject matter, need for, 16–17
charity property, 168–169

Trust property – *continued*
  condition not to dispose of, trust void where, 28
  different beneficiaries, held variously for, 16–17
  generally, 14
  identifiable, must be, for tracing claim, 150–151. *See also* TRACING
  insurance of, 115
  lifetime trust, creation of, 12–13
  protection and security of, 114–115
  resettlement, 14
  sale of, to trustee, liable to be set aside, 111
  settlor's death, trust taking effect on, 11–12
  sub-trust, 14
  trustees' duties and powers in relation to –
    accounts, as to, 115–116
    appointment, on, 114–115
    distribution, as to, 116–117
    generally, 114
    investment, as to, 117–125. *See also* INVESTMENTS
  various beneficiaries for concurrent interests, divided among, 17
Trustees
  also beneficiaries –
    liability of, for breach of trust, 146
    possibility of, 5
  appointment of –
    court, by, 102
    duties and powers in relation to trust property on, 114–115
    effect of, in relation to trust property, 102–103
    first trustees, 98, 99–100
    new trustees, 99, 100–103
    see also number of, *below*
  buying equitable interest from beneficiary, 111
  charitable trust, of, 170–171
  choice of, 98–99
  custodian –
    appointment of, 96–97
    charges of, 110
    role of, 96
  delegate, power to –
    generally, 108
    liability of trustee when agent employed, 108–109
    restrictions as to, 108

Trustees – *continued*
  discretion of, standard of care as to, 105–106
  duties and powers of –
    active, duty to be, 107
    delegate, power to, 108–109
    derivation of, 106–107
    generally, 105
    maintenance and advancement of beneficiaries, as to, 127–134. *See also* BENEFICIARIES
    not to profit from trust, 109–113
    standard of care, as to, 105–107
    trust property, relating to, 114–126. *See also* TRUST PROPERTY
  expenses of, 110
  fiduciary, as, not to make an incidental profit, 112–113
  first –
    appointment of, 99
    disclaimer of interest in appointment as, 99–100
    incomplete transfer to, supported by consideration, 64–66
    judicial, 97–98
    liability of, for breach of trust. *See* BREACH OF TRUST
    more power, having, 46
  new –
    appointment of, 99, 100–103
    court's power to appoint, 102
    effect of appointment in relation to trust property 102–103
    statutory powers in relation to, 100–101
  number of –
    generally, 103
    increase in, 104
    reduction in, 103–104
  paid, standard of care of, 105–106
  power of appointment, having, 42–46. *See also* POWER OF APPOINTMENT
  property transferred by settlor to trustee, 60, 62–64
  Public Trustee –
    charges of, 110
    office of, 95–96
  remuneration –
    authorisation for, 109–110
    court's powers as to, 110
    custodian trustees, 110
    duty to act without, 109
    Public Trustee, 110

Trustees – *continued*
remuneration – *continued*
solicitor-trustee, of, 110
trust instrument, 109
sale of trust property to, liable to be set aside, 111
secret trust, role as to. *See* SECRET TRUSTS
selling property to trust, 111
settlor declares himself, 59–60, 62–64
sole trustee –
Public Trustee as, 95
settlor as, 9
trust corporations as, 97
trust property, duties and powers as to. *See* TRUST PROPERTY
Trustee Act 1925, powers confered by, 106–107
trustee de son tort, 98
unpaid, standard of care of, 105
who can be a, 95

Trusts
administration of –
charitable, 167–175. *See also* CHARITABLE TRUSTS
maintenance and advancement of beneficiaries, 127–134. *See also* BENEFICIARIES
remedies for breach of trust, 144–152. *See also* BREACH OF TRUST
variation of trusts, 135–143. *See also* VARIATION OF TRUSTS
characteristics of, 5
charitable. *See* CHARITABLE TRUSTS
concept of, 3–6
constituting. *See* CONSTITUTING A TRUST; GIFTS
constructive. *See* CONSTRUCTIVE TRUSTS
corporations, as trustees, 97
courts, relevant, in matter relating to, 6
creation of. *See* CREATION OF A TRUST
deceased's estate and, 6
discretionary. *See* DISCRETIONARY TRUSTS
express. *See* EXPRESS TRUSTS
fixed. *See* FIXED TRUSTS
functions of, 6–8
history of, 4–5
implied by equity. *See* CONSTRUCTIVE TRUSTS; RESULTING TRUSTS
land. *See* LAND

Trusts – *continued*
perpetuities, rule against. *See* RULE AGAINST PERPETUITIES
powers as to –
distribution between several beneficiaries, settlor's powers as to, 41–42
mere power, excercising of, 46
power of appointment, 42–46. *See also* POWER OF APPOINTMENT
protective trusts, 46–47
property taking effect on settlor's death, of, 11–12. *See also* TRUST PROPERTY
protective, 46–47
resulting. *See* RESULTING TRUSTS
secret, 85–89. *See also* SECRET TRUSTS
setting aside. *See* VOIDABLE TRUSTS
sources of legislation, 4–5, 6
statutory, 7–8
variation of, *See* VARIATION OF TRUSTS
void. *See* VOID TRUSTS
voidable. *See* VOIDABLE TRUSTS
without a beneficiary, 40–41

Unincorporated associations
non-charitable, as beneficiaries, 37–40

Variation of trusts
authority of the court, by –
application for, 125, 135
compromise jurisdiction, 137
emergency and salvage jurisdiction, 136–137
inherent power, 136–137
statutory powers, 137–143. *See also* statutory powers of the court, *below*
beneficiaries on whose behalf court can approve, 139–140
benefit of each benificiary, must be for, 141–142
charitable, schemes for, 169
family provision and, 31–32, 142
informal, 135–136
matrimonial proceedings, in cases of, 31, 142
settled land, in relation to, 142–143
statutory powers of the court as to –
generally, 137
other statutory powers, 142–143

Variation of trusts – *continued*
  statutory powers of the court
    as to – *continued*
      Trustee Act 1925, s 57,
        under, 138
      Variation of Trusts Act 1958, s 1,
        under, 138–142, 143

Vesting, remoteness of
  rule against, 20–24

Void trusts
  condition not to dispose of
    property, 28
  divorce, in relation to, 27–28
  effect of, 28
  generally, 18
  illegal purpose, to promote, 27
  marriage, in relation to, 27–28
  public morals, contrary to, 27
  rule against perpetuities,
    contravening, 18–27,

Void trusts – *continued*
  rule against perpetuities, – *continued*
    See also RULE AGAINST
      PERPETUITIES
  void condition, effect of, 28

Voidable trusts
  court, set aside by –
    bankruptcy, where, 32–33
    family provision, 31–32
    general powers, 33–34
    generally, 30–31
    matrimonial proceedings, 31
  generally, 18, 29
  settlor, set aside by, on general
    equitable principles, 29–30

Will
  gifts by, 129
  mutual. *See* MUTUAL WILLS
  trusts of property made by, 11